Astrology
secrets *of the* moon

Astrology
secrets *of the* moon

Discover your true life path and purpose

PATSY BENNETT

ROCKPOOL
PUBLISHING

A Rockpool book
PO Box 252
Summer Hill
NSW 2130
Australia
www.rockpoolpublishing.com.au
http://www.facebook.com/RockpoolPublishing

First published in 2015

National Library of Australia Cataloguing-in-Publication entry
Bennett, Patsy, author.
Astrology: Secrets of the Moon / Patsy Bennett.
9781925017762 (paperback)
Includes bibliographical references.
Astrology:
        Horoscopes.
        Human beings—Effect of the moon on.
133.5

Cover by Jessica Le
Edited by Megan English
Editorial assistance by Katie Evans
Typeset in 11.5/15pt Bembo by Post Pre-press Group, Brisbane
Cover image by Shutterstock
Printed and bound in China

10 9 8 7 6 5 4

Author note: Calculations in the table, The Moon's North Node Signs 1921 to 2025,
on page 10, are set to the mean nodes.

'Go further than you planned. Ask for the moon: you will be surprised how often you get it.'
—PAULO COELHO

For my family, who remind me why we're all here.

Acknowledgements

Many thanks to my publishers and the staff at Rockpool Publishing, my friends and my many teachers, especially Sue Tompkins and Melanie Reinhart, whose enthusiasm for astrology led me to become an astrologer.

My deep gratitude also goes to Martin Schulman, whose research into the moon's north nodes kickstarted my own interest in the subject.

And last but not least, I have my clients to thank—it is your enthusiasm and interest in astrology that has led me to write *Astrology: Secrets of the Moon*. I hope this book proves to be a useful guide throughout your life and the lives of those you love.

Contents

Preface

Are you looking for happiness? Searching for your life's true purpose? This book will help you unlock your hidden potential and find fulfilment.

Astrology: Secrets of the Moon is for anyone who's secretly wondered if they can be more than they are. It's for anyone who wants to know why they're here and what their unique, wonderful contribution to this extraordinary world is; for anyone who wants to discover their hidden talents and gifts—and make these talents and gifts work for them.

When I read my client's astrological charts, it is invariably the moon's north node that provides the key to their happiness as it explains so succinctly which actions will lead to fulfilment—and a more productive and satisfying life.

In the same way, *Astrology: Secrets of the Moon* will explain and reveal *your* moon's north node sign and pinpoint your unique spiritual quest; your true life purpose. Much like a sun sign book, *Astrology: Secrets of the Moon* lists each north node sign from Aries to Pisces. You'll learn about yourself and those close to you, including your children. And you'll discover your potential and the deeper meaning of your life as well as how to feel truly fulfilled. With the help of this book, you can be all you've ever wanted to be—and much more.

Introduction

In this fast-paced world we rarely have time to look up our friends, let alone up at the night sky. And if we do look skywards at night we only see a murky reflection of streetlights, especially in the city. So many of us miss out on seeing the moon and stars in all their majesty, in the darkness, that being in the countryside or out at sea can provide.

In our instant information culture of texts, broadcasts, podcasts, tweets and posts we've forgotten our ancient shepherds and muses, our divine messengers and our solar system, including the stars we called our guiding lights. We've forgotten that the concepts, beliefs and ideas that were attached to the heavens used to inspire us every day. Now our smart phones, tablets and headsets—wonderful inventions that they are—have plugged us into an altogether different worldwide web.

We've forgotten that the concepts, beliefs and ideas that were attached to the heavens used to inspire us every day.

THE SUN AS LIFE-GIVING FORCE

In our modern society we no longer give the star at the centre of our solar system, the sun, a second thought. Yet it is our life-giving force. As recently as 400 years ago the sun was the cornerstone of our everyday lives, helping us to tell the time before pocket watches became available in the 1500s. Now that we have wrist watches and phones to keep us up to date and on time there's very little need to pay attention to the sun.

In fact, if we do think about the sun it's generally in a fearful context. We see the sun's solar flares as potential disruptors of our satellite and communications systems and, even more negatively, we see the sun as the precipitator of deadly rays that will cause skin cancer. We see it as a vengeful, terrible and dangerous mechanism rather than the life-giving, time-keeping force it has been for millennia.

AN ANCIENT INFLUENCE

It's little surprise that we have forgotten that the sun and our neighbouring planets are named after gods and goddesses, or that until as recently as the Renaissance the planets had a mighty influence over our earthly domain.

The connection made by philosophers and scientists thousands of years ago between our planets, the gods and our own wellbeing is a significant one. Indeed, long before the Greek and Roman Empires, the Venus of Laussel carving that survived from the upper paleolithic period depicts the goddess holding a shape resembling a bison horn or a crescent moon with notches cut into it. Anthropologists believe this represents a lunar calendar, which indicates the moon was used as a kind of marker of time or as a monthly time-keeping device as far back as 22,000 years ago.

Megaliths (such as Stonehenge in the UK, which dates back to approximately 3000 BC) are aligned to the summer and winter solstices, which again confirms that the sun and planets have been significant markers of both time and seasons for thousands of years.

Over time scientists have recorded significant political and geophysical events and gradually correlated this information with specific planetary positions. This has been tabulated to the point where astrologers are able to predict events by deducing the relationship between the movement of celestial bodies and events here on earth—and our individual lives.

Astrologers are able to predict events by deducing the relationship between the movement of celestial bodies and events here on earth—and our individual lives.

'As above, so below'

The premise that everything that occurs in the skies will be mirrored by events here on earth was most notably put in writing by the Ancient philosopher, Hermes Trismegistus (purported to be living c 1900 BC). His book, *Emerald Tablet,* contained the concept of 'as above, so below', which principally dictated that our microcosm on earth is an exact reflection of the macrocosm of the universe above.

Trismegistus's beliefs were accepted for thousands of years and came to be known as the Hermetic tradition. His ideas were echoed in Plato's works (c 400 BC) as well as in the work of many other philosophers of the time. Ideas from the Hermetic tradition were revived most recently during the Renaissance (14th to 17th centuries), and while it has been all but forgotten in our everyday lives it continues to thrive in one particular area: astrology.

A celestial science

Astrology—the science of the relationship between celestial bodies and life here on earth—has survived over millennia and is gaining popularity and credence once more. Although taught in many universities around the world, astrology is still popularly dismissed as entertainment. Yet it is an empirical science—one that has been studied, recorded and tabulated throughout the centuries and even millennia.

Astrology is an empirical science—one that has been studied, recorded and tabulated throughout the centuries and even millennia.

Indeed, as a science it not only works, but is extremely useful. Each individual astrological chart is a snapshot of the planets' whereabouts at a particular time and place (usually a person's birth), and can answer significant questions.

In this way a basic knowledge of your astrological birth chart will give you more insight into your potential than the best computer, search engine or program.

More specifically, and as discussed in *Astrology: Secrets of the Moon*, knowledge about the placement of the moon's north node in your astrological birth chart will deliver a unique insight into your life. Personally I consider the moon's north node as the key to contentment because this astrological point represents your spiritual path, illuminating what your true purpose is on a metaphysical level. You're on a unique path in this lifetime and are about to find out what it is.

The moon's north nodes

What is your purpose in life? How will you feel truly
fulfilled? When you are able to answer these questions,
everything in your life will fall into place . . .

The eternal dance between the earth's two most powerful guiding
lights—the sun and the moon—can give us clues to the meaning of our
existence here on earth. We gain insight by ascertaining where they were
on their celestial path at the time of our birth. And we refer to the points
where the moon's path around the earth intercepts the sun's ecliptic, or
apparent path across the starry background as seen from earth, as the
north and south nodes.

Nodes literally means 'knots' in Latin.

As beings of celestial energy—souls, spirit, light and sound incarnate
on earth—our lives are also a journey. In this way, the south node
represents where you've come from, showing you your path and
everything you learnt in your last lifetime. (If your imagination doesn't
stretch to past lives, then the south nodes can be seen as markers of your
subconscious tendencies—those patterns of behaviour that you fall back
on in times of stress or those you may be proficient in, but no longer
stretch you to your full potential.)

Your north node represents your soul's path in this lifetime. It can
show you where in your life you can move along most easily and how

to feel fulfilled. The north nodes are a gateway to divine inspiration. When you understand your purpose as you journey through life, the universe and your very life force itself will combine to support you in your efforts.

'Many astrologers believe that the nodes hold more importance than the rest of the chart.'
Martin Schulman

DISCOVERING YOUR NORTH NODE

Once you know which sign your north node is in, you're ready to know how to make the most of your life and talents. To find out which zodiac sign the north node was in when you were born, simply look up your date and year of birth in the table, The Moon's North Node Signs (1921 ro 2025) on page 10. Then look up the section in this book that corresponds to that sign. For example, if you were born on 6 July 1992 your north node is in Sagittarius, and you can refer to Sagittarius on page 185.

READING YOUR NORTH NODE

Each of the 12 zodiac signs depicts psychological archetypes and within each zodiac sign there are 12 sub-sections. These sub-sections explain in detail your values and self-expression—the secret you—as well as how to make the most of your talents within various areas of your life such as your home and family, work and relationships.

You'll also see that each section has a list of Approaches, Talents, Interests, Challenges and Potential pitfalls among others. These subheadings list key words and career suggestions that will help you focus on your own special talents. In short they will show you how to play to your strengths, which will help you progress.

As above, the Challenges and Potential pitfalls sections are intended as a guide for what to avoid and are not an excuse for bad behaviour! I am very much of the positive astrology mindset that believes the intention of astrology is to help us be the best we can.

There are also affirmations included to help you maximise your own potential in a positive way. They will help you in the many areas of your life, especially when you feel under stress.

As you read about your own archetype remember that you have free will (see *Making the most of your talents*, below). This is the key to turning your life into a labour of love—and success.

NOTE TO ASTROLOGERS: *the 12 sub-sections under each star sign can be read as the house position of the north node, so Your unique approach will be read as north node in the 1st house for that particular sign, Communication will be read as north node in the 3rd house for that particular sign and so forth.*

MAKING THE MOST OF YOUR TALENTS

Our free will enables us to be the best we can be, and this journey of the soul typically involves struggles and challenges. From Greek myths to modern-day real-life stories our lives embody the search for the hero(ine) inside. It is the journey of the evolved soul to strive and overcome the shackles of fate, triumphing as a conscious, awakened and proactive person.

With this in mind, *Astrology: Secrets of the Moon* pinpoints character flaws and challenges with the intention of enabling your inner hero(ine) to rise to the challenges of life. It is done in the safety of knowing that the more you express and motivate your inner hero(ine), the more you'll evolve—not only as an individual, but also collectively as a member of the human race.

In fact, the more your insight into your soul allows you to grow, the more you'll blossom—and the more you'll feel fulfilled. It's an exponentially increasing curve. With this in mind, the north nodes will add another dimension to your understanding of yourself—and *Astrology: Secrets of the Moon* will provide information you'll wish you had years ago!

1921–1949

26 Feb 1921–23 Sept 1922............................Libra
24 Sept 1922–6 April 1924............................Virgo
7 April 1924–24 Oct 1925 ....Leo
25 Oct 1925–5 May 1927 ....Cancer
6 May 1927–26 Nov 1928 ....Gemini
27 Nov 1928–25 June 1930 ....Taurus
26 June 1930–2 Jan 1932 ....Aries
3 Jan 1932–23 July 1933 ....Pisces
24 July 1933–20 Feb 1935............................Aquarius
21 Feb 1935–3 Sept 1936............................Capricorn
4 Sept 1936–24 Mar 1938............................Sagittarius
25 March 1938–14 Sept 1939 ....Scorpio
15 Sept 1939–24 April 1941........................Libra
25 April 1941–23 Nov 1942 ....Virgo
24 Nov 1942–5 June 1944 ....Leo
6 June 1944–16 Dec 1945............................Cancer
17 Dec 1945–11 July 1947............................Gemini
12 July 1947–29 Jan 1949............................Taurus
30 Jan 1949–20 August 1950..........................Aries

1950–1999

1 Jan 1950–20 Aug 1950 ....Aries
21 Aug 1950–10 Mar 1952 ....Pisces
11 Mar 1952–24 Sept 1953............................Aquarius
25 Sept 1953–23 April 1955..........................Capricorn
24 April 1955–28 Oct 1956 ....Sagittarius
29 Oct 1956–21 May 1958 ....Scorpio
22 May 1958–8 Dec 1959..............................Libra
9 Dec 1959–26 June 1961..............................Virgo
27 June 1961-10 Jan 1963 ....Leo
11 Jan 1963–6 Aug 1964 ....Cancer
7 Aug 1964–22 Feb 1966 ....Gemini
23 Feb 1966–11 Sept 1967............................Taurus
12 Sept 1967–28 March 1969 ....Aries
29 March 1969–11 Oct 1970........................Pisces
12 Oct 1970–6 May 1972 ....Aquarius

1950–1999 (cont.)

7 May 1972–20 Nov 1973 .... Capricorn
21 Nov 1973–13 June 1975 .... Sagittarius
14 June 1975–30 Dec 1976 .... Scorpio
31 Dec 1976–20 July 1978 .... Libra
21 July 1978–6 Feb 1980 .... Virgo
7 Feb 1980–27 Aug 1981 .... Leo
28 Aug 1981–20 Mar 1983 .... Cancer
21 Mar 1983–1 Oct 1984 .... Gemini
2 Oct 1984–22 April 1986 .... Taurus
23 April 1986–10 Nov 1987 .... Aries
11 Nov 1987–29 May 1989 .... Pisces
30 May 1989–17 Dec 1990 .... Aquarius
18 Dec 1990–5 July 1992 .... Capricorn
6 July 1992–23 Jan 1994 .... Sagittarius
24 Jan 1994–11 Aug 1995 .... Scorpio
12 Aug 1995–28 Feb 1997 .... Libra
1 Mar 1997–20 Sept 1998 .... Virgo
21 Sept 1998–6 April 2000 .... Leo

2000–2025

7 April 2000–16 Oct 2001 .... Cancer
17 Oct 2001–5 May 2003 .... Gemini
6 May 2003–28 Nov 2004 .... Taurus
29 Nov 2004–22 June 2006 .... Aries
23 June 2006–4 Jan 2008 .... Pisces
5 Jan 2008–22 July 2009 .... Aquarius
23 July 2009–20 Feb 2011 .... Capricorn
21 Feb 2011–1 Sept 2012 .... Sagittarius
2 Sept 2012–25 Mar 2014 .... Scorpio
26 Mar 2014–15 Oct 2015 .... Libra
16 Oct 2015–28 April 2017 .... Virgo
29 April 2017–10 Nov 2018 .... Leo
11 Nov 2018–4 June 2020 .... Cancer
5 June 2020–28 Dec 2022 .... Gemini
29 Dec 2022–10 July 2023 .... Taurus
11 July 2023–25 Jan 2025 .... Aries

Aries

The hero(ine)'s journey

SITUATION

Your quest is to achieve single-minded action and self-assurance. Your life will present you with choices and obstacles that you will be asked to negotiate. You'll have to call on your inner hero(ine) to assert itself in order to do this, but one of your true talents lies in your ability to rise to a challenge through decisive action, and to implement solutions to conundrums.

You will find, though, that you are predisposed to being indecisive. Because you like to be a peacemaker you're constantly in search of harmony and balance, and you'll look for resolution and peace at all costs. This makes you likely to sway from one idea and opinion to another, which can mean you become trapped in a constant state of indecision—and the hero(ine) inside remains dormant.

Trying to create balance and harmony—both in your own life and the lives of others—can mean you are constantly trying to keep everyone happy while satisfying no-one, least of all yourself. You'll eventually become assertive once you tire of this situation, but as a child you can be shy; a typical lamb. The process of becoming assertive will involve bursts of energy as well as outbursts. (Imagine a lamb beginning to stand up and walk for itself—this process comes in fits and starts, and can be frustrating.)

As you mature people will see you as fiery, daring, open and gutsy, even challenging. You have a subconscious understanding of how easy and delightful—and balanced—life can be, but may become impatient or easily annoyed when it isn't.

Your dynamic energy, combined with your refreshing ability to be assertive and enthusiastic, is impressive. You will enjoy injecting your considerable arsenal of energy into your productive activities, but as a child harnessing this may take extra effort.

> NOTE TO PARENTS: *keeping this child physically active and involved in team activities will be excellent for channeling their energy into healthy pursuits and building assertiveness through cooperation.*

Over time you will learn to integrate your vivacious sense of self and your need to be proactive with a more balanced expression, thereby displaying the qualities of the true hero(ine) you are: brave, courageous, and self-confident.

PURPOSE

When you exercise a balanced outlook and show single-pointed vision your sense of purpose will blossom. Your self-confidence and resourcefulness will grow from seeing the effect your independence and willpower has on the people around you—and on yourself too.

Indecision and attempting to please others is a hallmark of a north node in Aries, but when you step into an understanding of your own individuality and purpose you will gain strength as a separate, independent and effective individual. Paradoxically this will help you attain the harmony and integration you so crave in your relationships.

You'll accept that being the best person you can be is pleasing not just for you, but for those closest to you and the world you live in as well. You'll express your values, and sparkle in an open, honest way—and you'll be appreciated and valued for it. You're one of life's pioneers, both in your personal life and within your career.

You may be fiery and independent, but your fulfilment derives from your understanding that respect, compassion and kindness are the bedrock of human harmony and that being assertive can bring these qualities to life for you. Believe you will succeed and take that first step—the future is in your hands.

Affirmation

I am happy to assert myself. I am loved and I love in return.

Famous people

Richard Branson, Bruce Springsteen, Carl Jung, Jay Leno, Natalie Cole, Kylie Minogue, Sean Connery, James Dean, Peter Gabriel, Larry Hagman, Jennifer Aniston, Princess Margaret, Neil Armstrong

Your unique approach

You gain a sense of purpose from being independent, self-sufficient, pioneering in some sense, and by planning and fulfilling your own destiny. Your natural impulse (especially in childhood) is to acquiesce to others' demands, primarily because you're in two minds about what you really want or think. As a result of your fundamental uncertainty you lack self-confidence and can risk living vicariously through other people.

In doing so you inadvertently relinquish your chance to be yourself: outgoing, adventurous and independent. You also risk forfeiting the chance to find happiness and achieve the greatest sense of fulfilment from living life on your own terms, being true to yourself and encouraging others to do the same.

When you are daring, courageous and stand up for yourself, you'll not only feel at ease with who you are, you'll also be in a position to help other people by the example you set. By achieving openness and transparency in your relationships and being honest about who you are, your life will become peaceful, deep and aligned with your true nature. What's more, a self-confident individual will attract other self-confident people!

The type of activities you're attracted to will reflect your dynamic energy. You're a trailblazer through and through, and your purpose is to learn how to translate your eager, fair-minded and vibrant energy into positive action. You're curious, young at heart and a real go-getter!

Perspective

Bold, pioneering, innovative, independent, fiery, can be shy when young, inquisitive

Talents

Initiator, coach, motivator

Interests

Self-expression, sports, self-help, self-development, human rights, new escapades, mediation

Challenge

To believe in yourself

Potential pitfalls

Indecision, self-doubt, self-deprecating, aggression, temper tantrums, impatience

Affirmation

I am certain of myself.

Values and self-expression

You pack a powerful punch. Your robust energy and vivacious desires will spur you on to exert your influence over others, and your ideas will spring to life through proactive endeavours.

You'll fight for your values and won't hesitate to speak up as you mature, but as a youngster and behind the scenes, you may question yourself and your core values. You're prone to take a back seat, be this with close family members, partners, work colleagues, and even with the world.

When you fail to express your feisty nature, you risk succumbing to aggressive outbursts, self-doubt, temper tantrums and passive-aggressive behaviour. The feeling of being indebted to others is a constant reminder of your underlying sense of inadequacy, indecision or guilt over past actions but, luckily, as you mature and your natural ebullience bursts through, you become assertive (as opposed to aggressive), and your path opens up clearly before you.

Your love of the finer things in life (such as good food and well-made products) and your appreciation of the beauty in nature and the simplicity of the purest thoughts and feelings will guide you to understand that true values—such as kindness and the desire to be helpful—are fresh, simple and remarkably easy to sustain.

The impulse to repress your true self will diminish as you become adept at establishing your own set of values. Effort, experimentation and outgoing research will free you from the underlying indebtedness you feel to others and their opinions.

You may find that as you mature you become adept at setting standards for others by being a forerunner or a pioneer in an area that advocates new laws, customs and scientific developments, for example. You're one of life's leaders and you won't let other people down.

Perspective

Intuitive, deep-thinking, spontaneous, impulsive, vivacious, dynamic, fighter

Talents

Public speaking, analysis, innovation, perseverance

Challenge

To be assertive as opposed to aggressive

Potential pitfalls

Rebellious, feelings of guilt, indebtedness, insecurity, melancholia

Affirmation

I express my free will assertively and compassionately.

Communication

As a young person you may be shy, but as you grow and mature you'll find you have a talent for networking, socialising and communication in general. Your single-pointed quest is for correct, direct and straightforward communication, forward-thinking and progressive negotiation, and interactions that translate ideas into action.

This may be challenging initially as you're constantly in two minds about what you think, let alone what to say and, still less, what you'll do especially as a youngster. You may even experience periods where you find speech and general socialising challenging because of shyness, indecision or reticence.

Early on you may be encouraged to choose your words carefully as you're likely to speak before you think, but as an adult your gift of the gab will lend itself to a pioneering, bold and courageous arena.

Once you find your voice and locate that inner hero(ine) who is bursting to have a say, you'll overcome any shy streak. And by taking the first step and drawing on your resources, speaking your mind, making an important but daunting call or setting up a meeting, you may be surprised by how quickly your projects fall into place.

You crave freedom of movement, and you may resent feeling boxed in. You'll take off on journeys and adventures without a second thought and you'll take along just about anyone who wants to come with you. You're also happy being alone on life's journey as you're a self-sufficient soul. Should you meet a soul mate, it will be someone who will share your love of adventure, your buccaneering attitude and your joie de vivre.

With a north node in Aries, you're the ultimate explorer discovering and conquering every new frontier with increasing vitality. You'll also enjoy reporting about events with little or no embellishment simply because they are so exciting, and there is no need for exaggeration at all.

Perspective

Assertive, daring, restless, chatty unless shy, direct, straightforward

Talents

Writing, study, negotiation, sales, inventions, patents, science

Challenge

To find your true inner voice

Potential pitfalls

Bluntness, arrogance, tactlessness, impulsiveness, hesitation

Affirmation

I have a voice. My life is an adventure and I'm writing the script.

Home and family

You're an innovator and will excel at instigating new ideas and approaches, particularly within family relationships and at home. As an adult, hands-on work with property, construction and real estate will appeal.

You'll attempt to break new ground in domestic matters, perhaps even in the way you live your private life. Your interests in domestic or property matters result from a childhood in which your home was fulfilling and harmonious—or the opposite.

Once you're happy with your domestic circumstances you will feel the need to expand your influence to your career or direction in life in general. Your impulse to succeed in the world is strong and you will want to recreate the loving feelings you so appreciate at home in the outside world—a mighty task indeed, and one that can exhaust you.

You are at risk of overworking, which can precipitate a lack of enjoyment both at home and at work. Feelings of not having attained your goals will spur you on to create a stronger role in both worlds, but can lead to a vicious cycle where you lose the very qualities you're striving for in the first place: recognition and contentment.

You can only do so much, but rest assured you will feel satisfied and empowered in life. You will attain a sense of happiness, strength and importance by achieving a place of harmony and ease in your home and family as well as among your peers.

True strength and authority will radiate from you once you accept—and believe in—your inner strength. You will not gain strength or happiness by being forceful or aggressive, largely because you are already a strong character and a force to be reckoned with. You are a bright spark who will encourage many people to see your way of doing things: bravely, courageously and with spirit. Realising this will be your key to success.

It is possible, after all, to be both feisty and loving; to be assertive in the home without losing your temper or having a tantrum. Your true power and influence will come from expressing your inner might, enthusiasm and spark in a proactive, inclusive and caring way.

Perspective

Competitive, vivacious, enthusiastic, caring, feisty, motivated, groundbreaking

Talents

A good influence, peace-loving but can be a fiery leader, innovative

Challenge

To build enduring inner strength

Potential pitfall

Being domineering, controlling, rebellious

Affirmation

I attain my goals calmly and assuredly.

Creativity and life force

Your energy level resembles a seedpod bursting forth with vitality and the impulse to grow. Your intention to make something of yourself and your life is powerful indeed. You're innately attracted to work within groups and organisations, but your challenge in this lifetime is to express your fiery, gutsy, bursting wellspring of life in your own unique, independent way.

Your journey through life will progress in a cyclical manner as if you're constantly reinventing yourself. You may find this frustrating as you're driven to constantly update your ideas about who you are and what you want to create in your life. Those close to you can find this frustrating, too, and may be confused by the ever-changing kaleidoscope of your interests and activities.

Your tendency to constantly update your life, however, is precisely where your creative talents lie. It's because your circumstances continually change that you have a unique perspective. You understand what makes things happen, what life force is, and what your unique role is in creating the life you want—largely because you learn to mould your energy and life into a bright plan of action.

You are aware that you are the motivator within your own circumstances, whether you express this in your ability to take action without too much fuss or simply through your own dynamic yet practical approach to everyday life.

You're a pioneer within the creative realms of innovation, music and dance. You can fire up other people's imaginations too, and will discover that you are the creator of your own happiness and that your life itself is your particular work of art.

Perspective
Imaginative, gutsy, innovative, dynamic, achiever, enthusiastic, powerful

Talents
Art, music, sports, creativity, taking command, practicality

Creative career
Artist, musician, performer, actor, advertising, PR, publicity, design, inventor

Challenge
To create the vibrant life you want

Potential pitfalls
Self-critical, easily distracted, absent-minded, anxious

Affirmation
I am the seed. My activities are the soil.

Work and daily life

You're a dynamo. You want to see your ideas and sparkle expressed within your daily activities and work. You're an impassioned innovator and you'll act upon your insightful ideas and principles vigorously and with resolve.

You'll be particularly attracted to work in areas that enable you to express your individuality and your dynamic take on life. You're likely to prefer being self-employed once you mature and have chosen your line of business. Where you can supply a better idea or a more useful approach, you'll do it. You're a trendsetter and may be a frontrunner within human rights or a policy maker, even if simply within your family or immediate community.

As a child you may prefer to stay behind the scenes, immersing yourself in everyone else's work and business. You may prefer to look after everyone else before you consider your own position or begin to look after your own interests. This is partly due to a fear of exerting your own influence and presenting your own abilities and insights. There is also a lack of self-confidence and indecision that prevents you from choosing your activities.

Your natural disposition is to make like a sheep and follow others rather than discover your own unique talents and ideas. You may be tempted to give in to your fears and may be extremely shy or even inhibited.

NOTE TO PARENTS: *give these children extra encouragement to be themselves and find out what really fires them up!*

If at first your attempts to assert yourself fail, give yourself a pep talk—you have a powerful role to play as an innovator, worker, caregiver and communicator. If you don't assert yourself you risk becoming aggressive and prone to temper tantrums, but once you're ready to express your ideas through your actions you'll find they will be well received and even welcomed by others, especially in the workplace. You may in turn become a powerful motivator of others, helping them express their inner spark and ideas in their own daily life and deeds.

Once you overcome your shyness in the workplace you'll find you become a well-respected worker. You'll enjoy helping others find balance and harmony in their lives and will thrive in areas where you connect people together or perform some kind of service either within the medical, beauty-related or even public sector.

You will also be attracted to activism or mediation at some point in life, largely due to your wish to see fairness and harmony in the world. Your task is to put your ideas into action and what better place to see a balanced outcome than in your daily endeavours?

Perspective

Daring, caring, sporty, impetuous, energetic, intuitive, self-effacing, can be quiet, contemplative

Talents

Reasoning power, insight, innovation, determination, proactive, trendsetting

Type of work

Self-made, self-employed, health, fitness, beauty, veterinary, animal care, team leader, human-rights advocate, adventurer, pioneer, self-help, self-development, inventor, mediation

Challenge

To turn ideas into action

Potential pitfalls

Uncertainty, inactivity, self-destructiveness, fearfulness, self-doubt, aggression

Affirmation

My work is valuable and appreciated.

Relationships

Although you like to be independent, dominant and individualistic, like many people you also crave harmonious relationships. Paradoxically, when you initially try to form balanced relationships you can feel the need to put yourself and your needs second, but in doing so you negate your independence. As a youngster you can be innocent and gullible, and this can place you in potentially vulnerable situations.

Clearly there is a discrepancy between the assertive person you are on the one hand, and your inclination to play second fiddle in relationships in the name of harmony on the other. You may even display a strong tendency to merge completely with your marriage partner in an attempt to become one and the same person, all in the name of togetherness. In this scenario, you will experience tension within relationships when you do eventually assert yourself.

Your inclination to play second fiddle can be a stumbling block in a social group as your propensity to immerse yourself in the group dynamic means you become trapped in a situation where you lose your identity, especially as a youngster. This will clearly cause you significant unhappiness and could also lead you to become rebellious.

The tension you feel within your relationships stems from being happy to identify yourself with others while wanting to exert your own influence and autonomy. You may seesaw between passive and subsequently aggressive behaviour, only to find that this does not create the equilibrium you crave.

In your quest to understand relationships you may prefer long-distance relationships during some periods of your life in the mistaken effort to create long-standing relationships. In the process you potentially sacrifice intimacy for longevity.

Once you have discovered how to be number one while also being in an equal, balanced and fair relationship, you will discover how to attain true happiness and gain a sense of purpose. You will come to know that this is possible, it is simply a matter of honouring your better self— the one that seeks to bridge differences and identify with other people on some level—while asserting your independence and sense of identity.

Once you learn how to do this you will enjoy the respect, freedom and true love you crave. You will progress at work and within your chosen profession. You will excel at being both a team player and a team leader.

Perspective

Friendly, kind, private, individualistic, independent, dynamic, spontaneous

Talents

Networking, socialising, teamwork, compassion, mediation

Challenge

To be both an individual and a people person.

Potential pitfalls

Introversion, melancholia, aggression, domination, indecision, rebellion, gullibility

Affirmation

I am number one and so are you!

Motivation

You are motivated by success, but in order to achieve it, you must call on your inner resources. You must have a clear goal to channel your considerable energy into your pursuits because without direction, your intense power and drive can do a lot of damage by becoming aimless, haphazard and even self-destructive.

You are likely to have considerable funds pass through your hands throughout your lifetime. It will be important to be clear about what you truly want from life and relationships at home, work and in your broader circumstances, especially where financial negotiations and shared responsibilities are concerned.

Deciding what is important to you is part of what will make you happy. By discovering what's truly valuable to you—especially in relationships—you'll instinctively pursue your goals and the significant people in your life (albeit assiduously and without forethought in some cases).

You will accomplish goals quickly, but if you haven't researched your options and are unclear of what your goals are, you may fall into the trap of not truly valuing your success. In turn this can undermine your sense of accomplishment and inner strength, leading to a lack of self-esteem.

When you discover what—and who—you truly value you'll enjoy an extremely fulfilling and dynamic life. You will have clear goals and will respect your inner spark and feistiness. You'll know that these qualities will help you to attain your goals and that they are a true gift.

You are likely to be interested in social dynamics, personal vitality, self-help and any form of human understanding, including sexual dynamics. You will pursue these areas vigorously and with great success, especially when you combine your enthusiasm and drive with respect, forgiveness and compassion not least for your own efforts.

Perspective

Wilful, dynamic, can be secretive, driven, forgiving, flirtatious, charming

Talents

Analysis, research, sport, compassion, determination, drive

Challenge

To be motivated by your values

Potential pitfalls

Lack of self-esteem, quick-temper, restlessness, selfishness, disloyalty, indecision, aimlessness

Affirmation

I am powerful. I create a beautiful life.

Seeking . . .

As one of life's true pioneers you're constantly chasing new horizons, forever pushing forward with daring activities. From abseiling to mountaineering you'll seek out thrilling activities that will set your heart aflutter.

You may be daring beyond reason with regard to your own safety as you believe that all things in life are fair and equal. When you push yourself to extremes, life may teach you that security and safety are the result of prudent decisions, and they are not a guarantee.

In fact you learn that your brave quest for new experiences—and your propensity to push forward with daring activities to attain quick thrills—can be counterproductive and even put your life at risk. Instead you come to learn that what you are actually looking for is that hero(ine) inside yourself. You know subconsciously that this hero(ine) must be awakened in order for you to be the best you can be.

You'll ardently pursue studies sometimes independently of recognised educational institutions. You'll enjoy entering uncharted waters and will not only travel, but will experiment with ideas, philosophies, religions and spirituality. You may also experiment with different types of relationships as your studies will span a broad spectrum, including social interaction.

Your attention span may be short. You become easily bored without a constant supply of new horizons to conquer. As a youngster you may easily dip in and out of various circumstances until you're found what you're looking for. Be careful not to drop circumstances or people too abruptly, leaving behind valuable ties and connections.

You'll absorb and disseminate information rapidly and fervently. News, gossip, travel and knowledge in all their forms will attract you and you'll pursue professions in which words, actions and facts speak loudly.

As you mature and your need to swap information and be super busy diminishes you'll see that the one true message you need to learn, discuss and pass on in life is relatively short and easy. You will come to understand that your own courage and ability to take action are the true delights you were looking for all along, and they weren't far away at all.

Perspective

Gregarious, adventurous, impulsive, original, courageous, shrewd

Talents

Sports, study, intellectual assessment, conversation, debate

Interests

Sports science, cultural studies, travel, exploration, business, commerce, defence strategy

Challenge

To discover deeper meaning

Potential pitfalls

Restlessness, lack of discernment, recklessness, bluntness, extreme risk-taking

Affirmation

I seek new frontiers out there and in my heart.

Career and direction

While you're comfortable taking the lead in life the impulse to make your mark on the world could be daunting. This challenging paradox could spur you on to great success even if secretly you feel more comfortable cocooning at home than putting your stamp on the world.

At heart you're fully aware of your urge to prove yourself, to make your mark and promote your own talents and strengths. As a child, despite your shyness, your inner monologue is, 'I will succeed, just you wait and see!'

When your inner lamb becomes the ram you know you were always meant to be you'll assume your role as the self-confident, proactive, dynamic and authoritarian person you know you are deep down.

You admire the dynamics of a functional family because you come from a happy one or just the opposite. This will fuel your worldly success as you strive to recreate functional dynamics in the wider world by disseminating the attitude that the world is, in a sense, a global family.

You may learn through the school of hard knocks that success in the world differs dramatically from the happiness you derive from pleasant family dynamics. This will lead you to become increasingly assertive in the workplace in an attempt to create a more harmonious working life. Simultaneously you will become increasingly appreciative of family or domestic life. Indeed the care and attention you lavish on your home and work life will be testament to your inner strength and sense of caring. In this way you will eventually make your mark on the world.

Learning the ropes of a new career at a young age may be challenging as you will not appreciate being told what to do. Be patient with those who teach you as well as the process of fulfilling your potential to be the best you can be. There will be time and scope in your life to prove yourself, although it will require you to pace yourself, follow a long-term plan of action and rein in your powerful, dynamic and potentially rebellious self.

Characteristics
Brave, although potentially timid as a child, driven, energetic, a leader

Talents
A good worker, supportive of others, a good homemaker, proactive, can take charge

Type of career
Self-employed, architect, scientist, inventor, family-rights advocate, corporate, homemaker, carer, publicity, PR, inventor, family advocacy, business person, creating empires, property, corporate, mediation

Challenge
Patience, especially when young

Potential pitfalls
Impatience, underachieving, self-doubt, lack of motivation, antagonism, loneliness

Affirmation
I am the best I can be.

Goals, groups and humanitarianism
You have a wellspring of creativity, love and plain old life force at your fingertips. You're bursting at the seams to share your perspective on life, the universe and everything. You're an ardent lover of life itself and you lead from the heart.

You'll make a great team player and also a formidable leader, precisely because you know when to take the lead and when to back down. You will win whatever battle comes your way with your bravado and, later in life, your finely tuned intuition.

You'll be inclined to take risks far too freely, so some self-restraint is necessary, especially when young. You can minimise your potential for harm in this regard through honing your intuition from a young age.

You may believe subconsciously that all good things will come to you naturally, yet you may find you need to work a little harder than you initially thought to attain your goals, especially when you are young. Naturally this will be frustrating, but if you're patient with yourself and those around you, you'll find that your willpower and sheer drive will see you succeed.

As an adult you're a good people person and will be a charming addition to any group, club or organisation, an attribute to anyone's team and a positive addition to a group's dynamics, even if somewhat easily distracted.

You're imaginative and you'll enjoy putting the creative touches to enthusiastic endeavours. The arts and music will attract you as much as intuitive, Aquarian-age projects. Equally, corporate work will keep that bright mind sparkling.

As you learn to channel your particular brand of creativity into a manageable and cooperative sense of self and self-expression, you'll venture far afield in your areas of interest and achieve your personal aims.

You're an engine room of successful initiatives and you'll pursue your interests with passion. You'll affect everyone you meet with your infectious enthusiasm and ability to see concrete results. You will naturally excel when you take the lead within the group dynamic, although you'll be seen as the hero(ine) who has risen through the ranks rather than a domineering, cut-throat achiever.

You're likely to enjoy expressing your dynamic energy through sports. (This is an area that youngsters will enjoy, too, as it enables them to let off steam.)

Perspective

Sociable, outgoing, networker, enthusiastic, risk-taker, passionate, driven

Talents

Liaison, networking, influence, perceptiveness, compassion, taking control

Interests

Art, design, music, theatre, charity, networking, socialising, sports

Challenge

To avoid taking extreme risks

Potential pitfalls

Temerity, impatience, distractions, temper tantrums, imposing control

Affirmation

I am a valuable, dynamic part of the big picture.

The secret you

You'll enjoy working behind the scenes in some capacity, especially as a youngster. You're comfortable working for someone else when you first start out in the workforce, providing them with the diligence and loyalty they require from an employee as long as you're able to express your energetic self.

If you're not enabled in this way you'll feel repressed or put-upon, which will be unfulfilling and stifling, possibly leading to aggressive outbursts. Teaching yourself to see the long-term picture will help you to manage your temper and aggressive behaviour. You can overcome your fear of failure by trusting that your inner hero(ine) *will* help you out.

Your unique, proactive energy will find fulfilment by providing services to others, performing voluntary work and making charitable gestures. Work in health, medicine, self-development, psychiatry, metaphysics and spirituality will appeal to you, although you may pursue these interests quietly in your own time when you're young, principally as a form of self-help. As you mature you may produce some truly pioneering and groundbreaking work in these areas.

You may feel secretly frustrated when you try to take control of your life, be proactive or take dynamic action. You may feel that your actions and intentions are somehow doomed to fail; that you will only ever be a sheep and not the hero(ine) you know you are. This can lead you to work in secret or in an underhand way—even working with the occult (anything that is hidden) in ways that will only benefit you—but this will be counterproductive.

Your drive towards self-fulfilment will be fruitful when you make the most of your talents, which include being discerning, principled and courageous enough to exert yourself. You also have an innate radar and intuition that, when you tune in to it, will always guide you towards the right decision and the right action to take.

The secret you seeks to hide your light, largely because you are at the beginning of your journey as a hero(ine) and the accompanying timidity, self-doubt and fear can be daunting. But your task in this lifetime is to reveal the enterprising, determined you that is bursting to come out so that you can be a vital, effective and positive force.

Your challenge is to learn to understand your part as an individual in the big picture, to understand how order is born out of chaos and how we as humans emerge from the cosmic soup to live our lives and contribute our unique role within the whole.

Once you establish what your unique role is in the bigger picture, you'll understand how your dynamic contribution is integral to the functioning of the whole. You'll blossom as a result of casting off your secret fears and doubts, your aggression and frustration, and draw on your resourcefulness to reveal the truly adventurous and courageous hero(ine) you really are.

Characteristics

A late bloomer, resourceful in maturity, loyal, steadfast, perfectionist, aggressive, rebellious, frustrated

Talents

Insight, intuition, research, discernment, loyalty

Interests

Medicine, healing, self-help, charity, psychiatry, forensics

Challenge

To let your light shine

Potential pitfalls

Inhibitions, fearfulness, underhandedness, deceit, indecisiveness, self-doubt, apathy

Affirmation

I let my inner hero(ine) out.

Taurus

The impassioned realist

SITUATION

You'll experience intense events in life. Your challenge is to work through strong feelings by exercising self-control and a sense of perspective, understanding that the drama in your life is manageable even if it appears overwhelming at times.

By simply embracing the still point within each kaleidoscopic, chaotic event you'll discover that no matter how destabilising it may initially appear, there is a constant that is secure and safe. You'll realise that in the same way that nature always changes while still following a pattern of seasons, so too birth, death and transformation follow a pattern that establishes order over and above the apparent disorder.

Your circumstances in life will, at some point, dictate that you detach yourself from a pattern of instability or drama that has led to inertness or even stagnation within your life. You may find that certain experiences and circumstances take place in a repetitive pattern and that you're trapped in a virtual groundhog day of ancestral proportions.

Through your life journey you will learn that the strength of your convictions and the impact of your actions will lead you to a deep, automatic desire for transformation in the same way a chrysalis is transformed into a butterfly.

You'll gain strength, self-esteem and self-worth as you strive toward a new approach to the wonders of life—even amidst its constant chaos and change—while succeeding at staying within the confines of a stable pattern. In this way you'll become down to earth, realistic and adept at analytical, judicious and compassionate thought, which is a rare and valuable combination.

PURPOSE

You will find fulfilment and gain a deeper appreciation for your life when you understand the still point within change. As transformation churns and we evolve as human beings there are certain laws of the universe—of nature and existence—that are eternal and unchanging.

A sense of peace and security comes from knowing and experiencing these universal laws. Where previously there were only intense emotions, chaos and uncertainty, you'll eventually be able to establish stillness and moderation in your life.

Your gift in this lifetime lies in understanding the never-ending thread of energy and creativity inherent in the universe—and knowing that you are an integral, creative part of this life force. You'll gain a strong sense of purpose from understanding that your own actions, which are initiated in your thoughts and feelings, impact considerably on your environment, on those around you and on your future.

When you honour common values and choose respect and honesty over drama and neediness, you will find happiness and project positive outcomes into your future. Channeling intense desires and emotions into practical, positive actions can only help you carve out a better way.

It is your choice alone whether to be a feather in the wind (being blown this way and that by drama and random events) or be the wind itself, which carries things here and there but by its very nature, never changes. Within this choice lies the understanding of your role within your life—that your choices and actions determine your future. Your ability to marry pragmatism with compassion spells a bright future ahead.

Affirmation
I am the still point within the chaos. I am calm and creative.

Famous people

Mother Teresa, Barbara Walters, Hillary Clinton, Al Gore, Prince Charles, John Belushi, Kurt Cobain, Pamela Anderson, Lulu, Olivia Newton-John, Yusuf Islam (Cat Stevens)

Your unique approach

You have a deep, passionate approach to life. In the area of relationships, life will appear particularly intense and chaotic. You may be tempted to blame other people for your own shortcomings (especially as a youngster), simply because it's sometimes easier to deal with complex circumstances by blaming others. In addition you may not initially see that other people's experiences are not as dramatic as yours. A perceived lack of understanding or support from others can create feelings of resentment.

As you mature you'll realise that your unique perspective on life enables you to approach drama in a practical way. You're able to create a stable environment, especially within relationships, principally because you're able to locate the eye of the storm and remain within it, establish peace in times of flux and discover that there is stability even within a constantly changing panorama of dramas.

Your temptation will be to take control within your relationships or within a broader context, forcing things to happen the way you want them to. You'll find that imposing your will on another person or situation will backfire and only create more chaos, upheaval, drama and instability in your life. Once you realise this you'll be halfway to creating a happier, more stable future for yourself.

You'll find the quickest vehicle to happiness is understanding that the energy inherent in the universe is both static and dynamic at the same time, and that your desire to carve out your own future within this state holds the key to happiness. Because of this desire (as opposed to your will), and with the help of your sensible, moderate approach, you have the motivation and ability to imagine a better way, thereby creating your own, improved, destiny.

Your connection to the eternal is something you already feel inside you. Giving your full attention to the eternal source of life (whether you call this God, spirit, Buddha or the universe) and being willing to allow this to work through you will provide the clearest path to happiness.

You will love surrounding yourself with art, beauty, luxury and treasured people. They give substance to your appreciation of everything in life that is beautiful. Nurture the eternal beauty you feel inside yourself and listen to your deep understanding of what truly matters in life—love and compassion—and be true to their expression.

Perspective

Sensitive, intense, sensuous, caring, wise, practical, down-to-earth, dramatic

Talents

Constancy, dependability, calm, creativity, imagination, pragmatism, organisational skills

Interests

Food, fashion, style, luxury, art, music, beauty, gardens

Challenge

To understand chaos and create calm

Potential pitfalls

Self-destructive, stubborn, domineering, critical, manipulative, obsessive, dramatic

Affirmation

I give substance to my dreams.

Values and self-expression

You will have the opportunity in your lifetime to create a sense of stability and self-esteem through your possessions, desires and finances. Your belongings and status will matter to you because you see them as expressions of your values and self-worth. This may result from having been brought up in a particularly wealthy background—or the opposite.

Being wealthy will appeal to you as you see finances as a valuable resource. Even if you do express your values through your surroundings, possessions and valuables more so than others, not everyone with a Taurus north node will seek to accumulate money above all else. You will pursue relationships with particular people who embody your values—again, more so than others. You will value comfort and luxury and your home will be sumptuous.

You have the considerable ability to transmute your own desires and energy into a material manifestation. In effect you can give substance to abstract attributes. This is partly due to your practical approach to life combined with a deep understanding of life's process itself, giving you the ability to achieve your highest goals.

This is precisely your gift. You can create and manifest whatever you desire. This means it is all the more crucial to be careful how you spend your time and energy. The intensity with which you invest your energy in your activities and the people you associate with will make waves, which will ripple out endlessly as you are actively creating not only your own future, but also a future that impacts everyone around you. Your self-expression and values emanate on a non-verbal level as well as a verbal one. Your every thought, emotion, attraction and impulse creates waves, even as you read this.

As a young person you may be attracted to money and all the shiny outward signs of success, but as you mature the more enduring values and expressions of value will appeal to you such as peace, contentment, love and a happy home life. The dramas associated with accumulating and manifesting your material desires will soon give way to creating a satisfying environment that sustains the deep-seated contentment you strive for, which can only come from inner peace and harmony.

Perspective
Tactile, caring, determined, earthy, practical, goal-oriented

Talents
Making money, enabling others to do so, making dreams come true, creativity, analysis

Challenge

To value what you do

Potential pitfalls

Egoism, materialism, manipulation, unscrupulousness, obstinacy, obsession, greed

Affirmation

I feel nurtured by peace and harmony.

Communication

You will strive for meaningful interactions—pointless banter is not for you. You comprehend life and communicate on a direct, earthy, physical and practical level, deriving meaning from your fingertips as they touch the world around you and soak up information.

You're motivated to understand the practicalities of communication and interaction and how they apply to relationships, especially those with siblings and within your neighbourhood and community. Your drive is to discover the worth, value and importance of being connected with other people and of understanding, on a fundamental level, the inner workings of the human condition.

You feel a connection to other people and with life itself intensely. You may travel through the dark night of the soul that will take you to places—whether real or metaphorical—where you lose contact with the sacred and higher dimensions of human intent, leaving you with the belief that life, relationships and you, yourself, have no soul and no worth.

As you mature you will come to see that the one true common thread—love—is what binds people in your life together, and that communication enables the free flow of love. You'll understand that certain relationships are deep, strong and enduring, despite initial doubts to the contrary, and you know that the currency that binds people together is sometimes simply words. They have a unique value—and power—of their own.

Through this understanding you will become one of the most anchored and practical people, as well as an extremely effective communicator. You will understand the power of the word through communication and the impact that carefully chosen words can have. Ultimately you know that elevated thoughts and positive intentions (carried through to compassionate actions) are the driving force behind what makes both your life—and the lives of those close to you—rosy to the extreme.

Over and above these traits, you communicate in a hands-on, practical way through your actions. You're a sensuous person who also appreciates the value of tactile and direct communication. Your gestures and deeds will have even more impact than the spoken word especially on people close to you. Your smile speaks a thousand words.

Perspective
Inquisitive, methodical, practical, curious, hands-on, realistic, reasonable

Talents
Research, investigation, insight into relationships, psychoanalysis

Challenge
To avoid distractions

Potential pitfalls
Lacking trust, self-worth and/or morals, materialism

Affirmation
I communicate my values.

Home and family
You understand the value of property as a family base as well as an investment, whether in a financial or emotional sense. You also appreciate the value of property as a meeting place in the community and as a functional shelter, pure and simple.

You'll develop a broader understanding of how a house functions as the outward expression of your values. This could naturally lead you to work in real estate and in construction, architecture or interior design.

Positive family dynamics will be the bedrock of your success story. If you come from a household that was chaotic, busy, large or unusual in any way you'll work hard to establish a sense of calm and stability in your own home. The nurturing you derive from family and domestic dynamics—and from having an active family role—will have a profound effect on you.

Your home life as a youngster will be a topsy-turvy place involving power struggles and/or intense and dramatic changes in your life (such as moving house frequently or other changes due to the departure of significant family members). As you mature your desire to make your home a more stable area of your life will bring fulfilment.

As an adult you'll strive to feel sustained and supported by your family and home life. The common ancestral thread—or lack of it— that runs through your family history will also influence your direction in life. You're likely to strive to prove yourself a success through your career or status if only to make a point relating back to your family circumstances.

As you mature you'll enjoy creating a sanctuary from the busy or chaotic nature of your career or general status in life. You'll enjoy creature comforts at home and your home may come to resemble a resort as you endeavour to feed your inner need for comfort and security through comfortable, sumptuous surroundings and the peace created by your own private haven.

Perspective

Family-minded, boastful when young, proud, enjoys creature comforts and luxury, ambitious, materialistic

Talents

Sensitivity, caring, creating calm, goal-oriented, adventurousness, kindness

Challenge

To create an oasis at home

Potential pitfalls

Feeling unstable, intense, vengeful if provoked, obsessive, egotistical, inflexible, stubborn

Affirmation

My home is my castle. Calm radiates from my heart.

Creativity and life force

As a youngster you'll love being the centre of attention. You're dynamic and understand your own power. Your need to be the centre of attention is based solely on your desire to be gratified—it is not egotistical—and this desire may be hard to shake off even in adulthood.

As you begin to mature and dispense with the impulse to gratify, you will find that a whole new world opens up to you. As a result, your need as a child to be satisfied through food, play time and toys—and as an adult, through sex, distractions or even addictive behaviour—will diminish.

Some of the self-indulgent behaviour arises from basic insecurity. There is a faint fear of being plunged back into chaotic or dramatic circumstances that you have either lived through or fear might occur. Once you learn to identify with a still, stable and calm sense of self your compulsions will diminish. Activities such as meditation and yoga will help you find this inner calm.

You'll find you have a great deal to offer creatively and that you're able to appreciate the finer beauty in life more than many. Self-expression through the arts and plain old fun will appeal to you as you experience these activities in an immediate, physical and sensuous way. They will have a stabilising and soulful effect on you as you find that your appreciation for the lightness of a feather and the flight of a butterfly have far more appeal—and a far more positive influence—than the need to self-gratify.

You have a strong need for self-expression and creativity. As you express your creativity you'll find that a new approach to life will unfold—one in which activities just for the sake of self-gratification become a misuse of your considerable talents. You'll attain fulfilment by having a cause or an end goal to work toward within your daily activities.

You'll enjoy expressing your talents in group activities and your ability to accept responsibility will mean that work within groups (from parents' groups to the boardroom) or corporate and managerial endeavours will suit your temperament.

You have a deep understanding of the nature of life and beauty itself. Combined with your love of family and the fundamentals of good living, your everyday existence becomes an artistic tapestry in the making.

Perspective

Artistic, capable, self-confident, selfish when young, constructive, practical

Talents

Insightful, able to make something out of nothing, creative, responsible

Creative career

Builder, designer, artist, musician, work with children, advertising, management

Challenge

To overcome self-indulgence

Potential pitfalls

Egotistical, aimless, self-gratifying, self-destructive

Affirmation

I am beautiful and I can create beauty.

Work and daily life

You're a perfectionist at heart. Whatever you try your hand at—from tidying the house to looking after children, to working at the office—you'll strive to be the best you can possibly be.

You derive a sense of wellbeing and fulfilment from being good at what you do. The potential pitfall is that your pursuit for perfection can stifle your creativity. In addition, your need to conform to—and excel within—an institution or group dynamic could quash your individuality and sensuous spirit leading to endemic laziness and lack of interest.

As you mature you'll realise that goals, restrictions and conditions are only as restrictive as you make them. You are able to turn what others see as a limiting situation into a productive one. You understand the intrinsic value of work itself and having a practical, daily routine.

You have keen insight into the true value of objects, activities, routines and people. What's more you have the ability to understand the value of accomplishing goals.

You derive value from having values. And in those circumstances where you feel you must bow to other people's demands, such as the workplace, you're able to understand your own role and support others' needs because you understand the huge value that your own contribution—and everyone else's—makes to the group endeavour. You're able to see the bigger picture while paying strict attention to the minutest detail at the same time.

As such you're able to be of service to other people and be a supportive and valuable member of your community. You'll be attracted to hands-on, practical or methodical work as it helps you feel that you're truly immersed in your activities. For this reason you're likely to be a hard worker, but can risk over-working. Holidays and pleasure time may need to be scheduled and adhered to so as to avoid burnout.

Perspective

Hard-working, willing to please, caring, principled, perfectionist, supportive, sympathetic

Talents

Meticulousness, professionalism, helpfulness, productiveness, resourcefulness

Type of work

Service industries, hospitality, medical, caring, event organiser, agriculture, vintner, beauty, fashion, mortuary, finances, insurance broker, motivational speaker, gardener, life coach, media, philosophy, teaching, law, religion, trade, commerce, engineering, property, design, relationship counselling, homemaker, power broker

Challenge

To balance perfectionism with practicalities

Potential pitfalls

Fussiness, neurosis, fanaticism, fixation, laziness

Affirmation

I accomplish my end goals gracefully.

Relationships

You'll enjoy expressing your core values and sensuality in your intimate relationships. Your core values include the understanding that basic human needs are an expression of the life force and therefore human needs are to be respected. You take for granted that trust, love and compassion come from the heart and sense that sharing these feelings is the seedbed for future contentment in relationships. The words mutual respect are an integral part of your relationship vocabulary.

You'll not only discover your own worth through close relationships, but also the worth of others and the love you share. As you will learn so much through your relationships you may be tempted to succumb to the impulse to change your friends, and potentially even partners, in rhythm with your own development, especially as a youngster. You may also attempt to impose your will on other people. The latter will clearly backfire and as a result your first practical lesson about the importance of mutual respect will have been learned.

A residual fear of being plunged into chaotic circumstances or losing control over your circumstances could lead to restlessness or extreme emotions. The feeling you must constantly move from relationship to relationship, chopping and changing your choice of friends and even partners as you go through life may be unsettling.

Important friends and relatives may come and go due to the demands of their own circumstances. And yet, with the intention of enjoying giving and receiving love you can establish some of the most enduring and loyal relationships humanly possible, not only in your personal life but also professionally. You will make a powerful ally and proficient business partner.

As you mature, you'll find more stability within your personal relationships rather than feel that you must constantly move on or that others' movements will disturb your peace of mind. The more you learn in life the more you'll develop your own feelings of stability—and be able to enjoy steady relationships without expectations or demands over and above the exchange of respect, love and compassion.

It's in the exchange of love in all its forms that you will find true fulfilment in this lifetime. The true power and vitality of positive, mutually nurturing relationships contains the life force that will help you accomplish your most potent goal—finding the stillness and peace inside yourself that can only be found through expressing, giving and receiving love and kindness.

Perspective

Grounded, nurturing, steadfast, loyal, respectful, earthy, helpful, affectionate, sensual

Talents

A keen eye for beauty, good provider and nurturer

Challenge

To give and receive love without fear of loss

Potential pitfalls

Obstinacy, inconstancy, instability, controlling, fearful, lacking in self-esteem or self-control

Affirmation

I am loved and I love.

Motivation

You have strong emotions and your desires and impulses can lead you to a life of fulfilment and happiness, but all too easily these same emotions and desires can lead you to a life of self-indulgence where you are enslaved to your passions and cravings.

Self-indulgence, addictions and the pursuit of luxury and money could take a lot of your focus and energy in this lifetime. The accumulation of possessions for the sake of it could even dominate your life and you risk running into debt as a result.

You will come to understand that it will be more productive to live a balanced and less intense life. Being a slave to your passions is against your natural instinct to be in control of your own impulses and to feel secure and stable.

Fulfilment in this lifetime will not result from satisfying constant cravings. With a little perspective and self-discipline you will miraculously (it will seem this way at first) transform your life into something beyond expectation.

Purely by keeping your feet on the ground and your eyes open you will understand, through your own experience, that within each action there is an equal reaction. The law of karma dictates that everything you do will come back to you. So pandering to unquenchable impulses will only result in more unquenchable impulses. And the more you feed your addictions, impulses and unfulfillable desires, the more they will dominate your life.

To avoid being overcome by chaos, lack of self-control, temptations, jealousy and envy, learn to turn your focus towards self-fulfilment on a more enduring level and you will find you're capable of creating a wonderful, enriching, nurturing life.

You have an innate talent and aptitude for meditation and yoga as your uniquely sensuous nature can easily tap into the calming effects of the essential life force that lies just beneath the surface of your skin.

You have the self-discipline and self-control to create your own destiny. You're able to effortlessly take control of the seeming chaos around you (without being controlling) by setting the intention to make sense of it all and to live life in that still point of the storm where your thoughts are clear as a bell and your actions clear as a diamond.

Perspective

Adaptable, empathetic, understanding, intense, compassionate, spontaneous, passionate

Talents

Meditation, foresight, helpfulness, compassion, self-discipline

Challenge

To avoid being a slave to your desires

Potential pitfalls

Drama, scheming, calculating, addictive behaviour, controlling, inflexibility, unreliability

Affirmation

I can turn chaos into calm. I am self-controlled.

Seeking . . .

You're on a quest to understand the bigger picture. This means not only understanding how the world works, but also understanding what it all means, intrinsically, so that you understand its worth—and what it's worth to you personally.

You'll dig deep to find value and meaning in life and this quest can manifest in all kinds of ways. You may seek meaning in relationships, study, religion or travel and exploration. You're always looking at how objects, circumstances, events and people can benefit you and, as you mature, the world. Ultimately you're searching for ways to be the best you can be and to anchor yourself in the chaos of life.

If you find after short investigation that something has no intrinsic value or meaning to you, you're liable to discard it or to disappear in a cloud of dust so quickly it'll seem you were never there. And yet you can be the most loyal, patient and avid follower of whatever interests you—to the point of distraction. Once you're on a path there's very little that will deter you because your intensity and focus is all encompassing. What you're looking for is security and stability, which incidentally you know you'll find in your heart.

Because you approach your activities with such intensity the lesson in your lifetime is to be careful what and who you get involved with. A little research before you dig in will always help because you will dig deep. Once you've found what you're looking for you'll enjoy transforming the object of your attention into its highest possible potential in an intense and dramatic way.

Your ultimate quest resembles that of the alchemist turning the base metal of your life to its highest possible form: gold. And to feel that you belong there—lock, stock and barrel.

Perspective

Practical, explorative, appraising, secure in knowledge, intense, loyal, patient

Talents

Organisation, accumulation of knowledge, steadfastness, resourcefulness, insight, perspicacity

Interests

Cooking, self-improvement, beauty, fashion, finances, trade

Challenge

To maintain perspective

Potential pitfalls

Obsession, selfishness, compulsiveness

Affirmation

My life is a treasure. I belong.

Career and direction

You have a well of motivation and desires that will help you to succeed in your life and career. You'll be inspired to stay a few steps ahead of everyone else. This impulse will help you to succeed, especially materially, but it can potentially cause you to lose sight of what truly pleases you, especially when you become fascinated by your career, direction and status. For this reason it's important to regularly check that you're still on the path you know is the most productive and beneficial on every level, including spiritually, not just for you, but for those you interact with as well.

You'll enjoy working steadily towards an end goal within your career, so planning a step-by-step project is something you're adept at. You may be extremely charismatic and influence people purely by setting a good example. You'll find that people will freely follow your lead, so again, regularly check that you're on a positive path as this will help you to avoid misleading people who have put their trust in you.

Looking after others in a practical way will appeal to you on a fundamental level. Much of your pleasure and fulfilment will come from being a nurturer, whether you're the chief breadwinner in the family or if you literally feed people for a living by working, for example, as a chef.

Tension in your life may be caused by your relentless drive to satisfy your own needs and ambitions and your need to satisfy the needs of those you hold dear. In addition you have a perennial fear of sudden change, which potentially makes this an additional source of anxiety within your relationships, especially those at work.

Yet as you mature and learn that nurturing yourself actually helps you to nurture others—and vice-versa—you will overcome this inner tension and fear. Once doubt is banished you'll be free to work your magic: simply and practically.

Characteristics

Capable, nurturing, motivated, reasonable, sensible, intense, determined, charismatic

Talents

Strategy, motivation, good organisational skills, caring, role model

Type of career

Beauty and health industry, business, care industry, domestic/property industry, nutrition, hospitality, homemaker, carer, chef, massage, holistic, self-improvement, mining, plumbing, debt collector, educator, lawyer, administrator, religious leader, inventor, writer

Challenge

To self–nurture

Potential pitfalls

Burn–out, misleading others, selfishness, subservience

Affirmation

I am happy. My happiness radiates.

Goals, groups and humanitarianism

As a youngster, you'll have powerful energy levels that are best channelled into sport or other energetic activities such as dance. As you mature, you'll enjoy club activities and group endeavours in which your strong artistic and musical abilities will fuel many of your interests with like-minded people.

During childhood you'll have the urge to lose yourself in creativity and music. As you mature this tendency could lead to a similar urge to lose yourself through drugs and alcohol. Your sensuous nature can be all consuming, leading to addictions and over-consumption unless you direct your passions and sensuality via productive group interests and activities such as performance and team sports.

Once you put your mind to a task you'll accomplish anything, especially if it involves careful planning. You may well take a leading interest in human rights and enlightening activities that improve the human condition over the long term. You'll be attracted to charity or voluntary work during some phase in your life as you like to back a cause you value. You'll enjoy working behind the scenes in a philanthropic capacity.

Your sense of purpose will flourish the more you channel your creative and high energy levels into productive pursuits in the group dynamic and within the community. Your sense of humour is infectious and this will bring fresh insight into your best way forward on a daily basis. Your most profoundly moving moments will stem from your passions, your creativity and your enjoyment of your personal life. They will fuel your every move, aim, hope and action.

Perspective

Passionate, community-spirited, determined, creative, realistic, humorous, energetic

Talents

Music, arts, sports, self-starter, empathy

Interests

Fashion, community-based interests, inventions, poetry, inspired speaking, corporate, charity, PR, publicity

Challenge

To channel strong energy into productive pursuits

Potential pitfalls

Inflexibility, self-obsession, selfishness, self-indulgence, greed

Affirmation

Let's work together.

The secret you

You'll derive deep and lasting fulfilment from feeling that you're anchored in life. This deep-seated impulse could be expressed in a multitude of vocations and being helpful may be especially rewarding.

As a youngster you fear that you will find nothing of any true worth in life. Conversely you fear that you are unable to be of any effective use yourself. Secretly, insecurity and a fear of chaos are your crosses to bear even once you've gained status, direction and respect in life. Engaging in activities that keep your hands busy, your feet on the ground and your senses in touch with everyday life can help to diminish these feelings.

Your need to be useful and practical will cause your life to undergo several periods of upheaval or extreme change, which can include the need to adapt to a new daily routine or work schedule. You'll work hard to prove your worth even if only to yourself.

You're likely to work behind the scenes at some point in your life. Whether you are in service with government departments or in the underbelly of life. The choice will be yours.

Your challenge is to work out how you will develop your talents and how you will make them work for you both realistically and practically. You fear your talents will remain hidden in the unseen corridors of life, the intrigues of the underbelly of life or worse in addictions or behind prison bars because you know deep down that if you pander to your basest emotions rather than aspire to your highest self you will fail.

You may be attracted to the occult, which literally means the hidden, but care must be taken that you do not lose your integrity, or worse still yourself, in the complexities of the hidden realms.

When you work at being anchored and stable in life you will find that your capacity to do good deeds—and even to be a healer of sorts—emanates from your natural good sense.

You know that your gift lies in being a selfless person who willingly gives their time to the service of others and that you can reach your highest potential in this way. Once you're on a positive path you'll be fully aware of the sacrifices you make in your life to make the world a better place and this conscious awareness will motivate you to succeed.

You are an impassioned realist and will always maintain a sense of perspective. Knowing that you are fundamentally able to do this will steer you straight through chaos and into that safe harbour that allows reason, stable values and actualisation to reign.

Characteristics

Intuitive, secretive, sensual, charismatic, compassionate, caring, self-effacing

Talents

Healing ability through intuitive means, psychic ability, helpful, giving, effective, practical

Challenge

To let your inner light shine in practical ways

Potential pitfalls

Pandering to the lowest base emotions, falling foul of the law, talents remain hidden, ineffectual, distracted

Affirmation

I can reach my highest possible potential.

Gemini

The messenger or go-between

SITUATION

Circumstances in your lifetime will encourage you to develop your communication skills primarily in order to exchange the vast amount of information that will come your way. Multitasking will become second nature as you'll naturally seek to broaden your horizons to assimilate and in turn deliver information.

You may be particularly studious and you'll enjoy conveying your knowledge through teaching and research. You'll have a passionate interest in knowledge in general. You're the zodiac's natural-born communicator and you'll disseminate information whether as a journalist, broadcaster, researcher, academic and for some, in less salubrious ways, as a backyard gossip!

Mercury, the planet that rules Gemini, was named after the Roman god who was given the task of delivering messages from the other gods to humans. Similarly you have the capacity to deliver important messages either in a practical or esoteric way as a channel delivering wisdom to the earthly plane beyond even your own experience or comprehension.

You're particularly qualified as a messenger because you're able to deliver information impartially and without prejudice—unless you're one of life's gossips, in which case your communication style will more accurately resemble Chinese whispers!

On the whole the way you communicate is characterised by your sense of fair play. This is what gives you the ability to deliver clear, concise and impartial messages. In fact your involvement in communication can be so unprejudiced that you're unable to comprehend the true impact words, speech and human interaction can have. As such you can appear heartless, flippant or even cruel to people who infuse their words with emotion and personal meaning. In this sense you can be seen as a bit outside the norm, a little wild, aloof or indecisive and maybe even socially inept, especially as a youngster.

You'll be drawn to commerce and international trade as you are a natural bridge between cultures and customs. This type of interaction will appeal to you because of the service you deliver (much like Mercury, the winged messenger). You're likely to engage in travel at a young age with your family, gaining a broad knowledge of other cultures and languages.

PURPOSE

You'll gain fulfilment by being a channel for information and knowledge, a bridge between different areas or people or by exchanging goods. A great deal of wisdom, information and thirst for knowledge will fuel your lust for life. You'll discover how to do many things at once and will have multiple talents, twin or complementary interests.

The key to your happiness lies in how you disseminate information. Your quick wit and impressive intellect will help you to learn and study. But will you be the neighbourhood gossip or will you learn many languages, travel and study cognitive science? Will you work in the media or with children who need additional help with their own communication skills? Will you become adept at trade between different countries with different values and customs?

You are a messenger and go-between. The messages you deliver and the way you deliver them is your choice and will colour your entire life. The qualities of fair play and justice will help guide you along and in this way you'll avoid one of your major pitfalls—becoming distracted by the many messages and interests that your life journey will expose you to.

Instead, the qualities of fair play and tolerance will help you focus on the importance of the service you're providing. Ultimately this is to connect various ideas, cultures and people; to be the bridge between different worlds, ideologies and attitudes. You are the glue and positive connection between the realm of the gods and the earthly domain, and the conduit for new ideas and circumstances to flourish for the good of everyone you encounter and your own personal relationships.

Affirmation

I speak the truth. I live the truth and I am the truth. I speak and communicate my higher purpose.

Famous people

Uri Geller, Burt Bacharach, David Bowie, Andy Warhol, Bill Clinton, Dolly Parton, Sandie Shaw, Elton John, Charlie Sheen, Donald Trump, JK Rowling, Mark Zuckerberg, Steven Spielberg, Vincent Van Gogh

Your unique approach

You're comfortable being the centre of attention although as a youngster you may be shy and nervous. You may talk uninterruptedly or seldomly. Shyness in this case is born of feeling ill at ease or different in some way socially. For example, due to a background of international travel with your parents. You may need to learn to be tactful as you mature or learn additional social skills.

As you grow older you'll be happier putting yourself and your ideas forward, perhaps blazing a trail in the area of communications. If you're a stay-at-home parent you'll be happy to chat and entertain children all day long as you enjoy laughter, fun and joviality. Your enthusiasm will remain child-like until a ripe old age.

You have a playful side that will help you remain youthful and attractive. Your sense of humour helps you convey happiness and wisdom, connecting people in a joyful way.

The temptation is to ignore others' opinions and attempt to lead a conversation with the sole objective of having things go your way. This tends to trivialise your unique talent, which is to connect people to each other and yourself to them.

Using conversation and communication as a two-way street (rather than as the mundane exchange of daily gossip or as a channel for your own personal agenda) is far more beneficial to you. Learning to communicate on a one-to-one basis as opposed to work-related, group or community-based communication is a key aim.

By educating yourself and pursuing valuable information you'll feel far more fulfilled as a channel and source of information. By being well informed your tendency to be indecisive can also be avoided.

You're likely to be attracted to larger-than-life personalities who complement your quick wit. You'll enjoy exchanging witticisms and discussing world events. You're a philosopher in the making—and a philosopher of the people. You'll vigorously pursue the company of others and are unlikely to be a loner, especially once you overcome shyness. As you mature you'll become a loyal partner and your lust for life and sense of adventure, joy and humour, are unlikely to ever leave you.

Perspective

Chatty, versatile, adaptable, changeable, humorous, quick-witted, generous

Talents

Good communication skills, writing, mathematics, public speaking, coaching

Interests

The news, travel, reading, writing, socialising, networking, club activities, sports, religion, spirituality, acting

Challenge

To integrate your ideas socially

Potential pitfalls

Aloofness, flippancy, verbal cruelty, distractedness, inattentiveness, flightiness, indecision, gossip

Affirmation

I communicate for the best possible outcome.

Values and self-expression

You're a multifaceted individual and gifted in many different areas. Your inner values will determine which road will truly fulfil you in life. As you progress you'll become increasingly aware of what's valuable to you—money, honour, prestige or relationships for example—and these priorities will change and grow as you yourself grow and learn.

You'll become increasingly adept at attaining your goals and will enjoy doing so once you've decided what you truly feel passionate about. This will depend on which values mean the most to you as well as how straightforwardly you feel you can express yourself through a particular medium.

You're a determined and inquisitive individual, but you can lose interest quickly once you've attained the knowledge, object or even the relationship you desire. All the more reason to be sure about your values and act on them (rather than the latest trends or taking action due to peer pressure), otherwise you may find yourself unfulfilled and unhappy despite being busy and productive.

As the perennial bridge between people you'll come to appreciate what's truly of value to yourself and others. You'll discover this quickly and your path resembles that of a bee—tasting nectar here and there and moving on—because you're in the process of deciding the true value of various experiences. You'll potentially earn the label of being superficial and may appear self-indulgent because not only will you deeply savour experiences, once you have what you want you'll unceremoniously move on.

You may appear to be a social butterfly, but once you identify the heart of a matter you'll prove to be one of the most loyal and understanding people imaginable because your sense of self is built on the bedrock of honesty and respect.

As a youngster you'll learn through trial and error how to apply these qualities to your life and will measure your success by what you're able to secure as your own, such as accolades, friends or possessions.

You may come from a family who is wealthy or attains possessions easily or the opposite, but once you discover what activity truly works for you you'll excel, infusing your every action with enthusiasm and joy. As an adult you're adept at earning your own living.

A chameleon at heart and a go-between, you can adapt to new environments and deliver other people's messages without changing their meaning or context. In your lifetime, you'll appreciate not only the currency of successful interactions and negotiation on a larger scale such as through trade or education, but also the currency of successful personal and intimate relationships through love, respect and tolerance.

Perspective

Curious, joyful, fast-talking, efficient, focused, interested

Talents

Quick learner, compassion, courage, mimicry, acting ability

Challenge

To find your true passion

Potential pitfalls

Procrastination, superficiality, no direction, easily influenced

Affirmation

I am true to myself and to you.

Communication

As a child you're largely chatty and inquisitive. You'll learn to express your curious and alert mind through speaking multiple languages (perhaps due to a childhood spent travelling or a bilingual parent), having a passionate interest in reading or a natural ability for writing.

As an adult you'll enjoy leading in all kinds of areas of research. You have a vast capacity for learning and disseminating information. This may have been gained through a broader education or from travel that has opened your mind to different belief systems and lifestyles.

Higher education will appeal to you unless technology becomes an increasingly attractive area to work in. Distance learning or keeping up to date with news and discoveries on electronic devices will appeal as you're always on the move. You're the true global citizen. Networking, communications, the media, technology, computers and travel will all synthesise to make you a true international resident of the global village.

You're such a fast-talker that you may need to learn to listen and try to understand both sides of a story. You may also need to learn to be tactful, particularly with people from different backgrounds or customs and within your personal relationships.

Your interest in all things foreign, otherworldly and generally different could make you hard to pin down. Being in a committed relationship may work, ideally as a long-distance or on–off arrangement, as it would fit into your packed itinerary.

You'll disappear on adventures and escapades on a whim. While you're learning the art of diplomacy through various phases in your life you may appear to be superficial in the attempt to keep everyone happy. You may also be inclined to replace tact with white lies and deceit. Ultimately you may be accused of being a trickster. When this occurs you'll learn that the fine art of communication resonates best with you when you are transparent, honest and open.

Perspective

Fast-talking, inquisitive, chameleon-like, mimic, ambivalent, persuasive, knowledgeable, may talk with hands, capable

Talents

Acuity, intelligence, eloquence, adaptability, clarity, sympathy

Challenge

To be discerning

Potential pitfalls

Anxiety, distractions, deceit, trickery, shallowness, ambivalence

Affirmation

Knowledge is invaluable. Truth comes first.

Home and family

You'll aspire to greatness in the public arena. This impulse can lead to success in the world, but once you've attained some of your goals or gained public acclaim you may find that the lustre vanishes. You will come to know that true pleasure and the richness of life lie closer to home, where your heart is.

You'll blossom on a spiritual level in an active family role. As a child your family is likely to be a large, blended or extended family. You will travel or move around a great deal. Your younger self can be flighty, possibly quick-tempered and always on the go. You'll tire out your parents.

Your life lessons are tightly bound to your family, domestic situation or property. For this reason, as an adult, you may be attracted to working within other people's homes or with their families.

As you mature you'll find that your true interests lie in spirituality or the occult, which literally means 'the hidden'. Your fulfilment lies in implementing inspired spiritual ideas and practices in your daily life—both for yourself and your family—and you'll enjoy teaching your children the many valuable lessons you'll learn in life.

You're likely to develop a social conscience and will enjoy sharing this with your family too. Through your adventures outside the home you'll come to accept the value of having a strong social identity and how important it is to integrate into the fabric of society.

Yours is a progressive personality, willing and able to embrace all of life's wonders—and dilemmas—under the one umbrella of compassion. By striving for success in the world you'll simultaneously come to appreciate that it was your free will that motivated you to succeed in the first place—not other people, society or public acclaim.

Celebrating the power of your free will motivates you to succeed. You have a natural understanding that this is what liberates you and you will eventually experience the ultimate reward: a sense of freedom and wellbeing that inspires your heart and mind. However, you will come to understand through your domestic circumstances and their attendant responsibilities that even when you exercise your free will, certain values and parameters curb what is and isn't socially acceptable. With this understanding you will come to appreciate your role in life all the more profoundly.

Perspective

Outgoing, adventurous, pioneering, family oriented at heart, attentive

Talents

Persuasive, charming, compassionate, quick-learner, adaptable

Challenge

To be fully integrated in society begins in the home.

Potential pitfalls

Lack of commitment and motivation, prevarication, uncertainty

Affirmation

My free will sets me free. My values guide me.

Creativity and life force

You have a playful personality. Even as an adult you'll enjoy a fun sense of humour, slapstick comedy and pranks. Your catch cry is 'life is what you make it' and you're determined to have a fair crack at it.

The notion that we are victims of our fate will simply not wash with you. You'll shake the notion of a bad start in life like water from a duck's back. You'll easily accept the idea that as an intelligent human being you can create your own life from start to finish, much in the same way a child creates a sandcastle—with simplicity and joy.

You're able to move with ease from just about any circumstance—from boardroom to playground—but may be hard to pin down. You constantly flit from project to project or from ideal to ideal, but once you discover what truly motivates you, you'll be hard to ignore as you pursue your aims with such dynamic ease and zeal. The trick lies in identifying what really appeals to you and not frittering away your time and energy on superficial pursuits.

Your chameleon-like character will make acting an attractive career choice, and you'll enjoy performance especially as a child. Even if you're flirtatious and in danger of being superficial or a drama queen as an adult, your absolute love of life is what makes you the popular person you are. It shines through you and your enthusiasm is infectious.

This talent, in itself, passes positive energy from person to person, much like a bee carrying pollen from flower to flower.

Whether you're attracted to music, sports, the arts or simply and dynamically being the co-creator of a large family you are a bright spark, content to enjoy all that life has to offer.

Perspective

Playful, social butterfly, engaged, dynamic, quick, easily distracted, entertaining

Talents

Art, adaptability, charm, music, mimicry, multi-skilling

Creative career

Artist, craftsperson, sportsperson, entertainer, business person, musician, comedian, actor, working with children or social services

Challenge

To stick with an interest or hobby

Potential pitfalls

Capriciousness, fickleness, egocentrism, extremism, superficiality, thrill-seeking

Affirmation

My life is what I make it.

Work and daily life

You'll give everything and everyone your full attention—until you're distracted, which is when you'll move along to the next thing without a second thought.

NOTE TO PARENTS: *from a young age, encourage this child to see a project/plan/ sandcastle through to the end.*

As an adult, you're organised and able to organise others and respond quickly to their needs at work. You like to be helpful until something or someone else grabs your attention. Your behaviour may appear to some as uncaring, but in truth you simply lose interest.

This will be a stumbling block for you at work unless you can find out early on what your true passions are. Even these are likely to change though, and you're likely to adopt new pet projects in the blink of an eye. Ultimately your true potential will be realised when you fulfil your purpose as a messenger or a go-between, and many vocations will suit this ability.

You'll also find fulfilment and happiness in seeing a project through to completion and then adding a little extra on top—the bow on the present, the word of encouragement to a child, the polite manner with strangers. It's this extra gesture that will give you the satisfaction of having done the best you could rather than having done just what was required before you sped on to the next thing.

You'll enjoy periodically up-skilling so that you remain dedicated within your chosen profession. This sense of dedication means you can go beyond the call of duty when necessary. This natural quality is best deployed early in life to avoid the distractions from what will truly fulfil you.

You live your life through your nerves and may be prone to nervous exhaustion. It's in your interest to look after your health and your nervous system in particular. Taking the time to nurture yourself will naturally appeal to you and will help you to discover your own sense of commitment and staying power. Consequently you'll appreciate your own circumstances more, which will enable you to be a more proficient communicator and worker.

Perspective

Intuitive, curious, multi-talented, multi-faceted, capable, intellectual, communicative

Talents

Versatility, wit, compassion, cleverness, ingenuity

Type of work

Journalism, communications, media, business, academia, travel, law, publishing, performance, hospitality, accountancy, insurance, psychology, trade, medical, gardening, landscaping, agriculture, science, academic, interpreter, detective, forensic scientist, teacher, builder, homemaker, interior design, life coaching, real estate

Challenge

To avoid being distracted, and becoming accustomed to going beyond the call of duty from a young age

Potential pitfalls

Seeming uncaring, insincere, superficial due to restlessness

Affirmation

I care. I'm dedicated.

Relationships

Your love of life contributes to your playful image, and yet your purpose carries a more serious message, which is one of mutual trust. You seek to inspire people around you with your enthusiasm and your immense ability to give and receive love.

In your particular quest the risk is that you become the archetypal player. You move from one person to the next within personal relationships and even in business. You may never alight long enough to sample the nectar you would discover deep inside the core of circumstances and relationships beyond everyday or superficial interactions.

You know how important you are within other people's lives and don't feel the need to accentuate it, but may not be aware of others' need to be told how much they are loved and cared for by you. As you decide to leave the obvious unsaid—or even prematurely move on from relationship to relationship—you may appear to be lacking in true devotion and even emotion, creating trust issues within your relationships.

Your vast ability to love and be loved not only makes you a bridge between yourself and others but also between groups of people, couples, and even business people. You experience a child-like thrill when you take your place as a person who connects people and ideas together as well as making connections yourself and this will motivate you.

While your true pleasure and appreciation of life comes from being connected to other people, paradoxically once you've accomplished this connectedness you're apt to leave in search of making yet another connection. If you fall into the habit of moving on you risk missing the rewards of your actions.

Instead, when you take the time to savour your personal circumstances a little longer, you'll learn to develop these deeper connections. This in itself will create a sense of stability, which will produce a harmonious cycle: the more you stay, the deeper the connections; the deeper the connection, the more you'll stay and so on.

Once you find that special someone who mirrors your own interests you'll be unable to resist the urge to learn and study the benefits and effects of a close relationship, making you a loyal—if curious—partner. Siblings will be important to you, too, and a close filial relationship such as the closeness twins develop will keep your mind—and heart— engaged and alert.

The joy and fulfilment you'll attain from having profound personal relationships will surprise even you. In this way not only will the connections you make become much more secure and profound, but so too will your own experience and enjoyment of life.

Perspective

Light-hearted, charming, sociable, fun, flirtatious, quick-witted

Talents

Communication, the art of persuasion, charm, networking, respect, analysis

Challenge

To truly immerse yourself in a relationship

Potential pitfalls

Being a player, superficiality, lack of commitment, indecision, appearing cold, uncaring, duplicity

Affirmation

I respect my feelings—and yours.

Motivation

As an outgoing, light-hearted and communicative soul you'll enjoy collaborations both in the workplace and at home. You like to share and you tend to be generous in the process, but your generosity can also get you into hot water.

As you're naturally giving, you expect people to be the same. When they're not, the more duplicitous side of your nature can emerge to manipulate and trick people to do your bidding. After all, you may reason, that would only be fair since some people don't share and they seem to expect something for nothing.

Ultimately having realistic expectations will cancel out your need to be tricky. We all have free will, which is a quality you respect. What's more, the outgoing, trusting, playful and generous side of your nature is far more appealing to other people than your tricky side. And being appealing to others is vital to you because you can't survive without constant human contact. Feeling alone is total anathema to you.

Life is not a bowl of cherries, but with your quick wit, analytical mind, humour and charm you are better equipped to negotiate life's challenges than many. If you're realistic, mutually beneficial circumstances will simply fall into place. You'll attract fair-minded, caring people especially when you express these qualities yourself. You'll know when you've found happiness because you'll be surrounded by happy people.

Perspective

Upbeat, affable, adaptable, generous, objective, sociable, playful, wilful

Talents

Sympathy, compassion, intuition, sense of fair play, smart

Challenge

To respect others' free will

Potential pitfalls

Deceit, trickery, betrayal

Affirmation

I am the best I can be. I attract like-minded people.

Seeking ...

You crave information so that you can orientate yourself in life. You'll enjoy chats with siblings and neighbours. As a youngster and as an adult travel, religion, education and even legal studies will appeal to you as they will satisfy your craving for more information.

Your life is one big lesson in the attainment of knowledge in general and the wish to gain a grip on your own slice of life. You'll pursue knowledge and experience regardless of the cost, which could make you prone to taking risks. Ultimately, you're on a quest to understand the social fabric of life—how various cultures and human interactions function and exactly what your place is within that structure, down to the detail.

As a young adult, you're unlikely to want to be tied down by geographical or domestic circumstances. You'll enjoy a career that allows you freedom of movement and relationships will be sought with like-minded, outgoing, outdoorsy types.

You'll enjoy vocations that exercise your mind and stretch you to learn new things. You're more likely to want to be an author than a journalist, a filmmaker than a TV presenter. You want the big picture and the big experience and you'll enjoy challenging yourself and entering new environments.

Curiosity can lead to mishaps, but this idea is anathema to you because you want to experience life to the extreme. Learning temperance and moderation will help you fulfil your potential, even if you initially believe that your motivation and outgoing attitude will suffer as a result. If the prospect of being careful seems challenging, then sport and physically active pursuits will help satisfy your need for speed while you keep your day-to-day activities more realistic and down-to-earth.

True happiness will result from focussing on more localised and key activities rather than skimming over the top of grandiose and far-reaching plans. You'll gain understanding by applying knowledge to your circumstances, not merely flitting over the top of them. Your sense of fulfilment will arise out of understanding the relevance and everyday application of everything you do.

Perspective

Curious, goal-oriented, outgoing, fun loving, chatty, changeable

Talents

Research, adventure, sports, goal-setting, writing

Interests

Travel, media, languages, applied science, technology, socio-cultural studies

Challenge

To understand the impact of your pursuits

Potential pitfalls

Extreme risk-taking, restlessness, fickleness, egocentrism, irresponsibility, sense of futility

Affirmation

I understand life and my role in it.

Career and direction

Life is one perpetual merry-go-round. You're constantly on the move, especially at work, and you won't stop for anyone. Yet family values and a steady domestic life—one in which you take an active role—are equally as important to you as your active public profile or career.

As a multi-talented multi-tasker you're most likely to work two jobs—or more—at once. You may even try out various careers before deciding on one particular career at middle age that suits you best. Your multi-tasking is unrivalled, and when you channel your up-tempo energy into an inspiring career or your favourite activities you'll be a success, possibly even at a young age.

You're used to being part of a team at home so you can feel disheartened when you discover that team-playing is not always feasible in the world (especially when you're starting out as a youngster). Rest assured that you'll accomplish whichever goals you set yourself in life and your inexhaustible energy will see you succeed professionally. You are adaptable, affable and amenable. You're not afraid to take the lead if need be and you'll enjoy showing that your place on your particular cog in the larger wheel is indispensable.

You have the gift of the gab and you're not afraid to use it. You'll also be admired for it and will take your place on the world stage—or within your career—with style and panache. For this reason, you may be attracted to acting as a career at some point. You'll talk ten to the dozen, and sometimes say nothing at all. People will enjoy watching you perform because whether you have something crucial to say or not, you're a fireworks display in motion.

Characteristics

Fast-moving, nervous, fidgety, affable, good company, adaptable, bright spark

Talents

Communications, negotiations, team-player, positive attitude, endearing

Type of career

Business, IT, teacher, sportsperson, management, performance, mediator, psychologist, interpreter, marketing, PR, catering, psychic, financial, law, academic, human rights, travel consultant, explorer, scientist, author, film-maker

Challenge

To focus on one task at a time

Potential pitfalls

Dissipation of energy, naivety, selfishness, idle talk

Affirmation

I accomplish my goals.

Goals, groups and humanitarianism

You will enjoy collaborating and will gain a keen sense of purpose via cooperative efforts. You may flit from one group of people, activity or club to another until you find the one that truly suits your curiosity, energy and zeal. Then you'll enjoy immersing yourself fully in your activities.

For some, this level of zeal will translate into religious or spiritual fervour, especially if you come from an intensely spiritual or religious family that has instilled the necessity for congregation in your weekly agenda.

You'll frequently find yourself right in the brouhaha of passionate discussions over political, human interest and human-rights debates. Ultimately this will lead you to develop an interest in activism within these areas. You are outspoken and clear in your intentions, making an excellent spokesperson, campaigner, debater and conversationalist.

Your wit and quirky sense of humour are an appealing side of your personality that will be appreciated by the group dynamic.

You'll find being an advocate for many people including those who are underprivileged or have no voice of their own fulfilling. Your position as an advocate is a personal one where you're able to deliver the truth where others may not have the opportunity to do so themselves.

A sense of fulfilment will arise out of being able to mobilise large numbers of people, persuading and holding discourse over important matters and seeing yourself as a bringer of light, in some sense, to others less fortunate—or less able—than you.

There is a very real risk that you remain one of life's onlookers and spectators, though, largely due to your ability to appraise situations objectively and not to join in yourself.

You'll enjoy team sports as much as individual competitions, but as you mature the arts and music will be your sanctuary. You'll enjoy large family gatherings and happiness will come from one-on-one relationships. So to establish a more balanced outlook in life, make a conscious effort to be personally engaged as this will profoundly fulfil you.

Perspective

Outspoken, adventurous, zealous, compassionate, social butterfly, jovial, fun loving, helpful

Talents

Human rights, research, interpersonal skills

Interests

Activism, politics, negotiations, diplomacy, sports, management, admin, spokesperson, promoter, campaigner, religion

Challenge

To be hands-on rather than behind-the-scenes or a spectator

Potential pitfalls

Easily distracted, detached, being an outsider/onlooker

Affirmation

I shine a light of truth for others—and for myself.

The secret you

You'll enjoy fossicking and ferreting for information or any kind of treasure. You'll enjoy searching, leafing through books and even digging up the ground if need be. You'll shine a light where no-one has looked for a long time. Sometimes your research can lead you into completely uncharted territory, and it's wise to leave a contact point or marker that will help you to resurface when you choose to.

As a child you may be constantly in hot water for following people or trends that lead you nowhere fast. As an adult you will find that research, almost to the level of forensics or even espionage, will appeal to you.

Unfortunately your impartiality and lack of valued judgement about the outcome of your research could lead you to become mercenary—keen to do others' research for them with no qualms about the consequences until it's too late and you feel that you've let both them and yourself down ethically. The temptation to work for others with no true moral compass could lead you astray, much in the same way you were led as a child into hot water by mischievous friends.

The ultimate risk is that you become detached from a significant purpose and moral investment when you're engaged in the activity you enjoy the most—researching, digging or fossicking of some sort. This leaves you vulnerable to being exploited—and exploiting others too.

Your detached stance may also lead you to become isolated. As you mature there is a principle fear that you will be an outsider. And yet, you have a natural, in-built intuitive sense—to the degree of heightened psychic ability and spiritual or religious insight—which will help warn you, and even guide you, away from detachment.

Your intuition will lead you into more pleasant pastures and you'll gain kudos, happiness and wisdom from developing your psychic abilities, either through meditation, yoga or visualisations. Your intuition will also sound warning bells about areas that are simply too deep for comfort—or too detached to be of true relevance either to you, yourself, or to your fellow human beings.

Your true purpose is to be a messenger and a go-between, so even if this involves deep research and detachment from the message itself, you are still connecting with other people and connecting people together. Relaying information can only be of benefit if it's applied in a positive way and in a positive context, so by ensuring you remain engaged in the social fabric, that also includes a moral code, you will ensure your research—and function as a messenger—is put to good use.

Characteristics
Self-contained, can be a loner, helpful, perceptive, probing, curious

Talents
Research, psychic ability, compassion, impartiality, non-judgmental

Challenge
To remain engaged in the social fabric

Potential pitfalls

Lacking in morals and values, aimless, mercenary, duplicitous, trickster

Affirmation

I am discreet.

Cancer

The practical nurturer

SITUATION

You're a caregiver. Whether you work in the caring industries (such as the health and beauty industries or in aged care) or whether you're a stay-at-home parent or a teenager responsible for a pet, you will feel content when you're caring for someone or something. Sometimes the person you must care for the most turns out to be you.

You understand that material, practical and mundane daily concerns such as work are indeed important, but they are mere stepping stones to the core of the matter— nurturing, life-affirming and loving activities that best express your true nature.

You may feel you've already scaled a high mountain in some sense either ancestrally or within your own childhood, that you've already accomplished a great deal or that you come from a family that, all things considered, is accomplished. You feel that now it's your duty, or fate, to be the provider and carer of the generations to come—beginning with your own children or children in society in general.

You may find that your circumstances in life dictate that you must change course and break from family tradition in some way. This is primarily due to your perceived need to find a better path for future generations.

A strong patriarchal model is likely to accompany your life journey. Your father will have a strong influence either on you and your generation or on generations before you. For some, the absence of a father will be the distinguishing factor, and this in itself is the marker that causes you to place so much stock on the importance of a nurturing environment, both at home and in society at large.

You're likely to follow a more matriarchal archetype in this lifetime, one in which supportive, mothering and domestic-related duties are more relevant and appealing to you than those associated with patriarchal domains such as structure, tradition, rules and regulations.

PURPOSE

Your status and position in the world are important to you, especially as you may come from a family for whom status is particularly relevant. Your path in life, though, will time and time again teach you that status, material possessions and worldly power will not satisfy you. Your emotional and spiritual wellbeing requires nurturing just as much, if not more, than your desire for status and you'll derive fulfilment from nurturing your spiritual needs and tending the needs of others.

You may find that your life takes a double role—one of responsibility, authority and ambition on the one hand and the hat of domesticity and family on the other. But you alone will know that it isn't the work you do or the status you have that nurtures your inner life—it's the other way around. The support that stems from the love in your personal life feeds and inspires everything else, including your worldly ambitions and your desire to help or nurture others.

For you, love is an intelligence. Learning all there is to know about the practical application of love and all it entails, especially its caring potential, will fuel your heart and mind and lead you to enjoy an inspired—and wise—life.

Affirmation

I nurture myself because in so doing I can nurture others.

Famous people

Michelle Obama, Neil Young, Henri Matisse, Frida Kahlo, Mia Farrow, Queen Elizabeth II, Marilyn Monroe, Prince William, Hugh Hefner, Brad Pitt, Ian Thorpe, Allen Ginsberg, Johnny Depp, Richard Burton

Your unique approach

A parent or guardian in your household will have been an authoritarian, a stickler for tradition or just plain strict, and they will have instilled in you various disciplines designed to help you plan your adult life.

As a child, discipline may have appeared excessive to you, either at home or at school, but as an adult you're able to appreciate its relevance, even if it takes you several years in your youth to establish a form of manageable self-discipline of your own.

When you mature you're likely to crave a strong partner or authoritarian figure in your life and will be attracted to such people, either at work or in your personal life. Unfortunately this situation can lead to low-level anxiety and moodiness as it merely reflects your past, and spotlights your needy self or low self-esteem that stems from this disciplinarian background.

Even though you crave a strong partner or authoritarian influence in your life, your true happiness derives from being *self*-nurturing and *self*-disciplinarian and not having to rely on someone else to provide support or boundaries. In truth you're actually unlikely to need someone else to provide structure in your life or to tell you what to do.

NOTE TO PARENTS: *avoid being overly disciplinarian with your Cancer north node child as it may backfire when they lose the ability to self-nurture.*

As an adult, you may be tempted to mother or parent a partner or spouse and be a disciplinarian yourself. Conversely you may choose a partner who appears to be nurturing, but who turns out to be domineering and who will not appreciate being parented in the relationship. These scenarios will lead to a co-dependent or passive-aggressive relationship that is clearly counter-productive to the true spirit of a relationship that flourishes on giving and receiving pure love.

Once you allow your true nurturing soul to express itself and blossom, relationships will become more rewarding and loving. Once you've mastered the art of self-nurturing you'll find that nurturing someone else will be much easier and you will enjoy giving and receiving true love—not discipline or domination. This will extend to your career as well. You'll respect an employer who treats you well far more than an employer who has draconian, outdated rules and regulations.

Once you've embraced your nurturing side you will see harsh discipline for what it is—a control mechanism. This applies to any situation or relationship whether in your personal life, at work or in the world. And from that moment on you'll enjoy the fulfilment that true care will provide not only you, but everyone you meet.

Perspective

Inclusive, talkative, caring, considerate, loving, respectful, sensitive, intuitive

Talents

Nurturance, organisational skills, an eye for practicalities

Interests

Nutrition, cookery, design, architecture, building, storytelling, homemaking

Challenge

To be self-nurturing

Potential pitfalls

Being domineering, disciplinarian, timid, anxious, moody

Affirmation

I care deeply for myself and in so doing I care for you.

Values and self-expression

As a child you may measure a successful day by how good you feel, as many children do, but as a young adult you're likely to measure success and happiness in terms of personal wealth, possessions and your status, especially as you identify easily with predominant social status symbols— we do live in a materialistic society. You'll also judge your happiness by how well you can form stable relationships.

You're naturally drawn toward environments that are regulated and formatted in some way and people who achieve power through material incentives, who structure their day or who give rewards for good behaviour. You'll value and be drawn to work within professions that are structured and conform to a 9-to-5 routine such as office duties. Financial or corporate work will appeal at some point in your life.

As you mature your needs will dictate another scenario: you may feel less satisfied by strict guidelines and by material goods and you'll begin to crave satisfaction and inspiration on a deeper, more soulful level.

You are likely to appreciate and value food, and risk seeking emotional satisfaction through food, alcohol or drugs. Under-eating and over-eating can be a form of self-expression when you're under stress, and yet you'll gain happiness by satisfying your true sense of purpose and not by satisfying your cravings or desires. You know that cravings will only get stronger if you indulge them, leading to feelings of emptiness as well as obscuring what will truly make you happy.

As you mature you'll gain a strong sense of purpose that will satisfy your soul and spiritual needs, as well as your physical needs. You'll gain strength by listening to your intuition and your keen sense of values that are humanitarian and supportive, not ego-based, controlling, rigid or materialistic. Your true values and self-esteem revolve around your principles and standards and come from your heart—you are naturally compassionate and caring.

Your success lies in being able to put form and structure to your ideals and being practical and disciplined. Your high standards and motivation, straight from your kind heart, will meet with both approval and success. This enables you to feel true satisfaction and in turn promote this feeling in your friends and community alike.

Perspective

Disciplined, helpful, supportive, ambitious, practical, humanitarian, loving, discreet, measured

Talents

Professionalism, understanding, perceptivity, wisdom, organisational skills, sense of values

Challenge

To allow your caring self to dictate your values

Potential pitfalls

Materialistic, strict, tyrannical, unloving, cold, detached

Affirmation

I let my inner caring self shine.

Communication

You'll enjoy storytelling, reading and make-believe. You're the consummate creator, enjoying the rich rewards of the creative process—imagining a concept, constructing a plan, implementing it, discussing it and seeing it come to life.

You interact primarily through your senses and emotions, obtaining information as much from your intuition as through words. Your ability to build substance out of mere concepts means you are virtually able to perform magic: you can accomplish whatever you imagine, largely through the way you communicate from your heart.

Before you get to this stage a strict, authoritative or patriarchal influence will either hold you back in your youth and early adulthood or guide you into the world of hard work. As a result of self-discipline, endurance and potentially even hardship, you'll enjoy the wonderful results that application, endurance and sheer willpower can produce.

The discipline from a parental figure may be limited to one area of your life. You may have to endure a family dynamic that is archaic or even harsh, curbing your self-expression and even the way you communicate. But you're also likely to experience eye-opening adventures as a youth through travel, communication and religious, legal or cultural customs (or even restrictions for some), which will nourish your fertile imagination. An interest in foreign languages, fables and myths will delight your imagination.

Combined with iron-willed self-discipline, you have the seedbed for huge potential. Your wonderful impressions, ideas, notions, sensory perceptions, stories and hopes have the potential to bloom by way of your ability to structure, plan, relate information and stories and attain goals.

Such inspiration combined with structure and self-discipline spells inordinate creative potential. With the imagination to dream and the organisational skills to back up your ideas from inception to completion you can make your dreams come true. You're the designer of your future.

You will respond intuitively to stimuli, but you also risk being easily influenced so it's important to choose your activities and company carefully. You tend to mirror people's behaviour and messages, both verbal and non-verbal. Calming pursuits such as meditation and swimming will soothe your gentle soul and lead you to deeper insights into how to create happiness in your own life and the world.

Perspective

Imaginative, creative, talkative, inquisitive, curious, composed, gentle, kind

Talents

Research, storytelling, speaking, intuition, finesse, logistics

Challenge

To use your iron will to achieve your goals.

Potential pitfalls

Over-sensitivity, vulnerability, delusions, irrationality

Affirmation

I can create what I believe and wish for

Home and family

Your family, home and property are the bedrock of your existence. With a stable, secure and proud background to enjoy and live up to as a child, as an adult you desire in turn to provide the same. Family is your foundation.

As a youngster, proving yourself out there in the big wide world will appeal.

You'll be encouraged to do so through a strong patriarchal figure at the helm of your family (at least on one side of the family). For some, the absence of a strong family home or direction will provide the motivation to succeed as an adult at home and work as you attempt to attain the stability and security you lacked as a child.

You may feel the pressure to live up to certain standards and attain a level of status through your work, career and profile, yet your true sense of purpose and fulfilment will be derived from creating a happy family and a marvellous home life. As a nurturer, fulfilment comes from being kind, gentle and protective.

You may discover that your life will involve someone who is in need of special care. When this is the case you may secretly hanker after worldly success, but feel you're being held back by the demands of your family circumstances.

Still you will discover that your true satisfaction and heart's content lies in being useful, and applying your wisdom to practical, everyday family circumstances. If you're duty-bound to care for someone in your home or family, you will find feelings of fulfilment as you enjoy being loving.

You will be attracted to building homes and residential or commercial structures in many ways—from bricklaying to town planning or from building a safe home to helping build happy family dynamics for yourself and others.

The future you build for yourself and those you love will come full circle as the caring seeds you sow will germinate and return to the collective family home via your intention to spread love and nurturing in the world. In this way, the love and care you give will return to you one-hundred fold.

Perspective

Compassionate, considerate, protective, inventive, imaginative, proud, kind, gentle

Talents

Productivity, drive, motivation, self-discipline, helpfulness, confidence

Challenge

To love yourself

Potential pitfalls

Self-effacing, self-sacrificing, insecure, over-sensitive

Affirmation

In caring for myself, I care for others. My family comes first.

Creativity and life force

You'll create your own happiness. You were born with the building blocks of a successful life and you'll be aware from a young age that it's your job to put them to good use and create some kind of meaningful, dynamic and life-affirming structure.

The discipline you derive from toeing the line within certain institutions as a young adult will help you understand how you truly feel about being in the group dynamic. As an adult your collaborative projects with groups, organisations and humanitarian activities will furnish you with all kinds of opportunities to excel as an active cog within a bigger social wheel. You're able to assert yourself within a social mechanism and you're happy to work with corporate and group dynamics. A talented and inspired speaker and communicator, you are able to embellish a smart word with either a turn of phrase or gesture, which will help swing things your way.

Essentially a dreamer, your capacity to fuel your imagination with ideas and motivation will see you emerge as a true frontrunner in any activity you feel inspired to undertake, especially within group endeavours and humanitarian pursuits.

You're the definitive creative artist, able to turn your hand to artistic representation because you're aware that the creative process mirrors the process you undergo every day: to create a happy life.

As you mature you will come to understand this process more deeply. Your work within the group dynamic will be all the more urgent and fruitful because those you work with personally and professionally will provide the creative seedbed for your—and their—future potential.

Perspective

Creative, loving, gentle, attentive, playful, talkative, innovative, warm

Talents

Art, music, psychic ability, collaboration, design, swimming, acting, public speaking

Creative career

Actor, corporate, humanitarian, sports, arts, construction, writer

Challenge

To infuse every day with inspiration

Potential pitfalls

Rigidity, strictness, overly structured, fanciful, distracted, preoccupied, distant, melancholic

Affirmation

I'm a creator. I build a happy life.

Work and daily life

You're happy when you've pleased someone, and you'll learn that you're more appreciated in society when you do something that pleases someone else. The pitfall is that you can serve others regardless of moral context, leaving yourself open to exploitation especially within the workplace.

You'll feel that your ultimate goal is to be helpful. This can stem from a domineering parent, cultural structure or institutional regime that placed restrictions—or none at all—on the amount of pleasure you were allowed in your childhood.

As a youngster, without strict guidelines you can feel self-conscious and unable to function. You may also risk becoming rebellious or amoral as a young adult when you leave home and your daily routine allows you freedom of movement.

As you mature and become aware that your needs can be attained yourself, without strict guidelines, you'll learn that while great pleasure can come from pleasing others your first obligation must be to yourself, if only for peace of mind.

Jobs in the health and social sectors will appeal to you as potential vehicles to convey your own particular brand of caring. Involvement in de-cluttering, cleaning and clearing, in care-giving facilities or gardening, landscaping and volunteer work will all appeal to your sensitive, giving nature. Working within a family business is another possibility.

You're a talented storyteller and relating stories through images such as photography and film will entice. You may be particularly attracted to writing, performance and theatre.

During many phases of your life you may be loaded down by responsibility and duty, but you'll know that your first responsibility is to yourself. When you serve your higher self and only the highest and noblest causes at work and in your daily life, you'll enjoy fulfilling your purpose serving and pleasing other people all the more fully and completely.

Perspective

Amiable, compliant, self-effacing, humble, sensitive, kind, moderate

Talents

Diligence, organisational skills, instinct, practicalities, intuition, helpfulness, calmness, spirituality

Type of work

Institutional care-giving, health, veterinarian, refuge worker, landscape gardening, hospitality/food, beauty industry, public services, military, housekeeping, financial, family business, home care, family support, property realtor, architect, builder, midwife, writer, film, theatre, voluntary organisations

Challenge
To serve your higher purpose

Potential pitfalls
Being easily led and exploited, subservient, vulnerable, amoral, stubborn

Affirmation
I respond to the highest calling. It fulfils me at the deepest level.

Relationships

You'll feel fulfilled through happy relationships, but may believe at first that true fulfilment will come from status and money. You'll soon realise that when you feel happy at home and within your relationships you'll feel happy in all other areas of your life too.

As a child, a father figure was likely placed on a pedestal due to his absence or strictness at home. You pined for love when one parent or more was absent. As a result you seek stability in your relationships above all else. You may even attempt to live your life through your need to be under someone's wing and be tempted to marry for stability as well as prestige.

In turn you can seek to nurture or smother the people in your relationships, which could tip the scales into co-dependency. Paradoxically, your need for happy relationships can lead to clinginess, secrecy and manipulation.

You may become easily lost in your emotions and those of others. If you've had a bad day it's possibly because someone said or did something to upset you. You take it personally and dwell for hours over a word that was spoken in haste.

You'll gain a sense of purpose by asserting your ability to love yourself and understanding that in order to give and receive love fully, your own happiness must come from within and not from someone else. You'll feel fulfilled from learning to stand tall against the wind and not bend every time there's a breeze. To give and receive love demands a whole and stable heart—and you have this, if you stop and listen.

In your professional relationships you'll enjoy finding out how other people tick and sharing your wisdom about relationships as every true nurturer does. Studying psychology, human behaviour and science and romantic literature will appeal to you too. You'll use this knowledge to support your everyday relationships.

When you discover your own whole heart, your neediness and desire for closeness and security within relationships will diminish. In its place a mutual understanding will blossom between you and those close to you. You will stand tall and bold, secure in your self while still being receptive and caring of others.

Meditation and yoga will help you reach your inner light of peace and guidance.

Perspective

Loving, wanting to please, tender, instinctive, motherly/fatherly, attentive, sensitive

Talents

Understanding, sympathy, intuition, nurturance, generosity

Challenge

To give and receive love equally

Potential pitfalls

Clingy, needy, secretive or guarded, condescending, hypersensitive, lacking in self-esteem, dependent

Affirmation

I am beautiful. I love you, and my neediness will not predominate.

Motivation

You are insightful with a strong will and you'll learn to use this ability from a young age. Your understanding of others and yourself is invaluable, and you are motivated by your feelings, emotions and sensations.

You will find a way through life by learning to trust a deeper understanding of its daily rhythms as opposed to running your life by society's rules and out-dated traditions. Being the sensitive person you are you may feel that your gifts cannot be applied in daily life or that you are not respected for them, or that you cannot charge for your insights. This belief is clearly de-motivating.

As you mature you will find that your insight, understanding, sensitivity and intuition are valuable and you will be well remunerated, especially if you believe in yourself and follow your hunches. You'll enjoy researching interesting and offbeat subjects such as psychic phenomena, emotional trauma and deep mysteries such as near-death experiences or death itself.

You will have a natural insight into the depths of the human mind and soul, so psychological research will appeal to you. You'll gain fulfilment from being independent and using your gifts, and you'll soon learn to express many of your skills and talents.

Yet you have a propensity to play second fiddle due to the misguided belief that your gifts come a poor second to those of more powerful, charming or logical people. You're naturally attracted to strong-willed and domineering types, and this contributes to your propensity to undersell yourself not only at work, but also in your personal life.

When you do put your unique gifts to good use, especially within collaborative efforts, you'll attain your goals due to your iron will. Your determination requires you to stand tall and prove that your unique caring abilities and emotional insights are as important as other qualities deemed more important by society.

In so doing you will not only grow spiritually, but you will also add invaluable input to the bigger social picture, which will benefit everyone. This in itself will be a fulfilling outcome as you are essentially a giving and considerate individual—one who will find giving much more rewarding once you've attained a strong, independent position that allows you to take your stand and then give all the more.

Perspective
Insightful, perspicacious, practical, inquisitive, intuitive, inspired

Talents
Discernment, psychic ability, generosity, empathy, initiative, determination

Challenge

To assert yourself

Potential pitfalls

Self-pity, self-effacement, delusions, inferiority complex

Affirmation

My gifts are valuable. I use them to help myself and others.

Seeking . . .

You're seeking inspiration and deep emotional peace. When you pursue materialistic tokens, status or prestigious relationships, what you're really looking for is peace in your heart, which only true love can bring. To find this, you'll study human emotions, sensations and impressions, often unconsciously, as this is the way you assimilate knowledge and seek to understand life.

Like all children you learn about your environment initially through sensory perception, although you tend to soak up emotional undercurrents more readily than most. As an adult you learn through your intuition, experience and hands-on, step-by-step practical means almost as if via osmosis.

People who know this gentler, sensitive side of you may be surprised when you express your adventurous, gung-ho personality, which can manifest spontaneously and sporadically. It can also make you remarkably courageous—if not impulsive—about the way you approach new experiences and forge ahead on your own particular learning curve.

You are an anomaly because the way you seek what you're looking for may be quite unexpected—sometimes gentle and loving yet at other times adventurous and eccentric. You have an in-built spiritual and religious wisdom balanced with a practical understanding of the necessity to believe in something greater than anything your five senses can reveal.

As a child your learning is methodical and practical, underpinned as it is with a deeper perceptivity than most children. You may also display a strong sixth sense that you'll enjoy using, and which will be a valuable tool later in life.

Even though your climb to the top of a mountain as an adult may be arduous, through your unique combination of methodical step-by-step planning and an exceptional knack of simply knowing what to expect you'll always get to the summit.

You have compassion for people from different cultures and beliefs and will enjoy learning about how other belief systems work.

You may lack staying power as you yourself are a changeable character and can easily lose interest and be led astray into other ventures. As you mature you will seek the inner workings and bottom-line reasoning before you can commit to a course of action, precisely because you realise you are so easily led and extremely receptive to persuasion and suggestion.

Your true gift is that you just know a great deal in life. This is something you can rely on and will be glad of.

Your sixth sense is your particular guiding light, especially when you put your neck out to learn about life's mysteries. Your passion for learning will unveil all manner of delights, and you'll find what you've been looking for isn't too far away after all. In fact love and peace are right inside you.

Perspective
Open-minded, sensitive, articulate, impulsive, garrulous, dreamy

Talents
Perception, diligence, methodology, instinct, sixth sense

Interests
Poetry, academia, nutrition, religion, spirituality, psychic phenomena

Challenge
To find inner peace

Potential pitfalls
Easily influenced, changeability, extreme risk-taking, impulsiveness, moodiness

Affirmation

I trust my intuition. It connects me with the divine.

Career and direction

Fulfilment in your life will result from trusting in your own power and life's journey as opposed to seeking power outside yourself. As a young adult you're likely to worry about stability, status and career, and you'll be intent on building a strong profile by pursuing career goals and material success.

If you let go of your expectations a little and trust in the process itself you'll find that enjoying and understanding the wonder of life is just as rewarding, if not more rewarding, than the pursuit and accumulation of status symbols and success in the world alone.

Clearly material stability is important in life, but as you mature your compassion will lead you into areas that do not represent traditional values—areas where you can't measure success in a traditional way, where you must trust that you're being guided for the best possible reasons; to come closer to what truly enriches you on a soul level as opposed to a material level.

As a caring individual you'll feel your purpose is best served by understanding the reason for creation itself and the mysteries of life. You'll feel content understanding the spark of life and the natural human impulse to feather your own nest through nurturing and mutual support. Your role as a parent, guardian and nurturer will be significant, in particular your role as a provider of care and love—rather than just the provider of material wealth and status.

Your career is likely to involve some form of care-giving such as health care, nutritional advice or even the provision of food and shelter. If you don't have children of your own, as a powerfully supportive figure you'll enjoy providing sustenance to other people's families.

You're an inspired and dreamy individual, able to imagine a life very different to the mundane nine to five. You may begin your working life within a strict nine-to-five regime, but as you mature you'll increasingly work hours and schedules that suit you, your ideas or your family more.

You are goal-oriented and your determination will see to it that you attain the status you crave in life. You will be admired for your contribution to others' wellbeing at work and at home, as well as to your community and neighbourhood as a whole.

Perspective

Goal-oriented, self-supportive, acquisitive and craving status when young

Talents

Provider of shelter, care, understanding, insight, efficiency

Type of career

Care-giving, food industry, film industry, management, mediator, counsellor, guide, PR, publicity, psychology, physiotherapy, massage, speech pathology, psychotherapy, dream analysis, financial, taxation, irrigator, farmer, adventurer, writer, communicator, publishing, academic, oceanographer, fisherman, philanthropy

Challenge

To trust your power.

Potential pitfalls

Materialism, mood swings, ambivalence, indiscretion, fear of failure

Affirmation

I create a cycle of caring that comes right back to me.

Goals, groups and humanitarianism

While you have a tendency to go solo or at least isolate yourself a little, you do enjoy socialising and networking. You have a natural empathy for people and a deeper understanding of the group dynamic than many of your peers, which enables you to take part all the more thoroughly.

You will fulfil your purpose thoroughly and with a great deal of satisfaction by integrating into group ventures, and you'll enjoy seeing projects take shape in the group dynamic. Theatrical presentations, musical and dance workshops will allow your inner light to shine.

You'll also enjoy following a story or a thread from start to finish, being thoroughly engaged as the project unfolds. You learn new activities effortlessly, but can be easily led. Choose what will suit you best by doing some research first and continually monitor how happy you are.

You're a naturally compassionate person and will enjoy working for a charity as you have the motivation to work in a team for a good cause and the benefit of all. Healing ventures will also appeal to you and you'll experience true satisfaction from feeling that you've helped in some way, that you've lightened someone's load or fulfilled someone else's dreams. This, in turn, will fulfil your own dreams. You're the practical nurturer.

Perspective

Team player, reasonable, sensible, intuitive, humanitarian, enthusiastic, disciplined

Talents

Cooperation, empathy, organisation, compassion, planning

Interests

Team-playing games, music, publishing, humanitarian, charity, reading, family dynamics, nutrition, theatre, writing, philanthropy

Challenge

To go with the flow without being led astray.

Potential pitfalls

Easily influenced, loneliness, isolation, staidness, stubbornness, timidity, retiring

Affirmation

Wishes do come true.

The secret you

You're willing to put yourself at other peoples' beck and call, yet you're hard to pin down. People who get close to you may find that your motives are difficult to ascertain, and that you're hard to understand.

You possess a natural reserve that can border on aloofness at best, and mistrust or unwillingness to integrate at worst. The secret you is truly protective of your own vulnerabilities and this can lead to a reluctance to try new experiences and learn.

You have a soft centre, and may therefore be reluctant to let anyone get close to you. You also have a hard shell and a tendency to be secretive and unwilling to step into the light. If you were to face new events and people with the gentleness and sensitivity you possess deep inside, you'd step into a rich wonderland in which being sensitive leads to strength and being vulnerable and gentle leads to courage and opportunity. This in turn will place you in a better position to help others, which is what truly fulfils you.

You're able to work hard, and your strong work ethic can lead you to over-work so you must avoid exhaustion. With a deep empathy for and understanding of people who suffer, you may be drawn towards work in which you protect or support the underprivileged. Fulfilment in your life will come from avoiding feeling that you yourself are underprivileged or a victim in some sense.

You are strong, but if you feel you are vulnerable self-nurture is a skill you must learn. Without being able to self-nurture you risk bending to other people's demands and becoming ever more vulnerable. By learning this skill you'll see yourself in a strong position to help others.

You are sensitive and may feel during certain phases in your life that you're vulnerable, easily tricked or taken advantage of. You may fear that you will be engulfed in a storm of feelings that will be difficult to navigate. You may also be afraid of being alone. Ironically that fear itself could thicken the protective shell around you and seal you off from accepting love—and you really will risk being alone. Thankfully you're aware of your sturdy backbone and strong sense of self, and protected by your own sense of self-preservation.

Your predilection for helping and nurturing people less fortunate than you dictates by the law of karma that you will be nurtured in turn during various phases in your life, and that you will be supported in everything you do, especially when you trust that this is indeed so. When you believe this you'll be in an even stronger position to support and protect the people you feel need your help because you will be ever more capable of helping yourself—and being the practical nurturer you truly are.

Characteristics
Sensitive, aloof, secretive, quiet, cool, moody, vulnerable, placid

Talents
Nurturing, empathetic, psychic ability, healing, helpful, considerate

Challenge
To be self-supporting

Potential pitfalls
Fear of being alone, aloofness, haughtiness, hardness, mistrustfulness, feelings of vulnerability or being unappreciated, overtly emotional

Affirmation
I am cared for and appreciated.

Leo

The crusading adventurer

SITUATION

You're an idealist, a visionary and an initiator—but you can act up too! You're a drama magnet, the centre of every situation. You're generous, fun-loving, giving, quirky, proud, attractor of the opposite sex and a real go-getter. Did I mention you're also fun to be with and charming? And you love to read about yourself, so sit back ...

You love to back a cause, and would consider yourself a humanitarian. You love to understand the inner and outer workings of the universe and the people within it. Those who know you may quibble with this as your self-absorption can border on selfishness (in their eyes only, of course, not yours). So how could you possibly be a humanitarian?

You'll gain kudos by consciously dispelling the idea that you're egocentric. And you'll gain advantage by making a strong distinction between being positive and being self-involved. Your confidence and positive attitude will automatically augment your sense of purpose, propelling you onwards and upwards. It's this trait, more so than your tendency to be proud or self-indulgent, which is the root of your success.

And in so doing you'll develop your assertiveness and self-sufficiency. If you put yourself in a better position to share the many gifts you have, can you be called self-centred? You're an initiator, a provider and a compassionate advocate of progressive ideas and values.

Purpose

You're the king or queen of the jungle. Recognising that you are indeed fabulous could be hard work though. How will you live up to everyone's expectations once you've revealed how truly magnificent you are? And how can you possibly live up to the high benchmark you've set yourself? By leading from your heart, by being a compassionate leader, an adventurer who enjoys promoting new and exciting ideas that not only validate your position but also serve to light up other people's lives too.

You're constantly in the limelight but as a youngster you may be happier hiding your light in the anonymity of groups and organisations, especially since this will help you avoid being called selfish.

You're motivated to back important causes and to campaign significant issues. You're a swashbuckling, blustering eccentric at heart and self-fulfilment will motivate you, principally because you'll see that by backing your own horse you're also backing everyone else's and creating better circumstances all around.

You'll gladly go where no-one else has been before, and you're happy to be at the forefront of innovation. You'll crusade new ideas and shed light on ventures which other, more faint-hearted characters wouldn't dare consider.

Your happiness radiates from you like the sun; you're very much the centre of your own universe. This is purely because you know that you create your own happiness, and this in turn shines on everyone else whose lives revolve around yours.

Your family will be important to you and, more precisely, your role within it as the kingpin. This position could be the source of considerable drama too. Being the centre of everyone's universe comes with its attendant responsibilities. Rise to these and you'll scale new heights. You'll also gain the respect you so dearly desire and deserve.

Affirmation

I create my happiness. I make my life—and yours—wonderful.

Famous people

K D Lang, Robert Altman, Lauren Bacall, Marcel Duchamp, William Blake, Barack Obama, Princess Diana, Jimmy Page, Jim Carrey, Dick Smith, Roger Federer, Jim Morrison, George Harrison, Billie Jean King

Your unique approach

You lead from the head and follow with your heart, but as you grow older this will reverse. When your intuition, common sense and mind work together as one you have an unprecedented lust for life and are passionately motivated to succeed. Finding the balance between your head (rational thoughts) and your heart (compassion, intuition and love) will be a major theme in your life as you may be tempted to act irrationally if you don't use all these faculties.

Through different periods of your life you're likely to think only with your head, and at other times only with your heart. But when you combine your head and your heart you have access to enlightened values and insight and will enjoy seeking new ideas and ways to put truly extraordinary projects into action.

You may be attracted to quirky or unusual partners, both in your personal life and in business, and would like to be progressive in your relationships. You may be attracted to an unusual line of work, which you will perceive as simply interesting. All things cutting edge will appeal as you like to feel you're blazing a trail and being explorative.

Your unreserved pride can be perceived as arrogance, and may also cause you to be blind to others' points of view until you begin to listen to your heart. You are a supremely compassionate person and your need for happy relationships and family will go some way toward preventing you from being led too much by your mind. Your love of family and intimacy will also curb selfishness.

You're a born leader, outgoing, dazzling and energetic. Coming from the centre-of-the universe mould you'll find putting others ahead of yourself difficult, preferring instead to be admired for your own abilities. Yet instinctively you already put others ahead of yourself through your love for your family and friends.

You have a lion's heart, and you'll let it shine. Mix this with your enlightened humanitarian values and your desire to seek the truth and you'll champion a bright and brave future indeed.

Perspective

Outgoing, can be oddball, dramatic, proud, upbeat, unusual, energetic

Talents

Can link your head and your heart, humanitarian, supportive, big-hearted

Interests

Sports, theatrical, entertainment, taking the lead, politics

Challenge

To see other people's points of view

Potential pitfalls

Arrogance, self-centredness, egotism, irrationality, selfishness

Affirmation

I am all that I want to be because I lead from the heart.

Values and self-expression

You let your light shine. You're clearly an individual, and you're not afraid to express your opinions, which may be eccentric or before their time. You are also adept at forging close ties. You have high ideals, and will align yourself closely with certain values and principles.

As a child you'll place particular value on your toys and can be picky about your food. Yet at times you are just the opposite: a big eater and generous with your possessions (and those of others).

Your family background may dictate that your values and customs differ to the norm. From a young age you'll have the opportunity to compare your circumstances with those that are radically different. You'll learn that happiness, values and customs may appear to be relative but that core human values come from the heart—not status, environment or customs.

The concept of ownership and possessions will be extremely relevant because your background will dictate that you have different values and therefore different possessions to many people around you. You may grow up being particularly generous—or just the opposite. What's yours is mine may be an attitude that follows you into adulthood (and one that will be swathed in humanitarian rhetoric). But secretly you may find sharing difficult, and as a result relationships may suffer from your preoccupation with—or lack of understanding of—the concept of sharing.

As you mature the value you place on life itself will become all-important, and loyal relationships will reign. Truly humanitarian endeavours such as charity work will set your heart alight. This in turn will help you to avoid succumbing to greed, and it will enable you to learn how to share and share alike. This will encourage you to form relationships based on equality and fairness.

You can excel in the life you choose especially if you follow your true interests, which you will discover by listening to your heart. Your niche in life is likely to be unusual, or in some way socially ground-breaking.

In sharing the rewards you'll gain in life with those close to you, you'll fulfil your potential as a dynamic, generous and loyal adventurer.

Perspective

Dynamic, humanitarian, compassionate, practical, progressive, independent, eccentric

Talents

Positive, proactive, goal-getting, generous, set a good example

Challenge

To learn to share and accept

Potential pitfalls

Greed, hoarding, miserliness, conceit

Affirmation

Love has the highest value. It makes me strong.

Communication

As a child you're bubbly and effervescent. Very little will hold you back. You're likely to be an outgoing toddler, and able to hold your ground in a crowd. You'll have high energy levels, and could leave others behind in the wake of your considerable energy. If you're born shy this natural reserve will diminish as you mature—you'll find true fulfilment through your ability to express yourself in dramatic and creative ways.

As an adult you'll be comfortable with verbal debates, public speaking, campaigns and any form of verbal presentation. Being in the limelight will appeal. You'll enjoy expressing your unique values and insights, effectively helping to bring about acceptance and tolerance.

You feel naturally that you have important information and insights to relay. The entertainment or media businesses will appeal to you as they are modalities where your voice will be heard and your face seen. Your humanitarian streak will ensure you keep your message positive, although your desire for the limelight and your dramatic delivery could cause you to forego principles in favour of creating spectacles or drama at some point in your life.

In your eagerness to get your message across you tend to dive without forethought into circumstances and speech. You may stumble over words in an attempt to get one step ahead of your thought process.

New challenges will present worthy adversaries for you, and you'll feel driven to keep up to date with the latest news and developments. Your passion for having your finger on the pulse will guarantee you don't rush headlong into areas you're unsure of.

You're brave, a true explorer and you lead with your heart. To ensure your mind isn't too far behind you'll benefit from regular reality checks that will keep you focused on your humanitarian goals rather than on satisfying your ego.

You have a tendency to be misled by grandiose plans and projects that border on the eccentric. Yet if you tune into the side of your personality that thrives on admiration, and therefore the approval of your peers, you'll keep within the bounds of reality and social norms. That is as long as your ego and pride don't get the better of you. Your projects, when kept within the bounds of reality, will be truly grand.

Perspective

Outspoken, eccentric, humanitarian undertone, impulsive, egocentric, positive, a real go-getter, adventurous, dynamic

Talents

Writing, entertainment, blogging, web engineer, technical or film work, sales, negotiations, PR, marketing, IT

Challenge

To keep communications real

Potential pitfalls

Pride, boastfulness, recklessness

Affirmation

My voice changes the world.

Home and family

You enjoy creature comforts, especially at home. After all, the king or queen of the jungle needs a castle and your home will be as impressive as if you were royalty. You're even likely to have regal bearing, preferring to walk the walk not just talk the talk!

You'll do what you must to retain your position in the centre of your world, your family's and of your household. To your mind, that's how it should be! You know your own worth and are likely to be respected—in your own home, at least. You may have an unusual family background or were born into a position others may envy. You feel that the love you have for your family is reciprocated.

This attitude will shine into the world, but life's various challenges (at work, for example) may show that not everyone shares your high opinion of yourself, and this can be humbling, naturally.

As a child you may suffer feelings of inferiority until you realise that criticism isn't necessarily something you must agree with. Instead, others' criticism may simply result from them mistaking your humility for incapability. You may therefore be treated as less able until, with maturity, you learn to express yourself more assertively.

> NOTE TO PARENTS: *teaching your child the difference between humility and inferiority from a young age will help these children feel self-confident, even in the face of the many hurdles they'll negotiate.*

You'll become more self-aware and comfortable with yourself as you mature. Your home and family do represent your kingdom and will provide you with a majestic setting of many comforts. You may even have a favourite chair, which could appear throne-like!

The perennial homemaker, as a working adult you may also be attracted to building, architecture, interior design and anything to do with domestic or family matters. You will lead in these areas and comfort and style will be a feature. You'll succeed in bringing attention to the validity of various models that show what makes a family a success, and what makes a house a home.

As you're naturally comfortable taking your seemingly rightful role at the helm of your home and family, this attitude will accompany you throughout your life. And make no mistake: your hubris will not be mistaken for arrogance at home where, to those who love you, you'll resemble a large cat—always happy to purr in front of the fireplace of your own making.

Perspective

Proud, authoritarian, enthusiastic, altruistic, appreciative of comfort and quality, graceful, noble, majestic

Talents

Good provider, protective, natural leader, inspirational

Challenge

To be powerful yet unassuming

Potential pitfalls

Domineering, tyrannical, superiority/inferiority complex, arrogance, self–serving, extreme humility

Affirmation

I am strong. I am courageous. I am humble. I am modest.

Creativity and life force

You're a creative and imaginative individual and have the energy and determination to see your projects and endeavours through to completion whether you decide to create a family, an empire or a successful career. This is largely because of your strength of conviction and keen mind. You also have the creativity and motivation to put your ideas and options to good use, seeing projects through to completion in quirky, original and often groundbreaking ways.

Partly due to your strong role in the family dynamic, you're innately comfortable collaborating with others and will naturally enjoy club and group activities. More challenging is the fact that you'll feel propelled towards the number one position, and to sing your own, independent song, which some people will take exception to.

You will be put in the spotlight at various points in your life, and once you gain self-confidence you can truly shine in whichever arena you choose. Your courage, true compassion and love of life will take you on your dance towards success and you'll be guided towards a powerful kingdom only you know how to reign in.

You're a natural-born performer, and you'll be attracted to the limelight like a moth to a flame. Once you're the centre of attention you'll assume the place of a light bearer, and you'll draw people towards you. Yet you're unlikely to be driven towards prominent positions or even fame by pure ego or self-satisfaction, but rather by the thrill of being able to express yourself and the enjoyment of feeling valued (and admired) by your peers. This is largely because you're motivated not by vanity or superficial honours, but by an incredibly strong life force and your celebration of this in all its forms.

If you do not express your powerful sense of creativity, you can resort to extreme thrill-seeking behaviour such as gambling and other financial risk-taking. Team sports and individual sporting events are an ideal way to channel your excess energy into harmless activities. At some point extreme sports may appeal too.

Your creativity and dynamism will bring people together in wonderment, admiration and gratitude that you had the boldness, enthusiasm and strength (and a little quirkiness) to open your heart— and ideas—to them.

Perspective

Feisty, family-loving, child-like, fun-loving, imaginative, eccentric

Talents

Uplifting, entertaining, humorous, loving, creative

Creative career

Entertainment, sports, performance, self-promotion, blogging, inventions

Challenge

To put your unique talents to good use with constructive activities

Potential pitfalls

Risk-taking, narcissism, vulgarity, carelessness, gambling

Affirmation

I create the life I imagine. It is beautiful and filled with love.

Work and daily life

Your considerable energy levels will help you through gruelling schedules. Even though you have a keen eye for detail and can be pedantic (both as a school child and as a mature worker), you may feel the need to rush things in order to get them done, partly due to your enthusiasm.

You may even feel that you've come from a background of, or that you have a distant memory of, being confined, censored, restricted or limited in some way, and so you feel you must rush in case the opportunity to act and speak up vanishes as quickly as it materialised.

As such you may appear domineering, impatient or even superior as you go about your daily business with urgency. It's in your interest to choose your moment to speak, and your words, carefully, especially as the messages you generally have are positive. You have an innate desire to help people, but you can gloss over details in favour of the bigger picture and in turn diminish the vastly positive effect your speech, actions and intentions have.

You may find your work entails bringing to light unusual or unprecedented standards or ideas. You may be pushed into the limelight as you follow your interests and will be attracted to technology, design, inventions, IT and new-age products as you like to be at the at the forefront of cutting-edge ideas.

You have high ideals and will be attracted to implementing them through your work in practical ways that also highlight particular issues or causes. You are not afraid to fight for your rights and beliefs—and not necessarily just yours. You have a talent for tuning in to the zeitgeist and expressing other people's feelings and beliefs on their behalf.

As you mature you'll enjoy being a powerhouse at work. You'll enjoy being productive and cooperative and the sense of freedom you get from feeling you're being heard and understood. You like being useful in your daily life even if you must step outside your comfort zone.

You can attain a truly remarkable sense of purpose through your daily life and work, especially if you accept challenges, express your heartfelt ideas and keep an eye on the details.

Perspective

Energetic, purposeful, inclusive, supportive, compelling, helpful, enthusiastic, gutsy

Talents

Understanding, quick wit, conversationalist, optimism, enterprising, willing to help

Type of work

Business, entertainment, food industry, insurance industry, building industry, architect, engineer, politician, sports, new age, social media, gambling

Challenge

To channel your high energy into productive pursuits

Potential pitfalls

Restlessness, eccentricity, self-serving, superficiality

Affirmation

I am free to express new ideas.

Relationships

You're an enthusiastic and outgoing person who loves to socialise. You may be drawn to oddball characters as they pique your interests and satisfy your need to be entertained—and to be entertaining yourself. Eccentric people may attract you by virtue of their evident lack of inhibitions. You enjoy sharing a common strength of character and unbridled lust for life.

You're comfortable in intimate relationships, and being a part of collaborative efforts. You may see relationships as a worthy creative pursuit, one where the energy that two people share is far greater than what you, on your own, can muster.

For you the cornerstone of all relationships is respect, and you command—and demand—respect and admiration at work and home. You risk forgetting, though, that respect is a two-way street. In your eagerness, generosity and desire to be happy, you may forget that your own show of respect will be welcome and mutually beneficial.

In your natural exuberance you may (mostly unintentionally) risk upsetting the equilibrium of a fair and equal relationship. This can result in partners (both business and personal) feeling undervalued and less than equal with you. Your natural command and leadership qualities are often seen as domineering and may appear rude and disrespectful.

While yours is a fun-loving and generous soul, and you are eager to please and to be pleased, a measure of fair-play must always be uppermost in your mind. You must be willing to meet people halfway or you risk being seen as self-centred and losing what you seek to achieve: happy relationships.

Attaining happy relationships is, nevertheless, simple for you. You're a naturally pleasant, generally honest, pleasing and easy-to-please character: one of life's true nice guys. Let your true light shine.

Perspective

Vivacious, happy, oddball, generous, commands respect, self-confident, respectful, eager to please

Talents

Networking, socialising, initiating projects

Challenge

To achieve fair-play

Potential pitfalls

Self-centred, easily distracted, lack of respect, impudent

Affirmation

I share my happiness.

Motivation

You're motivated by your own dynamic love of life and your appreciation of all it entails, including its mysteries. You have more resourcefulness than meets the eye, but you're happier projecting your fun-loving side than your private thoughts, at least until you know someone well enough to reveal your deeper self.

Your adventurous approach to life will motivate you to leave your comfort zone and, on occasion, you'll be forced to take a risk, make a tough call or even gamble to achieve your greatest accomplishments. As a result you must be versatile, ready and willing to learn new ideas in your search to conquer new frontiers.

You're equally at home discussing finances as you are astrology, and as happy investing time in the local circus as you are investing money in garden produce. You have an open mind and it is this characteristic that truly motivates you to express your resourcefulness and the dynamic hero(ine) within.

Your genuine interest in every area of life means you're rarely bigoted in your views, unless you've been misled by negative ideas. People will naturally wish to consult you because your broad-minded, upbeat and individualistic take on events is not only refreshing, it's also well-informed.

Your high level of tolerance and acceptance gained through your curiosity motivates you to socialise across various socio-economic and cultural strata. While your attraction to out-of-the-ordinary characters will bring a great deal of joy and humour your way, you can be easily misled by charming, less than scrupulous characters into areas that are not as beneficial as they may seem. You will often find yourself drawn to investigate mysteries or quirky circumstances but, as long as you keep one toe firmly on stable ground, you will avoid being sucked into a situation that is not necessarily to your—or to anyone else's—benefit.

Your natural enthusiasm for life will shine a light on life's darker areas. At the same time it will keep you protected, especially as you understand that life is essentially a joyful and positive experience and one in which your own attitude will affect the outcome.

You, more than anyone else, will understand that your own contentment affects many others. In a sense you are duty-bound to be happy and feel contented, if only to demonstrate how this brilliant state of mind can do wonders for everyone who bathes in its light. And when you lead from your heart, the times when you must step up to challenges will prove to be worthwhile and your tasks will become as easy as breathing.

Perspective

Fun-loving, affectionate, open-minded, willing to take the initiative, charming, driven

Talents

Perceptivity, discrimination, sense of authority, enthusiasm, generosity, courage, resourcefulness

Challenge

To push yourself beyond your comfort zone

Potential pitfalls

Overly trusting, bigoted, egotism, intensity

Affirmation

I love life. My love strengthens me.

Seeking . . .

You are seeking the best possible way to express your strong sense of self and rise to life's challenges so that you can prove that you are a champion swashbuckling your way through life's adventures.

You'll be pushed by circumstances into the spotlight and asked to prove that you are in fact number one. Without being egotistical or trying to prove you're better than anyone else, you're seeking to express yourself from a purely existential point of view. You *are* the centre of your universe and it's a case of finding out how to be the best you can in an inclusive, compassionate way without alienating those you love.

You'll be attracted to esoteric and mystical studies, but you're unlikely to relinquish your own insights and personal power to someone else's doctrines. Instead you'll prefer to search for your own unique brand of knowledge and enlightenment—an ultimate truth that you've already delineated as your own. As such, you can, on occasion, appear to be distrustful and self-serving as the only information you'll truly trust is knowledge that you've sourced and experienced yourself.

You may promote unconventional practices that allow you to investigate your quirkier side, and you will enjoy spreading your wings and discovering your own true worth.

You'll be attracted to research through books, scripts, treatises and academic study. Psychological insight will draw you into all manner of realms of study but, again, you're unlikely to accept other people's research and ideas as fact, investigating ideas for yourself and not taking someone else's word at face value.

You understand the saying popularly attributed to Buddha that 'It is better to conquer yourself than to win a thousand battles. Then the victory is yours. It cannot be taken from you, not by angels or by demons, heaven or hell.'

You will want to see your work in lights. After all, it's your purpose to discover your own creative genius, and wouldn't it make a wonderful story—and in the spotlight, too! Your self-fulfilment will come largely from chasing a rainbow. If anyone can find the pot of gold at the end of it, it's you.

Perspective

Intelligent, curious, studious, dynamic, humorous, self-assured, inspired, inquisitive

Talents

Insight, productivity, sense of spirit, self-motivation, broad-mindedness

Interests

Psychology, reading, academia, research, sports, self-improvement

Challenge

To find your own truth and creative process

Potential pitfalls

Boastful, self-serving, flighty, lack of belief and trust

Affirmation

I'm guided by my inner wisdom.

Career and direction

At some point in your life you'll be challenged to prove yourself. This will resemble the magnitude of the trials King Arthur or Lady Guinevere underwent. What's certain, though, is that your adventures will put you in the spotlight. This will not necessarily be fame (although it could be), but it'll be a bright new realm in which you'll discover yourself and what makes other people tick too. You'll step into a new world that requires you to excel and vanquish your personal demons, seizing your own destiny to be the champion in your own particular fairytale.

This motif of rising to challenges will recur throughout your lifetime, especially in connection to your career and general direction, as well as your status (such as married/single or employee/employer). Your swashbuckling destiny is an exciting equation of exponential growth. It's up and up the whole way as minor setbacks will only serve to prod you on to ever-higher heights.

As a child you may feel like a fish out of water, having been put in difficult circumstances or made to become independent at a young age.

As an adult you'll be required to express your own true sense of self and creativity in the wide world with panache, style and conviction, flamboyance and positive charm.

Due to a fairly unconventional upbringing you're likely to have a non-traditional take on life as an adult. One of your challenges may be to muster the self-confidence to step out of an unconventional role and into the establishment through work, marriage or general circumstances. You're guaranteed—just by trying something new—to vanquish your inner demons and doubts.

You will assume your rightful place in the world because you are a force to be reckoned with, especially if you lead from the heart. Your mind will follow, it's just a heartbeat away.

You'll impress employers, but are unlikely to remain an employee for long as you're a natural born leader. You'll take your place and your troops will follow—and you'll be loved and respected for it.

Yours is a progressive mind with a talent for inventiveness, innovation and technology. You'll be attracted to work within social structures such as the public sector or industry. You're ahead of the rest in many ways, and may benefit from keeping people up to speed with your quick mind, or at least being patient with less-advanced thinkers and achievers.

Perspective

Influential, assertive, unconventional, adventurous, achiever, ambitious, original, quirky, dynamic, bright, charming

Talents

Resourcefulness, a born leader, entertaining, self-starter

Type of career

A leader in industry, the arts, music, dance, sport, business, entertainment, gambling, food industry, insurance industry, building industry, architect, engineer, politician, inventor, new age, social media

Challenge

To overcome your personal demons

Potential pitfalls

Fear of failure, self-doubt

Affirmation

I discover my path and follow my true passions in life.

Goals, groups and humanitarianism

You're a natural-born leader and will enjoy being involved in community events. You'll dazzle with your positive frame of mind and sense of fun, even if at first you feel safer in the group dynamic and need to muster that extra inner strength to take the lead.

While family and children are an absolute priority, your involvement, enthusiasm and zeal for a group or organisation could take the place of family during various phases in your life. You will not necessarily see this as a problem as you regard society at large to be one big family with you at the helm, guiding it as if it were a ship on stormy seas.

You're happy to aim for high ideals and you function best when you have goals, so you'll succeed all the more by setting them regularly. Despite being a humanitarian at heart you can, paradoxically, lose sight of the moral content of your activities and become virtually amoral, largely by being distracted or losing sight of the bigger picture.

You'll achieve a balanced approach in your lifetime by always coming back to and consulting your heart. If you lead with this wisdom you'll always win. And in your case, winning means being happy, fulfilled, at the helm and content. You're a crusader, the king or queen of the castle, and above all you are constantly in the process of redefining what is important—both to you and the world at large.

Perspective

Gregarious, magnanimous, adventurous, risk-taker, self-confident, goal-oriented

Talents

Leader and team player, community mindedness, self-motivated achievement, humanitarianism

Interests

Creative, entertainer, performance, new age, humanitarian, charity, research, psychology, acting, travel, aeronautics, sports

Challenge

To crusade a cause without losing perspective

Potential pitfalls

Distractions, self-defeatism, amorality, aimlessness

Affirmation

My heart holds the answer, and my truth shines.

The secret you

It's no surprise you're reading this book. All things self-help will appeal to you, largely because you know that the buck stops with you. You know that you must be on top form and that knowledge is the key to being the best you can be.

You'll enjoy boosting your energy with activities such as yoga, tai chi and karate. These focus your core energy and provide inner calm. This will relax your vivacious energy levels and help you get in touch with your inner self, which risks remaining dormant if you don't make the effort to wake your inner hero(ine).

As a child you may experience unusual health situations or out of the ordinary circumstances and your background could contribute to secret feelings of social alienation. As a result you may, when young, find sharing and relationships fairly challenging, and this may lead you towards unusual circumstances or unorthodox characters as you mature; or else you enter circumstances where you feel isolated. Both these scenarios risk augmenting your feelings of alienation, which are rooted in a fear of being different.

For this reason it's imperative that you consciously direct your energy into positive projects where you help others, where your high energy levels are expressed creatively, or where you avoid meeting charming but harmful characters who could potentially lead you astray.

As you mature and come to grips with your attraction to the quirky and secret side of life, you'll appreciate how strong you really are, especially your ability to create your own life path. You'll have every chance to discover the wonder of life and all it has to offer, and to know when to leave certain areas of life well alone.

The key to overcoming your secret fears of alienation and not being good enough is to believe in yourself and your abilities. Once you believe you can succeed, you will. In particular you'll excel at bringing many of life's integral parts into the light, such as its inner core or social failings, by drawing attention to them through your own interaction with unconventional people.

You'll enjoy revealing secrets and suggesting an enlightened approach to them, having unearthed them in your unique and courageous way or shining a light on causes and their merits. In this way you become the crusading adventurer, a bearer of light, who is redefining your own—and everyone else's—personal adventure in its best light.

Characteristics
Quirky, brave, inquisitive, potentially gullible, courageous if shy, intrepid

Talents
Research, forensics, archaeology, scientific research

Interests
Health, psychic ability, hypnotism, psychology, self-help, quirkiness, the unknown

Challenge
To be part of the whole

Potential pitfalls
Losing perspective, turning to crime, intoxication, fear of alienation, fear of inferiority

Affirmation
My inner light shines.

Virgo

The magician or fairy godmother

SITUATION

You're a truly inspired individual while remaining commonsensical at the same time. You may wonder where all your magnificent inspiration and spiritual ideas come from as your ideas have an otherworldly quality that is hard to pinpoint, but translates as your understanding that there is so much more to life than meets the eye.

You're able to take fragments of dreams, reveries and abstract thoughts, and mere nuances of ideas, and give them structure, new meaning and relevance. In a sense you're a true alchemist as you can turn mental images and inspiration into something solid, hopes into facts and dreams into events. In short you can breathe life into life itself.

Yet you're also a supremely sensible and methodical person. This is precisely where your true talent lies and what makes you such a standout character. You can implement abstract, spiritual ideas in beneficial, realistic ways. You're a magician in the classic sense: you can practically pull a rabbit out of a hat

You're also essentially ready, able and willing to be of service to others. You understand how important feelings of wellbeing are and like to help people attain their potential. The risk is that you become self-sacrificing, which is counterproductive to your purpose of inspiring others through your approach to life itself, and makes you subservient and no help to anyone, least of all yourself.

You're such an inspired individual that despite being practical and well organised, abstract and unrealistic ideals can sometimes lead you astray. During various phases of your life you're happy to pursue a spiritual or religious path with utter zeal, leaving all notions of practicalities behind such as how you'll feed yourself and your family. This can clearly be a failing.

Your idealism can also lead you to lose yourself in other people's agendas. Consequently you can lose the detachment that is necessary to analyse ideas and implement them. Yet critical analysis is one of your saving graces as it helps you to be a truly effective agent of positive change within your life and others' lives.

PURPOSE

Your purpose is to bring sense, applied structure and logic, to those areas that are, to all intents and purposes, merely impressions, nonsense or the stuff of dreams and imagination. You use this ability for the good of all, giving everyone whose lives you touch a glimpse of enchantment. Your ultimate purpose is to promote a sense of wellbeing, both in yourself and in those around you.

You're a brilliant poet at heart and have a deep understanding of life, the after-life and the various, seemingly unimaginable dimensions of the universe. You'll understand string theory without ever having studied physics, understand saints, clergy, philosophers and poets just as well as you understand mathematics or finance. This is the easy part.

Your deeper purpose is to communicate, demonstrate and make abstract, esoteric and spiritual ideals tangible and real. You're a true inspiration because you take the breath of life and shape it into real, con-crete activities and products, and you inspire productivity in others too.

You are health-conscious and will strive to promote feelings of health and wellbeing—and implement them in practical and beneficial ways. To this end you may be attracted to producing written work or learning hands-on healing, or just simply setting a good example. The modality is your choice.

You're able to see the sacrifices that previous generations have made so that you and your generation may enjoy the current standards and ideals. You understand that self-sacrifice has its place, but that being practical and realistic about life also has its part to play. You know that what you focus on becomes your future reality, and what you sacrifice is lost forever in the past.

Your purpose is to look to a new horizon of possibilities and potential, away from feelings of loss, fear or victimhood that has led to sacrifices, either your own, your family's or within your cultural history. The poor-me tendency is one that no longer serves your purpose. Your bright, incisive mind yearns to make sense of the world rather than wallow in feelings and sentiment.

You are ready to implement the lessons your ancestors learned and combine them with your own understanding of life's deeper rhythms, turning them into your own magical fairytale—one that will have a happy ending.

Affirmation

I am blessed with deep understanding. I will use it to create wonderful work.

Famous people

Christian Dior, Antonio Banderas, Aretha Franklin, Carole King, Salvador Dali, Barbra Streisand, Harrison Ford, Brian Wilson, Michael York, Anita Roddick, John F Kennedy Jr, Bob Dylan

Your unique approach

You will idealise people until you remove your rose-coloured glasses and see them for who they are—and yourself as the practical, methodical, analytical, intelligent and extremely helpful person you are. By idealising others you risk falling into the trap of losing yourself in them, and sacrificing your own life at the altar of theirs.

You come from a beautiful place in your heart in which the world is benevolent, almost complete. Although this is a personally enriching approach to life, you risk being seen as innocent and even ignorant as you appear oblivious to life's perils and challenges, especially as a young adult. You also risk being taken advantage of.

When life's challenges approach, which they invariably will, you can feel easily discouraged and defeated by the seemingly negative attitudes of people less idealistic and spiritually insightful than you. As a result you can lapse into the poor-me frame of mind that can cause you to self-sabotage.

As you mature you'll become more proactive, realistic and practical. This is partly due to the necessity to attend to the practicalities of life, and also to create your own happiness, which rests on your shoulders alone. Being actively involved in creating your own destiny will help remove the veil through which you idealise others and even life itself as you put in motion your own remarkable abilities to manifest your ideas and beliefs.

As you begin to see people for who they truly are, your appreciation of the wonders of life will increase because the intricacies of every person's soul—and the variety of life itself—is what makes life appear so wonderful to you in the first place.

When you become more realistic about what you and those around you can accomplish in a practical sense, especially within your relationships, the more proactive you'll become. You will also create the life and relationships you want built on inspired and healthy, real and fair, loving and practical, mutually beneficial sentiments.

You'll conceive ideas out of nowhere and you'll turn them into reality in the blink of an eye. In this way your life will reward you for your faith, compassion and understanding of its mysteries and its inherently potent force, which you are able to translate into reality just like a magician.

Perspective

Practical, realistic, reverential, sensitive, tidy, analytical, systematic, inventive, efficient

Talents

Intuition, precision, communication skills, imagination, inspiration

Interests

Poetry, news, blogs, politics, reading, housekeeping, arts and crafts, gardening

Challenge

To see life as it truly is

Potential pitfalls

Whimsical, forgetful, naive, self-sacrificing, idealistic, easily defeated

Affirmation

Life becomes more beautiful the more clearly I see it.

Values and self-expression

You have a logical, analytical mind and will attract material possessions fairly easily, but you may just as easily lose them, so a sound understanding of finances, especially those you share, is necessary.

You have a strong sense of self-worth, but can lose yourself in other people's ideas, lives, values and attitudes, especially people you're intimate with or share space with. Your key to success lies in being able to maintain your strong sense of self. You can do this by keeping a grip on your own values and morals as you enjoy and appreciate the (often intoxicating) company you're attracted to.

You will feel fulfilled when you enjoy and celebrate the beauty and life force around you, and express this through your actions and gestures. By understanding that you are not a reflection of other people—that they are a reflection of your own inner beauty, values and appreciation of them—you will become increasingly discerning about the company you keep, and more easily maintain your strong sense of self.

When you celebrate the uniqueness and beauty of other people, and of life itself, you'll realise that it's an aspect of yourself that you're celebrating too. In the same way you can create a wonderful relationship, you can also create a wonderful life: it is a reflection of your own thought processes, hopes and visions. And by maintaining a firm grip on your highest values and aims, you too can build your ideal life with your thoughts, deeds and imagination alone.

Perspective

Imaginative, poetic, analytical, hands-on, miserly/spendthrift, sensitive

Talents

Empathy, compassion, organisational skills, vision, logician

Challenge

To develop a strong sense of self

Potential pitfalls

Loss of identity, boom/bust cycle financially, self-sacrifice, gullibility, victim behaviour

Affirmation

I am an expression of the eternally divine.

Communication

You're one of life's natural-born communicators. The way you interact and gain information is likely to have a more profound expression and effect on others than most. You have knowledge and wisdom beyond your own understanding, which you may not be able to explain, yourself, let alone to less sensitive souls, especially when you are a child. Your insight may be beyond words, and you may appear vague when in fact you are the opposite—you are so clear that words may simply fail you at least until you master the art of self-expression. Some with this placement are natural-born psychics and mediums.

NOTE TO PARENTS: *listen to your children's stories, fantasies and theories, and allow them to express their innate wisdom. It will help them throughout their lives.*

As a child you may explore fairytales, inspiring cultures or religions due to your family's circumstances, but as you mature you'll get a handle on your own particular brand of insight that is truly profound. You've seen circumstances and places no-one else has. If people don't understand you it is not a reflection of your lack of insight (as you may believe), but simply a reflection of theirs.

As you mature you will become more comfortable communicating your insights and manage your particular talent: communicating knowledge and wisdom so that everyone can understand it and so it can be applied to life day-to-day.

Your heightened perception is what makes you such an adept communicator. Combined with your ability to convey this on a practical level, you're able to communicate complex ideas with people who are far less perceptive than you. This enables you to disseminate information on a broad scale.

Your interest in all things other-worldly will include delving into psychological or spiritual activities (such as psychological profiling, spiritual meditation or telepathy). You will do this in an attempt to attain heightened states of mind and learn alternative ways to communicate. Your thirst for knowledge will take you to wonderful places that you'll enjoy researching in detail. You're one of life's eternal scholars. Life's a lesson and you're a grade A student!

Perspective

Instinctive, organised, precise, curious, understanding, knowledgeable, hands-on

Talents

Communications including foreign languages, psychic ability, medium-ship, kindness, compassion, natural wisdom

Challenge

To value your abilities

Potential pitfalls

Lacking in self-confidence, misunderstandings, seeming vague

Affirmation

I turn wisdom into information.

Home and family

You'll feel most comfortable expressing your understanding of life's rhymes and rhythms within the privacy and supportive atmosphere of your own home and family, especially as a youngster. You know your insight is deeper than most, and your family is the first place you'll test some of your beliefs. In addition you understand that what makes life truly tick is close and loving relationships and these, for you, begin in the home, making this a particularly important area in your life.

You'll be inspired by your career and status, and will endeavour to inspire others through your work too. You may find that you go through periods when you need to sacrifice your career or chosen path for domestic concerns or necessities, such as looking after family members in need of nurturing. Yet you'll proceed through life with your own brand of wisdom that, as you mature, will become increasingly valued and valuable, especially within the home and domestic arena.

You have a deep understanding and/or interest in your family and ancestral history, such as family genes or the family tree as it has evolved through the ages. Your understanding of your present life will be fuelled by your appreciation of your family history, your family dynamic and the way in which this dynamic manifests through your own children and/or through your spiritual beliefs. You may find, in addition, that certain family traits will be best left in the past as you set sail on a new course of your own.

The theme of sacrifice may be noticeable within your family tree, perhaps due to hardship or cultural or political circumstances. In part your challenge is to overcome the pattern of self-sacrifice and the victim–martyr role ancestrally, and also to become practical about preventing its recurrence.

You'll enjoy being appreciated for the exquisiteness of your creations in the home and within your family. You may veer from bohemian chic to minimalist white. Individual rooms may be themed so you can express your various tastes in different areas throughout the house. You're a perfectionist at heart and, if this is expressed to the extreme in your home, excessive tidiness or even extreme cleanliness will result.

Values closer to your heart are as important to you as worldly success. Your activities, both within your career and at home, are likely to be aligned with some form of spiritual, religious or health-conscious activity. You believe that your every expression and action must be positive, beneficial and inspired as it contains the seed of creation itself—a mystical quality that inspires you to be the best you can be and to help others do the same.

Perspective

Inspired, sensitive, clear-cut, idealistic, wise, spiritual, particular, strict, a homemaker, neat

Talents

Nurturance, perception, discernment, helpfulness, methodical, health-conscious

Challenge

To put inspired ideas into action

Potential pitfalls

Dogmatism, obsessive-compulsiveness, self-sacrificing, victim behaviour, perfectionism, critical

Affirmation

My ideas and wisdom are appreciated.

Creativity and life force

A keen sense of the importance of your role in life's unfolding drama will help you focus your attention on your contributions so that, rather than being a sheep in a flock of many, swept up in the dramas of life, you are proactive and creative within your life.

Your creativity enables you to generate concrete results the moment you put your mind to a particular project. For you creativity has a much broader context than for many. It includes your ability to envisage the tangible results of your ideas, to turn mere whimsy into events and ideals into reality, step by logical step.

You'll enjoy mingling with like-minded people and supporting inspired charitable causes, even if you're not necessarily drawn towards activism. Your many interests and your ability to multi-task will take you into all kinds of diverse activities, and you may easily lose sight of your true aims and talents, so care must be taken to maintain direction.

Your musical, dramatic and artistic expression will demand that you turn your attention to these areas at various points in your life, if only to satisfy your desire to hone your creative skills in these areas.

As a fundamentally health-conscious individual, much of your creative expression will revolve around promoting a healthy approach to life. You'll enjoy sports and also earth-related, hands-on physical activities such as gardening.

Your bright mind will motivate you to get your hands dirty rather than to merely talk or theorise. As a youngster especially, you'll be happier behind the camera than in front of it, happier turning your hand to editing rather than writing, and towards production rather than pure art, although you will succeed at pretty much anything you decide to create.

Perspective

Well-organised, philosophical, realistic, sociable, original, practical, health-conscious

Talents

Making sense of nonsense, inspiring, multi-tasking abilities

Creative career

Meditation, yoga, design, production, editing, publishing, landscaping, vegetable gardening, water management, film, theatre

Challenge

To avoid dissipating your energy

Potential pitfalls

Losing direction and being easily influenced

Affirmation

I turn my creativity into actual events or objects.

Work and daily life

You're a hard worker. If this makes you or your friends and family laugh, then you have not yet found your calling. As a youngster you may be easily distracted, preferring to daydream rather than do anything at all. What's more, your strong sense of compassion could mean you become over-sensitive to the plight of others and life's challenges, causing you to retreat into a fantasy world of your own.

Yet if anyone can make something truly remarkable of their life, you can. This is particularly so within your daily routine and work because you can devise a plan, stick to it, and therefore see results. It's as easy as abc for you to turn your ideas, fantasies and even make-believe into reality.

Your daily life is likely to revolve around some form of ritual that may be religious, health-oriented or spiritual in nature. As you mature you realise this helps you attain your everyday goals. This ritual, belief or schedule acts as the skeleton on which you hang your various activities and work duties, enabling you to maintain a structure to accommodate your many interests and activities.

As a perfectionist you may deem chores and duties unworthy of your heightened abilities. On the other hand you may become practically obsessive about sticking to a timetable, a routine or to details. But if you envisage an end goal you will strengthen your resolve and character, and you'll be surprised by the wonderful results you can attain.

You tend to live off your nerves so being physically fit will help you maintain a healthy nervous system. You'll enjoy working in the health industry in some form because promoting wellbeing is your fundamental goal.

When under pressure you have a tendency to become regimented about your physical health practices. Paradoxically this can become a source of tension. You may go through periods in which you are simply too busy to indulge in sports or fitness regimes, but you'll generally find that you retrieve fitness levels fairly quickly when you return to your regime.

You're naturally drawn to help others, and may even have to sacrifice some of your time as a youngster to help someone in a difficult position or with a disability. You understand that your position as a helper is invaluable, but you may feel that you've had to sacrifice a part of yourself and may hold a grudge for this reason.

Becoming prey to the victim–martyr tendency is a major pitfall for you. The poor-me attitude does not serve your purpose. Besides, you're too savvy for that. As a perfectionist you risk demanding that everyone around you be perfect too, and subsequently you can become critical. Such unrealistic expectations are counterproductive and can create inner tension because you're a realist at heart.

If you keep perspective, that daydream place where life is perfect can become a real place in your everyday life, and a place of relaxation and fulfilment, rather than an escapist fantasy. If anyone can achieve this, you can.

Perspective

Perfectionist, helpful, inspired, hard working when adult, health-conscious

Talents

Administration, strategy, creativity, planning

Type of work

Medical, institutional care, work with animals, housekeeping, art, librarian, IT, research, academic, writer, translator, guide, teacher, health industry, environmentalist, psychic, religious, spiritual, nutrition

Challenge

To keep perspective

Potential pitfalls

Appearing lazy, disengaged, daydreaming, victim-like behaviour, self-pity

Affirmation

I work towards realistic goals and promote wellbeing.

Relationships

You know exactly what you want from partners, whether business or personal. You're highly analytical, and yet a rich imagination nurtures your soul. You appreciate the depth in others. You're respectful, loyal and likely to be naturally sympathetic. Your almost sixth-sense understanding of others is unique to you. You seem to understand every mood and emotion before a word has been spoken or a sentiment acknowledged. This makes you supremely supportive and understanding, but also highly sensitive.

You'll attract idealists, imaginative and poetic people, whose company is appealing and who take you to new spiritual levels, but you can also be practically enchanted by them, making the viability of a healthy relationship challenging.

The pressure you put on yourself to be perfect, especially within marriage and personal relationships, could be excessive. You may also expect others to be perfect, which clearly they are not. You could put huge demands on yourself to be super-human, and then fall short of the mark. You may then behave submissively in an attempt to be the ideal partner, mother, father or work colleague. This will prove frustrating as you are intrinsically a proactive person, eager to celebrate the positive results of your hard work and efforts in life.

When your relationship expectations fail to materialise you risk resorting to escapist tendencies, living in a fantasy world about your relationships. The worst-case scenario is that you cannot see yourself or others for who you or they truly are.

In this case you can set yourself up to fail because you will be repeatedly disappointed by others because of your exaggeratedly high expectations. The more this occurs, the more the cycle of failure will push you back into a world of fantasy in which your high expectations are destined to spiral into disappointment.

You may feel you must be self-sacrificing in order to achieve good relationships. But this negates your deep understanding of people, and your ability to create truly magical relationships based on deep understanding rather than expectations, fantasy or self-sacrifice.

Perspective

Romantic, imaginative, creative, inventive, analytical, poetic, respectful

Talents

Insight, earthy, deeply understanding, sixth sense, helpful, supportive

Challenge

To see others for who they are, and to see yourself for who you are too

Potential pitfalls

Over-analytical, idealistic, critical, submissive, demanding, self-sacrificing, escapist, naive

Affirmation

I trust my insight and instincts to show me the way.

Motivation

You're extremely motivated to attract and create wonder around you as if by the touch of a magic wand. You encapsulate the rare combination of being well-organised, down-to-earth and almost mystically inspired and creative at the same time. You'll have a practical interest in the occult (and all things hidden), and will be motivated to research this area as it will seem a natural part of your self-expression, especially as you mature.

Yours is the soul that brings into being beautiful art and inspired creations that others can't even imagine. You see the end result before it's even been considered, and similarly you can appreciate the depth in others before they have themselves. As such you may not appear to be driven or even particularly passionate. Instead you straightforwardly accomplish immense feats. In this sense you appear to be a realist, but essentially you're a true visionary with diamond clarity.

Yet you risk daydreaming to the degree of losing yourself in a fantasy world because you are motivated by high expectations and wish to see them materialise. Basic needs, rights and practicalities must be kept uppermost in your mind to avoid disappointment. Initially keeping things real may seem challenging, and you may feel that implementing your ideas on a practical level is truly difficult, or that your initial attempts will fail, just like a newborn lamb beginning to walk.

Trust in the fact that you will succeed. It is your destiny to be a practical, realistic proponent of visionary ideals. You'll enjoy being a catalyst in people's lives, applying your deep understanding of life on a realistic, day-to-day level, honouring your own sense of self and effectively adding your own touch of magic to the mundaneness of life.

Perspective

Idealistic, keen to please, mystical, gentle soul, philosophical, enthusiastic

Talents

Organisation, being encouraging, visionary, cooperative, attention to detail

Challenge

To believe you are a visionary

Potential pitfalls

Martyr-like behaviour, fantastical, subservient, overly trusting, withdrawn

Affirmation

I can implement my diamond clarity in life.

Seeking . . .

You have a thirst for spiritual understanding and seek to understand the intricacies of legal, governmental, cultural and societal structures. Ultimately you're looking for perfection in one or more of these areas.

You're a poetic soul at heart, and you're motivated to search for structures that can accommodate your unique, idealistic vision, and then build structures that will promote the same. You're looking for ways to create a kind of utopia in your own world—and put substance to ideas. Once you've accomplished this in your own life you'll seek to create it in others.

A clever combination of creativity and fact-finding will sate your incredible thirst for knowledge, but you risk entering domains in which you're misunderstood, in part due to language barriers or cultural differences. So to ensure you're understood in life you'll learn humility and to state your plans clearly and in a practical way.

Higher education will appeal to you as a way to deepen your knowledge and hone your analytical mind. The risk is that you forget to take the time to enjoy the spark that motivates you in the first place; the beauty and wonder of the world that is all around you and inside your imagination.

You're the quintessential networker and facilitator and will revel in connecting people from different backgrounds and researching ways to improve the human condition and environment. You have compassion beyond your years, and a deep understanding of values and customs, but you risk being distracted by being over-analytical on the one hand and glossing over the details on the other.

You may find that you go through phases in your life in which you pursue an ideal, a belief or a practice that may be extremely hard to attain and sustain. But by keeping your eyes firmly on your one true motivation, which is to create and manifest wonderful events and promote a feeling of wellbeing around you, you'll find you can do just that, as if by magic.

Perspective
Idealistic, curious, studious, creative, poetic, sense of fair play, kind, analytical, enthusiastic, thirst for knowledge, humble

Talents
Innovation, vision, enabler, facilitator, communications, healing

Interests
Science, studies, reading, writing, travelling, health, sociology

Challenge
To manifest your ideas

Potential pitfalls
Insatiable thirst for knowledge, lost perspective, unfocused

Affirmation
This is a wonderful world.

Career and direction

You'll enjoy being lost in a sea of domestic bliss, awash in the pea soup of contentment that makes domesticity so delectable. Yet during various periods in your life, as you mature, you will be attracted to an outgoing, very particular career or direction that requires you to become focused, ambitious, practical, methodical and very different to the person you enjoy being at home.

People who know you professionally may be surprised at how different your domestic life is to your public life. Your home is a place of relaxation and creativity, of sumptuousness and leisure, and the lush furnishings will reflect this. But at work you're professionalism and perfection to a tee. Your diamond-like mind will be quite a contrast to the ordered yet slightly bohemian, lackadaisical chaos of your home life.

You may enjoy mixing your domestic interests with your career and status by becoming an interior designer or professional housekeeper, for example, or by working from home. Your unique ability to be organised and practical, while being profoundly insightful and creative, puts you in a category of your own, able to combine artistic and caring inspiration with functional and practical output.

You are a naturally gifted healer as your innate understanding of people and your impulse to help them makes you intrinsically sensitive and perceptive. You'll take an interest in the health industry as a possible career. Interestingly you will enjoy the flow of money like water through your hands. For this reason you may be attracted to financial services too.

You instinctively understand what makes a person successful outside the home because you yourself will manage to blend the worlds of home and work into mutually supportive and yet very distinct categories. At some point in your life you may have to sacrifice your career or put it on hold to look after domestic matters. Once this phase is over it's unlikely to repeat itself as you may decide that no sacrifice need take place in either field, mainly because you'll work out a way in which both areas can work hand in hand.

You enjoy bringing people together over mutually enjoyable projects. You're a multi-talented, multi-faceted worker, and will enjoy sampling many different jobs. The one that grabs you the most is the one that will satisfy your purpose: to do something truly inspired, practical and worthwhile, both for you and for everyone you meet.

Characteristics

Professional, instinctive, precise, home-loving, realistic, diligent

Talents

Diamond-like clarity, inspiring, focused, good organisational skills, networking

Type of career

Interior design, personal care, motivational work, management, psychoanalysis, philosophy, mediation, business, finances, management, marriage guidance, health services, cosmetic, publishing, mystical, armed services, police force

Challenge

To find a vocation that expresses your creativity in a practical way

Potential pitfalls

Sacrificing home life or career, lackadaisical, head in the clouds, shy, retiring

Affirmation

I am all I aspire to be.

Goals, groups and humanitarianism

You like to generate beauty all around you either through inspired works of art or in a more general sense by adding a little sparkle to just about anything you do. Working within creative groups, organisations and collaborative, voluntary or community-based projects excites you. As a youngster you'll enjoy play and arts and craft groups. You're truly happy exploring your artistic and creative abilities in whichever way they present themselves. For example performance, music, painting or theatre. As an adult you'll be drawn to artists, gentle souls and musicians, and will enjoy socialising and networking with creative people.

The pitfall is that you risk becoming stuck in self-serving or the opposite, self-defeatist, activities. As you enjoy giving full rein to your imagination, fancies and reveries, you risk being swept up in daydreams and daily pursuits that serve no purpose at all. Being discerning about which groups and clubs you join and which people you mingle with is important, especially as a youngster.

You have a tendency to be drawn to people who indulge in recreational drugs or other escapist activities. The structure and organisation that productive, goal-oriented group activities can provide you with will help you to steer clear of self-destructive activities.

It's important to remember that you're part of the social fabric. This shouldn't be difficult as you have such a strong connection with the cosmic soup we're all a part of, but being community-minded will help bring your unique, personal talents out into society at large so that they may be of benefit to everyone. Ultimately your focus on healing and self-help activities will keep you engaged in group dynamics of an upbeat nature.

Perspective

Helpful, playful, creative, composed, realistic, expressive, enjoying group activities

Talents

Art, music, design, fundraising, charity

Interests

Design, music or stage production, art, publishing, voluntary work

Challenge

To avoid escapist tendencies

Potential pitfalls

Self-defeatism, melancholy, self-destructiveness

Affirmation

My creativity and contribution to the world is positive and nurturing.

The secret you

Illusion and reality are interwoven deep in your psyche, and the line that separates fact from fiction is a fine one for you. This makes you very good at storytelling, writing and art, but if you live your life blurring the line between illusion and reality, you risk being lost in an aimless world of fantasy or even immersing yourself in a world of lies and deceit.

Your compassion knows no bounds, but you risk falling into self-defeating or even vulnerable situations such as associating with nefarious characters or addictive personalities who can take advantage of your kindness.

Secretly you have a fear of illness. This may be linked with a fear of the unknown, although for some this may come from a childhood in which your health was delicate and you fear you may relapse. But as an adult you may simply come to see illness as impractical.

Your fear of not being perfect can lead to excessive self-criticism, which can lead you to inactivity or even stagnation, undermining your self-confidence and productivity.

A Virgo north node can indicate the most adept of healers and carers. You see the plight of the human race very clearly and with great compassion, and you humbly understand that you must be a source of help and assistance. Your imagination and deep spiritual empathy can then become the restorative well in which you dip your soul and receive inspiration and energy to do your particular brand of healing and magic.

You'll increasingly enjoy harnessing your compassionate side and channelling it into practical activities that are not only for your own good, but also for others'. The key to success lies in being vigilant about not blurring the lines between your hopes and wishes on the one hand, and your everyday life and reality on the other.

A keen interest in the occult (anything hidden) and the deeper human psyche will take you to places many people fear to tread, and a methodical approach will help keep your feet firmly on the ground. Being practical and realistic is the principle way that you can manifest your unique abilities and play to your strengths.

You're able to research depths others cannot reach, and in fact you do so almost subconsciously. Your vision is truly, and frequently unintentionally, profound. Bringing this to the surface and growing to your full potential for the benefit of all is your true gift, and in this way you fulfil your purpose as a true magician.

Characteristics

Excessively perfectionist, self-critical, sympathetic, trusting, distracted, forgetful, whimsical, humble

Talents

Discernment, healing, wisdom, perceptivity, good judgment, deep understanding

Interests

Secrets, the occult, philosophy, psychoanalysis, life after death, healing, spirituality

Challenge

To turn your weaknesses into strengths

Potential pitfalls

Undiscriminating, deceitful, delusional, out of touch, self-destructive, hypochondriac, unrealistic

Affirmation

I am a healing force.

Libra

A determined balancing act

SITUATION

Your life will frequently take you into daring circumstances that demand you step up to be the best you can be. You'll do so happily, and with natural flair too. You have the boldness, determination and courage to succeed, especially when you're under pressure. You're brave beyond even your own understanding, and have a strong independent streak.

Your quest is to create balanced relationships, but this can be in conflict with your independent streak. So how can the two exist side by side? You'll find that the answer lies in carefully balancing your independent side with the side of you that is looking for peace. In the process you will actively learn how to be a decision-maker and an accomplished mediator. This is partly because you're constantly in the process of debating the relative merits of your own approaches to circumstances as they arise, while always looking for the ultimate prize: balance and harmony.

You're adept at stepping from one environment to another, and do so with ease and grace. You would do well in politics and law as you are constantly searching for that elusive quality that makes things work out in life, and makes things and people connect and make sense. You're on the lookout for the keys that unite opposites, and you're able to communicate both the keys, and the common ground, easily.

Yet in doing so you can find yourself in extreme situations that are unbalanced to say the least. As a child you may seem to be argumentative, but this is paradoxically because you are searching for solutions and balance. You may find life perpetually precipitates you in situations that are simply too hot to handle. That is until you approach them with your particular brand of medicine: the intention to establish balance and harmony.

You're a true romantic at heart. The risk is that you continually seesaw from one drama to the next in your search for harmony and your attempts to unite opposites, boldly going where no-one else would dare. The gift is that you'll find true harmony inside your own self, and all you need to do is look for it there and communicate it to others.

PURPOSE

Your true purpose in life is to gain satisfaction from good relationships and communications. The key to attaining this is to understand that what creates the harmony and balance you seek in life is your own approach to it.

In your quest to establish good relationships you're liable to seesaw between various ideas and people, especially as a youngster, unsure as you are about how to manifest good relationships. As you're a bold, brave and determined person at heart you can risk lurching from one project to the next in search of the thrill or release that comes from new understandings and experiences.

When young you're likely to seek beauty and understanding outside yourself in the world. You'll seek justice outside yourself, yet the seeds are planted within you. You'll seek the perfectly balanced and fair relationship, but it's your own approach to people that decides the quality and value of your relationships.

You may have a faint memory of having been free and independent, so you crave the chance to recreate this feeling in your life. You'll be drawn to establishing partnerships and connections with people that promote freedom and individuality, and will also strive for happiness, love, closeness and trust. And it's precisely through allowing yourself and your partners (both business and personal) to express their freedom and individuality that you'll attain the most balanced relationships.

Affirmation

I'm beautiful, balanced and loving.

Famous people

Joan Baez, Neil Diamond, Placido Domingo, Al Pacino, Michelangelo, Tom Jones, Gene Roddenberry, Madonna, Michael Jackson, James van Praagh, John Lennon, John McEnroe, Alexander Graham Bell

Your unique approach

In your unswerving search for peace you are tempted to hide your independent streak and become one of life's sheep. You risk settling for half-hearted measures that sacrifice your own wellbeing and freedom, and possibly even that of others, in the mistaken belief that this is how you'll attain a peaceful ideal.

Powerful and dynamic friends and partners will appeal to you as you may subconsciously believe these partners can better express your own fiery side—the one that seems at odds with your peace-loving, balance-seeking self. Relationships with courageous, outgoing people also free you from the responsibility your fiery self requires, which gives you the freedom to express your romantic search for harmony.

The paradox is that dynamic or easy-to-anger friends and partners will doubtless cause you to fire up yourself, making the peaceful life you're searching for more challenging. And if you ignore your fiery aspects you will not attain peace at all. Instead your disregard for your assertiveness will slowly eat away at you and your self-esteem until you admit defeat and try again, and again, to find peace, establishing a pattern of never-ending inner conflict in your search for harmony.

There is no doubt that you are a peacemaker, able to establish harmony. But the ultimate question has to be how and at what price? You'll gain higher ground by being assertive (as opposed to aggressive), and by championing what's fair and right rather than settling for an easy solution. This will be far more successful than attempting to detach from your independent streak in your quest for balance in your own life.

Humbly accept that you can be both independent and in search of harmony at the same time. Yours is a unique balancing act, after all, and only you know how to do it.

Perspective

Peaceful, individualistic, seeking harmony, romantic, bold, determined

Talents

Strong appreciation of beauty, artistically gifted, good mediator, brave

Interests

Art, design, law, hospitality, architecture, beauty, fashion, agriculture, fiction, diplomat, politics, mediator

Challenge

To create harmony while being assertive

Potential pitfalls

Liable to play second fiddle, self-indulgent, half-hearted, wilful

Affirmation

Beauty and harmony are in my heart and all around me.

Values and self-expression

You value beauty, material possessions and status symbols. Attractive people will appeal to you, too, as you'll enjoy basking in their beauty. As you mature you'll look deeper and inner qualities such as kindness and compassion become the characteristics you admire more in people and yourself.

As a toddler sharing toys will either come extremely easily to you or it will be a challenge. The issue of sharing and partaking of joint resources is an area that will preoccupy you throughout your life. Your underlying appreciation of fairness, balance and harmony is expressed both in the way you seek to have good relationships, and in the way you share objects and resources. As a child you may frequently be heard complaining, 'That's just not fair!'

As you mature you'll gain insight into how important sharing is as it expresses so well your conviction that life must be just. The value you place on possessions you accrue, and the people who appeal to you, will change in line with your life experiences.

You'll be increasingly attracted to dynamic and powerful people in your close circle, and yet you will take the role of mediator attempting to smooth out the wrinkles that inevitably arise within circles of extremely active and dynamic people.

You'll pursue certain values and criteria with determination and, as you mature, you'll search for fairness and equality. You may be attracted to human-rights issues in your search for social equality.

Indulgence in fine foods and wines will also appeal as a means of self-expression as you value quality highly. You may be accused of having double standards as you appreciate the finer things in life while simultaneously understanding that some resources are finite and greed is counterproductive to your strong ethic about sharing. You have an appreciation of life's abundance that others may not fully comprehend. And you'll enjoy showing people just exactly what it is that makes life abundant, which is its inherent beauty.

You have an in-built appreciation of all things beautiful. You may be a gifted artist and self-expression through the arts will help you find balance and peace throughout your life. Beauty itself will enrich both your life and the lives of those close to you as beauty, to you, is the ultimate expression of the divine and the eternal qualities of harmony.

Perspective

Connoisseur, alternately peace-loving/aggressive, seeking fairness, dreamer, appreciative of art, music, imaginative, understanding

Talents

An eye for beauty and design, a deep appreciation of talent and others' abilities, justice-seeking

Challenge

To express the beauty you see

Potential pitfalls

Self-doubting, self-effacing, prioritising peace at all costs, lacking in values, greed, over-indulgent

Affirmation

I love life. It is abundant and nurturing.

Communication

You're the ultimate thinking machine. Above all your approach is intellectual, and people may wonder what you're contemplating or why you analyse data to such a degree. You're simply evaluating your environment and deciding your next step, especially as you're likely to up and explore an area of interest or go on an adventure at a moment's notice, especially as a youngster.

Your background will involve powerful or unusual educational or cultural influences that will guide you towards a profound understanding of the dynamics and inter-relationship of various cultures, people and ideas.

Your people skills go beyond the norm, and yet your empathy risks overshadowing your sense of self and your intellectual detachment. Your investment in your relationships is paramount, and you risk being easily influenced. You are able to establish strong relationships while retaining independent opinions, and in this way your caring side will blossom. You have strong impulses to be adventurous, outgoing and willing to try something new. You may be impulsive and have a short attention span, too, especially when young.

You'll search for the perfect relationship and good communications in every area you touch—at work, through education, travel and generally by being interested in spirituality and being emotionally invested in life itself.

You may also find that you have a particularly strong or relevant relationship with a sibling and a prominent position within your neighbourhood. You'll see yourself as an ambassador of good behaviour and right relations because feeling valued for your most positive qualities is the ideal you are working towards, and motivates your every move.

Perspective

Intellectual, gentle, fun-loving, optimistic, daring, enjoys quiet activities such as reading, meditation

Talents

A calm influence, mediation, research, writing, logic, peacemaking

Challenge

To communicate right relations

Potential pitfalls

Empathy can overshadow your sense of self, shyness, self-deprecating, easily influenced, mimic

Affirmation

I am a bridge to harmony through the way I communicate.

Home and family

You'll express your need for happy relationships at a young age within your own family and you'll naturally slip into the role of go-between or arbitrator. Your adult life will in some way continue to revolve around resolving and improving interpersonal dynamics. You'll see as you progress through life that many interpersonal skills stem from domestic circumstances, as do your own.

Your home environment will include strong or confrontational characters so you'll find out from a young age how to play the pacifist. And it's this role that will pervade your life in general. You'll make your mark through playing this role to its highest degree in virtually every area of your life.

At home you may need to engage combative people, but your role as the pacifist will increasingly enable you to bridge the antagonistic canyon that invariably exists around such characters. You'll manage to attain a degree of harmony in your own life because of this ability. You also learn to be diligent and potentially wilful because you learn to stand up to powerful characters.

As you mature new environments will appeal. You may move house regularly and pursue new experiences avidly, but amidst all this you're the person holding the fabric of many people's lives together (whether this role is recognised by them or not). You know yourself how important your role is, and you'll appreciate the immediate and beneficial effect you have on people.

Whether you become an architect, a builder, a homemaker, a full-time parent or literally a peacekeeper, you'll have every intention of getting out there into the world and making your mark. You'll also find that life's quirks and coincidences will always bring you back to the familiarity of your home because you're a romantic at heart. You'll seek to kindle and ignite warmth in a sumptuous home, and to take this feeling of comfort, light and kindness out into the world.

Perspective

Supportive, giving, optimistic, impulsive, adventurous, open to new ideas

Talents

Mediation, peacekeeping, pacifism, trouble shooting, go-between

Challenge

To marry romanticism with realism, being practical

Potential pitfalls

Being distracted by conflict, engaging in conflict

Affirmation

I create peace and happiness.

Creativity and life force

You're motivated by the concept of beauty and creating serenity in your surroundings and within your closest relationships. Beauty and love are prime movers in your life. As a youngster you'll try different ways to find these qualities in life by sampling diverse activities. As a social butterfly you may first try out one activity and then another in an attempt to discover where your true interests lie. You may be accused of being superficial—or even mercenary and greedy—in your whimsical and avaricious approach to the world as a youngster, but rest assured once you find what truly engages you creatively, you'll stay true to it.

You'll be attracted to the beauty of music and the arts. As you're naturally energetic you may be talented in sports. As you mature you'll be attracted to humanitarian causes, and may even consider becoming an activist. At the core of your sense of self, though, you are looking for the essence of beauty—that is what makes you beautiful, what makes other people beautiful, and how beauty expresses itself in life. Wherever you find beauty you'll pursue it with flair and vigour and will enjoy joining groups dedicated to art appreciation and/or the appreciation of beauty and life in some form.

In your search for beauty and harmony you're prone to take risks that the faint of heart would simply not contemplate. As a result you may encounter far-from-ideal circumstances, but they will only make you strive more to find what you're looking for.

You're an animated and attractive team player. If you channel your energy into beautiful outlets you'll create your own Garden of Eden. Your playful soul makes you the ideal companion for children. You're a Pied Piper at heart, leading those you love to an ideal world only you can imagine, let alone attain.

Perspective

Lively, enthusiastic, creative, playful, charming, dreamy, gentle

Talents

Art, music, imagination, being sympathetic, collaborations

Creative career

Theatre, the arts, music, dance, children's services

Challenge

To find beauty in all life

Potential pitfalls

Superficiality, sentimentality, frivolity, shallowness, mercenary, avarice, greed, risk-taking, burnt fingers

Affirmation

I find happiness and share it.

Work and daily life

You understand the rhythms of life, and the fact that we must find a work–life balance. You're a good worker and employee as you can be extremely well organised, understanding fully the concept of duty. You may have an overtly disciplined childhood (or an overtly untamed upbringing), and as you grow up you may baulk at society's morals as you point the way forwards to a new, more balanced paradigm.

Your rebellious side, should it persist into adulthood, is purely the expression of your own inner process which, by attempting to find some sort of order amidst the chaos, will constantly fight to understand your own role, values and position in life's kaleidoscope. To do this, pushing boundaries will be a part of the learning process. Your rebelliousness comes from an impetuous spark that, with age, will settle into a less unruly appreciation of life.

As you mature you'll gradually establish a new set of values and ideals. In the process they may create speed bumps in your life as you continually re-orientate yourself towards new standards that suit you and your own circumstances better. In so doing you'll try many new circumstances at work and in your daily routine to see if it fits the perennially evolving you.

You may go through periods in life where you're without direction, but your motivation and innate ability to stick to routine, structure and duty, as well as your ability to be disciplined, will always give you the capacity to work hard towards your goals. In addition, you'll find your true values and aims will at all times be underpinned by your natural flair, your sense of justice and joy, your organisational skills and your belief and determination that harmony and beauty will prevail—always.

Perspective

Diligent, good worker, capable, dutiful, conscientious, animated, energetic, adaptable

Talents

Organisational skills, fairness, self-belief, self-discipline

Type of work

Corporate, law, police force, diplomacy, administration, secretarial, mining, gemology, business, finance, trade, communications, mediation, design, family advocate

Challenge
To be true to your beliefs

Potential pitfalls
Amorality, rebelliousness, impetuosity

Affirmation
Order out of chaos brings beauty into being.

Relationships

You're a lover seeking the ideal relationship. Ideally you would marry your childhood sweetheart. Conversely you might spend your entire life searching for the perfect partner, jumping from one person to another until such time that you realise perfect people don't exist, and neither does the perfect relationship. The improbability that you'll find such a relationship doesn't deter you from your search because you know deep down that beauty is in the eye of the beholder.

You're one of life's true romantics, but you're also aware that your own approach to relationships is what will make them work. As such you can be extremely charming and persuasive.

Your search for an ideal person or even circumstance will accompany you throughout your life. So that in business, for example, you'll be forever on the lookout for the perfect deal with the perfect business partner. In your eagerness to spread harmony all around, you may become a philanthropist or a humanitarian, eager to make good contacts who'll help you.

Your desire to create unity and harmony will be expressed in your endeavours to bring two disparate qualities or people together. So you may become an art dealer attempting to find the perfect buyer to match the perfect painting, a mediator helping couples come together or a financial broker helping arrange deals between separate organisations.

In your personal life you'll be attracted to many different partners, and when you believe you've found the perfect one you'll pursue them with verve! As a youngster you'll search for status symbols and you may find that these are most easily appropriated by way of suitable marriage partners and shared assets.

You'll look for togetherness and union, but true satisfaction for you will arise out of your ability to create something beautiful and precious not just from joining two separate qualities together but from joining two separate ideas and turning them into a new concept. You'll enjoy seeing a new quality come from this union such as a new theory or approach to life. And when you bring people together you'll enjoy seeing the new entity this creates, for example two people becoming a couple, or literally two people creating a new life, such as a child that results from a marriage or union.

This drive to connect people, ideas and groups can develop into a kind of ego-centrism that borders on megalomania. You risk becoming so intent on creating an elusive yet appealing life that ironically you no longer hear, still less understand, the wishes of those you love. In turn this behaviour can lead to a lack of cooperation between people and a lack of harmony.

With age comes a more magnanimous approach as you begin to see that the beauty and unity you seek is inside yourself, in much the same way you understand that beauty is in the eye of the beholder. Unity and peace is inside everyone even if it takes some time, and a sprinkle of maturity, to discover.

Your restlessness and search for ideal relationships as a youngster will soon give way to contentment, in maturity, as you enjoy relationships that express your inner values and beauty. Living an ideal life is, after all, only a concept because what is ideal in the final analysis is your *connection* to beauty, art and love—and this comes from within.

Perspective

Optimistic, idealistic, romantic, fair-minded, well-meaning, innocent, willing to resolve conflicts

Talents

Resourcefulness, enthusiasm, motivation, charm, persuasiveness

Challenge

To learn balance through relationships by expressing yourself freely and allowing others to do the same

Potential pitfalls

Calculating, rebellious, restless, self-serving, ego-centrism, starry-eyed

Affirmation

Happiness comes from inside me.

Motivation

What better way to create beauty and harmony than through indulgence in the finer things in life, good humour and entertainment, and the pleasures of intimacy? At various stages in your life you'll appear a classic bon vivant, and you'll freely wish to share luxurious indulgences with those close to you.

Beneath the superficial, you are keenly motivated to overcome life's challenges and lack of harmony. You'll feel the need to constantly review what you believe is fair and just in your attempt to keep abreast of circumstances, and frequently change your mind to the extent that you may appear two-faced with your values, principles and morals. But your changeability constitutes your process of learning how to cooperate, and how to bring people together. Once you have sunk your teeth into a cause you can be quite the terrier, not letting go until you've succeeded with your task.

In life you're motivated to fight for values and principles. You can succeed under pressure as you have a wellspring of energy at your beck and call. You're a dynamo and can be competitive, thriving on direction and enthralling interests. But without adequate direction in life you can become fickle, restless, manipulative and potentially even depressed.

The key to feeling motivated lies in establishing stable, constant and benevolent values, and working towards expressing these in your immediate, everyday routine. To do this, cooperation, research and understanding how you yourself fit into the bigger picture will hold the key, and you'll begin by placing faith in your relationships as these are the foundations for your bigger picture successes.

Perspective

Serene, eager to please, compliant, willing to back a cause, peacekeeper, dynamic

Talents

Optimism, shrewdness, well-meaning, fairness, kind-heartedness

Challenge

To see your place in the bigger picture

Potential pitfalls

Meddling, changeable, obstinate/domineering, fickle, depressed, controlling

Affirmation

I create harmony by expressing my values that are based on fairness.

Seeking . . .

You're looking for your place in the bigger picture, and how your path relates to life's broader canvas. You're interested in the world and your neighbourhood too. Not just for the sake of it, but because you wish to understand how life is woven together, how it balances out and your place within it. You'll seek to express your opinions vociferously and you'll enjoy learning new information and studying new ideas and ideologies that will back up your claims.

As you come to understand your unique place in the world (whether from the comfort of home or at the frontline of communications and study), you'll see that your ability to value both the large and small, the insignificant and the invaluable in equal measure is what gives you your perspective.

You understand true value from the smallest to the largest detail because you understand that value in life comes from the way you approach it—from the heart as well as from the head. You have excellent perspective and are able to see both sides of the story on many fronts, and this is what helps you seek deeper truths in life and search for harmony.

At various intervals in life you'll be challenged to leave your preconceptions behind, to suspend your judgment and disbelief and discover life's contradictions and synchronicities. At these times you may be tempted to take extreme risks in the name of understanding life. You have a dynamic spark that, left untamed, can get you into scrapes. Luckily your search for harmony will keep you from excessively dangerous environments.

You understand the value of life in all its paradoxes and idiosyncrasies, the constant balancing act that constitutes its magic and beauty. Your deep understanding of these enigmas gives you the ability to derive a sense of peace, which is what puts you in a very beautiful place.

Perspective

Investigative, analytical, inquisitive, alternately outspoken/shy, genuine, risk-taking

Talents

Evaluation, affability, fair-mindedness, patience, willing to compromise, willing to resolve conflicts

Interests

Study, law, architecture, art, beauty, fashion, fine food, design

Challenge

To express your values in the world

Potential pitfalls

Presumptuousness, loss of perspective

Affirmation

I take my place in the world.

Career and direction

You're intellectually and emotionally invested in creating splendour in the world around you. In many cases you'll do this through the beautification of your own family, home or property. As you mature you'll be drawn to expressing your love of life, your appreciation of beauty and of simple indulgences out there in the world through your career and in your embrace of life's magnificent experiences in general.

While you'll feel comfortable expressing your more outgoing personality in the home or family setting, you'll grow to feel increasingly comfortable expressing yourself in the workplace and in the world as you mature. That is unless your enjoyment of comfort, good food and wine—to the exclusion of all else—dominates in your life. This is a tendency to be wary of as it can lead to laziness, inactivity and a lack of motivation that will lead you away from gaining a sense of purpose.

As you spread your wings in the bigger world you'll enjoy being the mediator, pacifist or bringer of comfort, wellbeing, love and beauty, just as you do at home. You enjoy working towards happy outcomes so you will be attracted to work within fields that involve conflict resolution such as marriage guidance or even the military.

You're able to excel both at work and home as your recipe for success in both is the same: the dissemination of beauty, harmony, love and fairness in your own proactive, gentle, charming and inimitable way.

You're a sensitive, artistic soul at heart. You'll enjoy immersing yourself in beautiful activities such as dance, music and art as these activities are ideal vehicles to disseminate your particular take on life: spreading magnificence and splendour wherever you go.

Characteristics

Family-oriented as a child, more outgoing in adulthood, aggressive as a child, fair as an adult, well-meaning, energetic, willing to create beauty and splendour

Talents

Beautifying your environment, art, broad-mindedness, mediation

Type of career

Artist, homemaker, designer, decorator, chef, beauty and fashion industry, mediator, counselling, brokerage, finances, business, trade, negotiation, diplomacy, marriage guidance, military, legal, psychology, peacekeeper

Challenge

To create beauty and harmony at work and in the world

Potential pitfalls

Lack of motivation, stay at home, laziness, self-indulgence

Affirmation

Beauty and love make the world go around.

Goals, groups and humanitarianism

You're comfortable being a leader in your field especially within the arts and family and child-related activities. When it comes to group activities you may at first feel that your particular brand of leadership will be swallowed up in the collective, especially as a youngster. But as you mature you'll find that the happiness you gain from teamwork and collaborative achievements will replace your need to take the lead.

Your fear that the group dynamic will engulf your personality is groundless, and your unique charm and creativity will blossom over time especially if you allow it to do so. You'll find that working cooperatively helps you shine brighter—much more so than working alone. After all, you are seeking to bring people together, and this includes you. Paradoxically immersing yourself in group activities will see you excel as an individual.

You'll work well within institutions and organisations. You're a sociable character, even if a little shy as a youngster. You're a valuable team member as you have a natural ease and understanding of others' situations. And once you are fully engaged in an activity you will keep at it until you succeed as you are a hardworking collaborator.

You'll be attracted to groups and activities that best express your desire to see love manifest all around you. Music, the arts, meditation, tai chi and gentle exercise will all appeal. Some of your friends may be surprised by your attraction for heavier interests such as loud music, the occult (anything hidden) and parapsychology, as you appear to be such a gentle character on many fronts, but you'll enjoy expressing the vital and insistent pulse that beats through your heart. You have a strong life force that demands expression!

Perspective

Independent when young, collaborative when mature, appreciative, friendly, sociable

Talents

Art, design, creativity, team playing, networking, music

Interests

Charity, music, the arts, dance, marriage guidance, peacekeeping, military, humanitarian, finances, gardening, politics, science, environment, media, research, academia

Challenge

To integrate harmoniously

Potential pitfalls

To be a loner, uncooperative, rebellious

Affirmation

I express the life force that connects us.

The secret you

You'll enjoy exploring the hidden side of society including those areas that are often kept separate from mainstream society such as prisons and hospitals. In these domains your unique talents will be invaluable, particularly because you can act as a bridge between the place people find themselves in at present, such as a prison or hospital, and the place they'd like to be in the future.

Rehabilitation and reformative work will appeal to you and you may do much work behind the scenes in society throughout various periods of your life. Your ability to connect people together will also be expressed simply through everyday gestures of kindness in your neighbourhood.

You're likely to be drawn to the occult, which literally means 'the hidden', such as spiritualism and magic, especially from an intellectual point of view and as an expression of human nature. Psychoanalysis will also appeal for the same reason. You're motivated to delve profoundly into the human psyche in your search for some understanding of what brings value to life, and also due to your interest in conflict resolution.

You'll value wisdom and inner peace as you find these qualities bring balance and harmony within yourself—and within the lives and the relationships of those you love.

Physical exploration of the deep such as diving, plumbing and digging of any sort will also appeal on some level whether this is due to an appreciation of the world's resources or the world's history involving archaeological digs, for example.

The risk is that you delve too deeply into places that are best left alone. You can consequently discover a dark world that is hard to escape from, such as the world of alcohol or drug dependency. Your bright-spark attitude that tends to jump feet-first into new situations could land you into a few sticky circumstances that could eventually transform you into someone you do not wish to be.

You secretly fear the inherent and underlying chaos in life, and that this will in some form inhibit the harmony you wish to create. The fundamentally rebellious and dynamic nature of the spark of creation holds particular fascination and potentially even dread for you as the big bang theory and the disorder in the universe that this premise suggests is the opposite of the concept of divine harmony.

Your inner rebel can also become a source of fear as it has a habit of emerging in your character at inopportune moments, but if you're able to channel this rebellious spark into productive activities your inner rebel will, in fact, become an asset rather than a hindrance. You are, after all, a determined individual, and this determination emanates in part from the harnessing of your inner rebel.

Your deep understanding and appreciation of all things beautiful will guide you away from circumstances and beliefs that lack harmony and love. You know that the beauty you see around you radiates from you. It springs from your own soul because you are a connector and a balancing force in the world; a determined individual who will seek to implement harmony above all else. You also understand the fundamental paradox that the spark of creation may indeed be erratic and dynamic in nature, but that within the grand scheme of things, balance will always reign.

Characteristics

Restless, deep-thinking, reserved, curious, keen to help

Talents

Ingenuity, inventiveness, fair-mindedness, exploration, intellect

Interests

Mining, space exploration, psychoanalytical, military, security, esoteric, rehabilitation

Challenge

To be a balancing force in your own life, as well as in others' lives.

Potential pitfalls

Slovenliness, apathy, self-indulgence, being misguided, addictions, presumptuousness

Affirmation

Beauty shines from my soul.

Scorpio

The passionate transformer

SITUATION

Your charisma smoulders just below the surface of your skin. And yet you will spend great swathes of energy trying to garner admiration. You may also feel motivated to gather resources such as money. This is all in an effort to replace what you feel deep down, and in moments of distraction, that you've lost.

Feeling you must recoup something that you no longer have, that is rightfully yours and which was perhaps taken from you causes you to appear almost feverish in your drive to succeed. Your obsessive pursuit of money or approval will mistakenly lead some people to believe you're materialistic and self-centred as they watch you strive intently to attain all that you can.

Deep down the feeling that something is lacking may stem from a sense of being undervalued, and this will be a source of anxiety and self-doubt. A natural query will be 'I feel I'm missing something—could this be because I am less than perfect myself?' When this question becomes too complex or too self-destructive to answer you may project the sense of lack onto those closest to you, and unintentionally devalue them in turn via inadvertent criticism.

You are passionate about succeeding at all costs. You're on a mission to be and have everything you know you once had and for some reason is now missing or hard to attain. A lack of self-esteem is the biggest challenge for you, and yet the irony is that you already have all that you could possibly ever want: deep-seated drive and intense motivation. Even if this drive is a result of your lack of self-worth, when you accept this powerful impulse you'll realise that you're at your most successful and powerful right now.

You're a power to be reckoned with. You do not need to chase something you feel you've lost as it is no longer relevant or necessary. It has been replaced by your own powerful life force that is immeasurably deep.

The secret to success in your life is to embrace your inner power and direct your energy into pursuits that take you away from your fears and self-doubt. You are able to transform anything you put your mind to, and you can transform it into exactly what you want it to be. Just look at how you transform your self-doubt into drive and motivation. The danger—and unhappiness—arises when you attempt to change people and circumstances that are not yours to change.

PURPOSE

You'll gain a sense of purpose by channelling your powerful energy into constructive pursuits that you enjoy because your intensity will otherwise be expressed through explosive emotions and strong desires. You will attract drama, and your life will include massive transformations within your own personal circumstances.

You risk spending your energy satisfying your immediate desires rather than pursuing and expressing your higher purpose. You'll feel increasingly fulfilled if you strive to emerge from every challenge stronger, more productive and more positive than before because without setting this intention you risk becoming self-destructive. Even worse you risk becoming destructive of other people, so it's important to be aware that your strong emotions can be the catalyst for positive transformation—and not just the opposite.

Another way to find fulfilment is to lose the faint memory you have of having had it all and now being inferior in some sense. Instead look ahead—never back. Rather live in the present with the intention that it will all turn out for the best. If anyone can do this, you can.

Yours is the quintessential journey of the hero(ine) who has seemingly lost it all. The challenge is to re-find the enchanted castle, to re-establish your place as the motivator, the prime mover. To do this in a positive way your purpose must include concentrated effort that will help you rise above everyday drama, chaos and passion. The hero(ine) inside you will find a way to the enchanted castle and take his/her place there, transforming your life into what you know it is and will be forever: perfect, powerful and splendid.

Ultimately the hero(ine) inside you will enable you to fulfil your highest purpose. But if you succumb to everyday drama, chaos, greed and passion you'll find you merely arrive at a shadow version of your castle where riches are illusory and life is a reflection of your own internal drama.

Affirmation

I am powerful. I can make a better future.

Famous people

Coco Chanel, David Frost, Henri Toulouse-Lautrec, Helmut Newton, Michelle Pfeiffer, Walt Disney, Abraham Lincoln, Germaine Greer, Tiger Woods, Ellen DeGeneres

Your unique approach

Self-centred, you? Not at all. Things can just look that way because you feel compelled to do everything you can to further your own agenda due to a lack of certainty or self-worth. You're likely to believe everyone is the same, too, that everyone is liable to promote their own agenda, so you'll be surprised when you're accused of being self-centred. Aren't you just the same as everyone else? Isn't everyone out for themselves?

You believe you're a great collaborator: the best partner. But as you may discover not everyone will agree with you, and a sad lesson you'll learn again and again is that you feel essentially alone on your particular journey. This realisation will lead to strong emotions and of feeling misunderstood. You may subsequently resort to controlling, manipulative behaviour in an attempt to gain a sense of stability or self-worth.

Strong emotions and feelings of being misunderstood will continue until you channel your energy into constructive pursuits that engage your sense of purpose. Your need to prove your worth through seemingly self-serving interests will eventually diminish as you begin to truly accept yourself as a powerful, independent and cooperative being.

Once you do you'll discover that you have a strong support system behind you, whether this was a dependable parent when you were a child or a dependable partner as an adult. And it's when you channel your energy into the enthusiasm and wonder you feel about life itself that people will be attracted to you, and this is what will enable you to feel no longer alone and to enjoy the bonds that signify you're not alone.

It's when you turn your mind outwards and away from yourself and towards other people, when you become genuinely interested in their circumstances and not only in your own that you'll discover your true purpose: you are a great collaborator when you show genuine interest in others. And when you dig deep and prove your own dependability, charm, inner power and strength to others, they will reciprocate. Together you'll transform your life and that of everyone you meet into something truly wonderful because this is collaboration at its best: mutually fulfilling and supportive actions that will transform your lives beyond what they are separately.

Your forte lies in your ability to approach your dreams in a practical, hands-on and transformative yet earthy way. You have the drive, the passion and the power to achieve your dreams. It's simply a case of believing in yourself and others, and your ability to work together. You are an enabler of your dreams—and others' too.

Perspective

Dramatic, passionate, indulgent, child-like, driven, powerful, enabling, instinctive

Talents

Drama, self-expression, cooperation when mature, diligence, focus

Interests

Psychology, self-help, romance, sex, theatre, music, drama

Challenge

To accept your own self-worth and power

Potential pitfalls

Being competitive, selfish, codependent, passive-aggressive, self-doubting, no self-esteem, manipulation, coercion

Affirmation

I believe in myself and in you.

Values and self-expression

Your life will revolve around the importance of your values and those of others. The value you place on life and feelings of self-worth are connected. If you feel you yourself have little or no value this will affect the value you place on other people and the outside world. In turn the value you place on an object or a person will predicate how well you can or cannot share.

The issue of sharing will be a focus in your life time and again. At the root of sharing is the question, what value do I place on this particular commodity, person or feeling? And what value will *I* have as a result of transacting with this commodity, person or feeling? This process will start early, whether you're an only child who doesn't need to learn to share with siblings at an early age or because you're part of a large family and must learn how to share toys, meals and love, very young.

You may sense that you're an outsider, the odd one out or the black sheep, and this will increase your need and desire to be accepted, loved and valued by other people. Your self-expression may appear excessively competitive or intense due to your need for acceptance.

As you mature during different times in your life you may find yourself in the position of having to provide, distribute or take care of vast amounts of resources or people. You may go through distinct phases in your life that are dramatic and wrench your heartstrings, and you will need to take your place in the eye of the storm and distribute products, food, love and resources to people around you. As a result you will develop strong values.

You'll be attracted to trade and commerce. The distribution of wealth or resources will be fulfilling in many ways: through banking, for example, or sharing information. You'll feel fulfilled by satisfying other people's needs too. To do this you'll enjoy finding out what they really want and supplying it to them in the form of food, resources, commodities, love or protection.

You'll find that others' needs and your own will constantly change. You will need to review your agreements with partners, at work and at home, but keeping on top of a changing scenario will not be a challenge for you. This is one of your fortes: adaptability as you stay on top of your—and everyone else's—changing values.

To establish what has true, lasting meaning for you, you'll begin by developing your self-esteem and self-worth. Once you truly value your remarkable life force and dynamism your self-assurance will ripple out from you like the clear tone of a bell, your charisma will radiate and you'll attract equally contented people who will share your mindset and values.

And you'll find that the only value that truly has any meaning is the one that you can share, because without the ability to share common ground, there is very little value in anything.

Perspective
Passionate, adaptable, intense, attentive, curious, principled

Talents
Fair-mindedness, networking, research, ability to share and provide

Challenge
To boost self-esteem and value others

Potential pitfalls
Self-centredness, self-doubt, anxiety, uncertainty

Affirmation
I am valuable and so are you.

Communication

The way you communicate will be remarkable in some way. You have a particular style, flair or manner of speech. You're charismatic and earthy, and you'll engage people mainly through your charm. You communicate initially on a non-verbal level through your strong, earthy or magnetic presence or your attractive smile.

Your intuition is strong to the point of being psychic and you're a deep thinker. Behind your charming self lies an intense person with powerful ideas. You may be prone to stubbornness, yet you will enjoy staying on top of the rapidly changing world of communications, technology and travel. You'll want to be in the thick of the latest news and developments, largely so that you can become a frontrunner in these areas yourself.

You're likely to be well educated, and not necessarily through the school system. You may have street smarts or you may have been home-schooled during periods of your childhood, resulting in a deep understanding of people at a grassroots level. Paradoxically this can lead to misunderstandings (because you're way ahead of the rest on many levels), but little will detract from your motivation to excel at communications.

Travel will appeal, too, as you'll find blending with different cultures relatively easy. As a result an interest in languages will accompany your travels, although your interest is likely either to be superficial or intense; one or the other extreme with nothing in between. The travel bug may take you by surprise at first as you're more comfortable in your own zone on many levels. Yet when you step out into a new environment you'll enjoy the sensory stimulation and, together with the intense experience that often accompanies travel, you'll feel more alive and engaged in life.

You're able to go with life's ups and downs, and with people's opinions and ideas even if you're sensitive and may sometimes feel out of your depth in conversation and interactions. You have the ability to blend and merge with any circumstance, making you the consummate chameleon and giving you the ability to experience many of life's various shades of experience.

Your life may be chaotic and extreme, but you'll live passionately, revelling in a whirlwind of adventures. You'll delight in interacting with people as you are driven to understand them—and in so doing, yourself.

Perspective

Sensitive, perceptive, intuitive, good communicator, adaptable, inquisitive, spirited, deep-thinker, charismatic

Talents

Sixth sense, research, taking responsibility, technology

Challenge

To learn and present new ideas

Potential pitfalls

To be stubborn, stuck or controlling

Affirmation

I am a vital part of my environment.

Home and family

Have you often felt you've had the rug pulled out from under your feet metaphorically—beginning at home as a child, and as an adult in the work arena? Then you've already had one of your first lessons and discovered your latent talent: not giving up!

Your tenacity will teach you how to live life to the fullest. And next time you feel the rug is about to be pulled out from under you, go with it and let the experience take you where it will—it could turn out to be a magic carpet ride after all!

Many obstacles are opportunities in disguise, and you'll appreciate that the intrinsic nature of life is continuous transformation both for you and those you love. Your role within life is to be an agent of change yourself as you are able to not only run with change, but also implement it yourself.

As you mature you'll feel better equipped to roll *with* life's ups and downs, and not roll over and give up. Domestic or family matters will demand your full attention every time you feel you're on the verge of a successful breakthrough, whether this is in your personal life or career path. As a result you'll learn and appreciate what it is to be loyal to those you love, and to the principle of love itself.

Many of your true achievements will come from a domestic or family setting, even if these areas are constantly changing or you must frequently move and adapt to new circumstances.

You understand instinctively that home, love and relationships are what's truly important in life, and by embracing the mundane and the everyday you'll experience a sense of belonging that you may feel is lacking in other areas of your life.

You'll appreciate this all the more by trusting the magic carpet ride, which can only take place if you accept the risk that the rug may, after all, be pulled from under you at the most inopportune moment. The faint-hearted never won anything, and the stronger you are the more you'll feel able to go with, not against, the dramatic changes in life, and be able to work towards positive outcomes. You are, after all, the pilot of this particular ride of your life.

Perspective

Changeable, intense, determined, persistent, tenacious, possessive

Talents

Being understanding, trusting, adaptable, capable, loyal

Challenge

To be resilient

Potential pitfalls

Becoming unyielding, unforgiving, moody, quitting, giving up

Affirmation

Change is the essence of life. I go with it and create positive outcomes.

Creativity and life force

You're the life and soul of any party or get-together, and you'll enjoy the pleasures of life to the max, especially when young. If you're less sociable you'll enjoy the thrill of the artistic process: creating works of art, music and dance. If not busy in a career, you will indulge your children, partners and families to the max.

Excess is the hallmark of a north node in Scorpio, especially in the area of creativity and life force. You have a strong link with a seemingly inexhaustible pool of energy, it's simply a case of tapping into it. Your lust for life as a youngster will include the temptation to experiment with drugs, excessive alcohol or food. You'll also enjoy sex, and you can risk becoming promiscuous when young, becoming addicted to sex or attracting promiscuous partners.

You'll avoid overindulgence, drama and excessive consumption and their attendant issues by channeling your taste for excess into productive activities. You'll find the results astounding as you'll succeed at the projects and initiatives you set your mind to.

Parents with a Scorpio north node become the ultimate in protective, indulgent parents. Workers become perennial workhorses and artists productive creators. Children may appear particularly self-indulgent or over-active, but will tend to grow out of this phase with adequate guidance.

Your life encompasses a richness and magical depth that only someone as extreme as you could hope to imagine, let alone to experience. You have the ability to transform obstacles into opportunities, weaknesses into strengths, and you'll begin your magical work of art on yourself, creating a fabulous person along the way.

Perspective

Fun-loving, vivacious, sociable, energetic, passionate, dramatic, emotional, intense

Talents

Drive, iron will, imagination, creativity, protectiveness, loyalty, steadfastness, hardworking

Creative career

Entertainment, music, dance, food industry, fashion, child care, art

Challenge

To avoid excess

Potential pitfalls

Overindulgence, extremism, selfishness, addictive tendencies, codependence, self-centredness

Affirmation

My life is what I make it—and it's fabulous!

Work and daily life

During various phases of your life you will find yourself immersed in secrets, mysteries or intrigue. As a youngster you may be accused of being secretive or of being insensitive for having revealed others' secrets, and as a result you may become deceitful.

As you mature you'll learn that managing the hidden side of life is something that involves skill and tact. You'll be attracted to work within areas of life that others may not usually see, such as rehabilitation centres or scientific research facilities. Research and analysis in every sense of the words will appeal as you learnt the value of information, secrets and hidden material at an early age.

Being aware that you have the propensity to be drawn to dark, intense or mysterious areas, you'll also know that sensitivity to others' feelings is important. In your lifetime you will discover—and hide—many secrets yourself, not least through the power of your own discretion.

You risk being your own worst enemy as being secretive or working with secretive information can attract intrigue and drama, yet you have a great deal of common sense and a practical approach to the sensitive areas of life. This is the key to your ability to broach taboo areas: you have your feet on the ground, and a deep understanding of the value of being realistic and sensible especially while you're wading in the deeper areas of life.

Contact with the underbelly of life can arise, and you will risk engaging in nefarious work or joining groups that use force, intoxicants or sexual favour as currency, but as you gain your sense of purpose from striving to transform the difficulties of life into something useful, you should manage to maintain perspective.

You'll be attracted to work that plumbs the depths either of human understanding, such as psychoanalysis or astrology, or of the human

173

condition, such as philosophy, health and social work. Your keen sense of values will be expressed through a strong sense of control, so you may also be attracted to work such as law enforcement.

Your earthy nature will encourage you to dig deep—literally! Mining, gemology, plumbing and tax collecting will all appeal to your forensic mind, which must get down to the substructure of matters at hand whether they are a psychological riddle or mine shaft.

Perspective

Inquisitive, prudent, eager, common-sensical, practical, secretive

Talents

Consideration, perceptiveness, helpfulness, healing and enabling ability, research

Type of work

Plumbing, forensics, mortuary, mining, tax, debt-collecting, nutrition, agriculture, finances, management, police force, sales, trade, investigative journalism, archaeology, travel, politics, IT, performance, social work

Challenge

Discretion

Potential pitfalls

Involvement in intrigue, drama, the underbelly of life, deception, being forceful

Affirmation

I'm passionate and practical. My work is beneficial.

Relationships

You're prone to indulge your desires and emotions before you've engaged your mind, especially in relationships. And should your actions be criticised your obstinacy can kick in, leading to further criticism including selfishness or even self-obsession.

As a youngster you will be sexually adventurous, and may be uninhibited sexually as you mature. As an adult this could lead to promiscuity or attracting promiscuous partners who mistake your earthy sensuality for unadulterated passion pure and simple. Drama and intrigue can arise to a fever pitch during various phases of your life.

You have unrivalled insight into people and the world itself, as well as its secrets. As such you can shed light on human relationships and the dynamics of human passions and desires that underpin all interactions. As you gain wisdom and perspective your insight will help you to form ideal relationships and create harmony in your life.

If you give full reign to jealousy, greed and lust you risk becoming a slave to your passions. To satiate these you risk being controlling, conducting codependent relationships, withholding affection and becoming destructive. Your lack of self-esteem is a breeding ground for cold, passive-aggressive behaviour as your fears of being undervalued cause you to effectively undervalue your partner and those close to you. In a worst-case scenario you may be tempted to be deceitful and display one type of behaviour while secretly harbouring another. You can then appear alternately cold and piping hot.

The key to a happy life relationship-wise lies in understanding the boundaries between people, in respecting others' opinions and their right to self-respect and simultaneously learning how to share and share alike. Allowing your mind and heart to engage sexually will also help you to avoid being a slave to your passions.

By walking this delicate line, the gift of understanding love in all its depths and beauty runs deep within you. When you discover this treasure you'll prove to be one of the most loyal people in mind, body and soul.

Perspective

Astute, obstinate, graceful, ardent, amorous, imaginative, jealous, private, appreciative of beauty

Talents

Understanding, imagination, nurturance, loyalty, responsiveness

Challenge

To achieve a balanced flow of love

Potential pitfalls

Passive-aggressiveness, controlling behaviour, codependence, deceit, slave to passions

Affirmation

I love with my heart, body and soul.

Motivation

You are driven to succeed and radiate charm. Your light shines and you could attract everything you want in this lifetime relatively easily from a young age, if only because your drive to succeed is so strong.

NOTE: *exceptions to the characteristics outlined here can occur due to astrological circumstances at birth. For more information see Notes for budding astrologers on page 281.*

You'll enjoy the relatively smooth acquisition of resources and a vast array of experiences. This may seem like an ideal circumstance, and yet such easy access to the vortex of human experience has its own challenges.

Discretion, choice and priorities become difficult to handle when everything and everyone gravitates towards you at high speed. The challenge lies in your staying power, and in making relationships work especially if your impulses and desires take the upper hand.

Yet you have strong values, and by developing a keen sense of self-worth you could discover an Aladdin's cave of delights in your lifetime. You understand the magic of the human experience that will enable you to share all of life's bounties with those you love.

Your loyalty to a higher purpose, whether it is spiritual or religious, is another motivator in your life. By allowing your sense of purpose to blossom you'll discover the true peace that lies at the heart of the theatre of life, which you can use as a building block to transform not only your own life to its highest potential, but also the lives of those you admire too.

Ultimately you're looking for communion in one sense or another, and whether you look for this in relationships, religion, spirituality or the mundane is your choice, so ensure you choose wisely.

Perspective

Charming, magnetic, zealous, attractive, competent

Talents

Understanding, generous, appreciative, supportive, loyal

Challenge

To let your strong sense of values guide you

Potential pitfalls

Over-indulgence, covetous, lack of discretion, calculating, compulsive

Affirmation

I create a beautiful future.

Seeking . . .

You'll enjoy the pursuit of passion, and when you realise this is because you're looking for a truly profound experience you'll begin to search for knowledge and wisdom as a means to stability and peace within the chaos of your life. Your ultimate goal is union, either with another person, a higher understanding of existence or with your own sense of purpose.

Your adventurous, emotional and dramatic approach to life can cause you to risk disappearing inside a tornado of activity, ironically never really indulging deeply enough to experience the wonder of a truly profound experience, still less a deep or existential union. Luckily you're unlikely to stop at a superficial understanding of anything. You will want to know the nuts and bolts, the psychology, the engineering and the structure behind just about every situation you encounter. You may appear obsessive as a result, but just as the penny is about to drop you'll whisk yourself off to the next project potentially missing the point all together.

Those close to you may feel they're under scrutiny when they're with you, that you dissect their psyches because of your need to know the details, the impulse and the passion behind their every move. You'll want to see how they feel, and to feel their passion. You'll find out the information you need through experience, by watching and making deductions. It's all in an attempt to understand life and rediscover a feeling of stability and contentment that you know must lie at its centre, and to connect on a deeply satisfying level.

You'll come to understand that this still centre and feeling of serenity is already within you, and if you stay still long enough and listen you'll hear it. When you locate this place inside yourself you'll know how to locate that still point of the storm for others, too, helping them access this vital and calming aspect of themselves.

Your search for the passion and spark in life will always come back to you, and the inner workings of those you care about. When you discover the peace within you that is separate from the chaos of emotions, drama and passion, you'll locate the building blocks that can transform your life into its highest, most productive and calmest form of expression.

Perspective
Driven, distracted, headstrong, observant, helpful, obsessive

Talents
Research, study, communications, psychology, logic, deduction

Interests
Adventure, travel, education, science, reading, people, information, the life process, finances, mortuary, law, tax, physical activities

Challenge
Through union find deeper meaning in life

Potential pitfalls

Over-analysis, inflexibility, flightiness, fickleness, disorganisation, chaos

Affirmation

The still point of calm helps me be the best I can.

Career and direction

You'll enjoy searching for a feeling of belonging in the world, such as being part of a team. You will put your every effort into your career and general activities so it's in your interest to find out early what you feel truly passionate about. You will be able to excel in your work life precisely because you approach it with such verve and zeal, wishing to embed yourself in the experience.

Your analytical mind along with your passion will steer you toward a career that engages both your mind and your morals such as police work, psychoanalysis and social work. You'll also enjoy fulfilling your need to be an agent of change in some way through your career and direction, so your choice of activity will revolve around how you can best achieve this. You'll appreciate the feeling that you're a positive catalyst in people's lives.

One of your tasks will be to learn workplace dynamics. Once you do you'll gain a sense of fulfilment due to the feeling of acceptance. Some with a Scorpio north node continue family businesses that have been passed down through generations. You'll progress through life by carrying forward your sense of identity through your family, but may wish to break with tradition and search for a sense of your own achievement.

Through your search for validation, belonging and acceptance you'll learn that your actions will be quickly rewarded, and your good intentions and the positive and constructive expression of your self-worth and values in the world will have widespread and positive ramifications. By planting a seed of good intention you'll enjoy watching it grow, and this will go a long way to provide you with the sense of achievement you desire.

You will also enjoy seeing the results of your actions manifest in real terms in the world around you. You aim to transform your world so that you understand your place in it. And in the same way you understand the ever-changing kaleidoscope of life's cycles of birth and death, you also understand your integral role in creating a healthy world.

The lessons you learn about the joys of professionalism and doing good deeds will translate back into your personal life as fulfilment. You'll enjoy this mutually beneficial cycle as it nurtures you and those you come into contact with throughout your life.

Characteristics

Outgoing, proud, practical, ambitious, cooperative, impassioned, intense, cooperative

Talents

Organisational skills, mentoring, dynamism, protectiveness, logic, self-motivation

Type of career

Psychoanalysis, social work, construction, design, tax, finances, business, fashion, admin, domestic services, strategy, politics, philosophy, commerce, sales, marketing, advertising, military, police

Challenge

To be a positive catalyst

Potential pitfalls

Dramatic, scheming, coercive

Affirmation

I belong. My contribution to life is valuable.

Goals, groups and humanitarianism

You're a dramatic, creative artist at heart. Your purpose is to share your talent for creating spectacle, enthusiasm and drama wherever you go, to present your wonderful creativity to the world through group endeavours, to raise your standards and at the same time raise those of the people you work and interact with. You desire to produce wonderful works of art in the broader sense whether they are musical, theatrical, sports-oriented, family, charity or work-related.

You'll feel fulfilled by indulging in the wonders of life, and to celebrate them and present them as something that will appeal to the masses, not just the few. When you interact with people in a group context your influence never goes unnoticed. You may not be the obvious shining star at the centre of every club, but you'll be a prime mover, a motivator, an enabler and at the very least a pleasure to have on the team.

You're a generous, loyal person, but easily distracted. You understand the passion that is at the heart of the human experience, and sharing and helping others to understand this is an activity you'll enjoy.

Your dynamic energy is well suited to sport as your desire to be part of a team truly motivates you to succeed. You're a keen tactician and strategist, which will enable you not only to partake in team sports, but also to manage them.

You may find family dramas underlie some of your experiences in life, but with a productive approach your experiences can help others in a similar situation. This will be a healing experience for them and you too. You may be attracted to groups and clubs that are self-help organisations, and you'll enjoy working within them. If you undergo challenging moments psychologically or physically you'll find the influence of support groups and organisations invaluable.

You'll look for new ways to understand life. Self-development classes such as psychic development will appeal at some point in your life as they could help you develop a deeper understanding of life.

Your compassion and willingness to help people evolve personally and spiritually involves the quest to evolve in some way yourself. This will largely manifest as a search for new ways to enjoy life, which is why fun groups will appeal to you the most: theatrical, comedic, dance and musical groups especially. Your reason to join a club or group will be based on practical reasoning: to celebrate, enjoy yourself and share the human experience with like-minded people!

Perspective

Sociable, cooperative, creative, charismatic, generous, eager, humorous, jovial

Talents

Influence, self-expression, loyalty, enthusiasm, motivation

Interests

Having fun, self-help, self-transformation, yoga, fashion, drama, charity, horticulture, sports, music, dance

Challenge

To bring joy to everyone

Potential pitfalls

Becoming lost in life's dramas, easily distracted

Affirmation

I celebrate life.

The secret you

You have an actively secret life. This is partly because you've learned to hide some of your strong passions and intense traits, especially those you feel are not socially acceptable like your strong sixth sense.

You're a natural-born clairvoyant in the literal sense that you can see clearly. You have psychic and even mediumistic skills. For you the other side, the paranormal and the other-worldly are not figments of your imagination; they are reality. As a child you're likely to have an invisible friend and be able to see fairies or magical people.

As an adult you have extraordinary insight into people's minds, which could lead to an interest in psychology. You may feel isolated from your peers as others do not share your insights, which may seem strange, unusual or unacceptable even to you.

But rejecting your talents and opting for a more realistic take on life is unlikely to fulfil you, as your depth of understanding does not lend itself to superficiality. You will later in life resume an interest in all things otherworldly as you will find it hard to resist plumbing the depths of profound study and self-knowledge.

You may wish to transform your life in a radical way during various phases of your life through travel and work, for example. A pitfall is that you may be tempted to take the fast track to deeper, altered states through psychoactive drugs. But you do not require them to attain highs as you have a natural predisposition towards heightened states. You'll attain these naturally and through meditation, prayer, self-knowledge and the deep bond you have with someone close.

You're secretly easily influenced by others. This can become perilous within sexual relationships when your strong passions dictate your actions, and you can be easily caught up in other people's dramas as a result. You also have a propensity to project your own undesirable personality traits onto other people, especially those close to you.

You have a hidden tendency to become obsessed with particular ideas such as the fear that your future is fated and you cannot escape it, or that you will always be alone and never attain a feeling of deep union, acceptance or intimacy with others. You may even feel that in some sense your repeated ventures and dramas that always seem to take you through Alice's looking glass will only end up with you staring down the same old rabbit hole.

Your health and wellbeing will transform in line with your secret life. Your every step, thought and emotion has a ripple effect through your body, and you'll experience this first and foremost physically. If you feel tired, for example, you can feel physically ill.

If you learn to listen to your body's signals you'll find the secret you—your powerful intuition—has a lot to contribute as a guide to the right path not only for you, but potentially also for others. So it's in your interest to nurture your physical, mental and spiritual health. You'll simply know when you're on the right track when your insight gives you a deeper purpose in life: to understand the meaning of the human experience and share this with people not blessed with such acute understanding.

Yoga, mindfulness, prayer and devotion to your higher self will enable you to be the best you can be, and these activities will transform your life, helping you avoid old, repetitive patterns. You'll find that even if the transformation you instigate in your life is motivated by your passions and desires, your life will flower when your passions are put to use in a calm, peaceful and compassionate way.

Characteristics

Perceptive, easily led, imaginative, thoughtful, conscientious, secretive

Talents

Insight, mediumship, compassion, clairvoyance

Interests

Spiritual, religious, medical, rehabilitation, pets, psychic ability, sensuality, sex

Challenge

To listen to your inner voice

Potential pitfalls

Being easily influenced, rejecting your own talents, being misunderstood, self-sabotage, fear of losing control

Affirmation

My inner voice guides me.

Sagittarius

The progressive seeker of the truth

SITUATION

You're one of life's adventurers always looking out for the next exciting escapade. But your curiosity, impulsiveness and free spirit can tie you down in superficial and self-indulgent activities that risk taking you away from your ultimate goal: to get to grips with the true grit and intrinsic meaning of your life.

You'll feel inclined to embrace the bigger picture, to push things as far as you can so that you can discover their essence. This is largely why you're so motivated by adventure and daring escapades—you want to know what's hidden behind the obvious.

You'll also derive greater meaning from life by learning to search for—and appreciate—other people's stories, not just yours. In the course of your lifetime you'll gather a great deal of information—from gossip to educational insight to facts derived from your own research. You'll enjoy sifting through the information and deciding what's truth and what's fiction, what's useful, productive information and what's trivia, gossip or mere distraction.

In the process you'll undergo various indecisive or seemingly aimless periods. You'll be too busy collecting information to make your mind up about the value of anything in particular. For this reason you may on occasion be described as shallow as you'll be seen to move from one activity to another, seemingly at random.

As a seeker of the truth, you'll enjoy sorting the wheat from the chaff, the wolves from the lambs, discovering facts and accumulating wisdom. As an adult you'll be attracted to fact-finding missions and even discoveries less outgoing and courageous people wouldn't even consider, let alone embark upon.

PURPOSE

Your purpose is to establish the truth of a situation, to find meaning in it and embrace the vastness of your experience, its intricacies and the bigger picture too. You will feel fulfilled by the sense of freedom you gain from knowledge. You may subsequently wish to shout your knowledge from the rooftops or publish your findings. Free speech will appeal to you. You'll also be drawn to vocations that enable you to discriminate between what's true and what's false such as work in the legal system.

You already know there are many facets to life, and truth can seem different depending on which angle you view it from. So you know that finding the ultimate truth is no easy task, but you have the deeper understanding that it exists.

The risk is that, in your search for the ultimate truth, you entertain so many different viewpoints that you become lost and distracted, never actually find any truth or meaning. As such you could lose sight of your purpose, becoming enmeshed in always looking for the next adventure or crusade, or in fruitless gossip and innuendo.

Your search for value and truth in life can paradoxically lead to a superficial, directionless existence, but you'll slowly come to understand that truth comes down to what matters the most to you: honesty, straightforward goals and a clear conscience. When you establish what— and who—matters most to you you'll find that this is your own ultimate truth as it gives you direction and a tingling sense of freedom.

Ultimately you'll judge your success by the degree of integrity and conscientiousness you can attain. You have luck on your side, which will keep you out of harm's way and enable you to adopt a progressive attitude to life's adventures, staying true to your own unique and liberating purpose.

Affirmation

The truth sets me free.

Famous people

Pablo Picasso, Drew Barrymore, Dustin Hoffman, Jay Rockefeller, Arsenio Hall, Tom Hanks, Whoopi Goldberg, Jack Nicholson, Bill Gates, Betty Ford, Leonardo DiCaprio, Nelson Mandela, Angelina Jolie, David Beckham

Your unique approach

Will you spend your time worried about people's expectations of you or do you have more important things to do? Will you follow other people's wishes or will you be your own person and discover what your life can be and how you can make things happen? Will you take the courageous step and be true to yourself, play to your strengths, gain direction and chase your own ambitious goals?

Rest assured, you'll make valid choices in life when you're faced with issues such as these. You'll always feel fulfilled by aiming high, and in this way you'll find success and fulfilment in life. You'll enjoy taking your activities to the highest point they can go, and even if you do not reach your goals you'll enjoy the journey. You're a flamboyant, larger-than-life personality and your positive attitude is infectious. You're likely to be an active sportsperson and you'll enjoy watching team sports.

Fundamentally truthful and diligent your forthright honesty can seem like blatant disregard for people's feelings, which can put people offside as they mistake you for a blunt, insensitive and even superficial person. State your intentions and your goals up front as this will ensure everyone is on the same page, minimising misunderstandings.

When under stress you can become a slippery fish in an attempt to avoid intense personal confrontation, side-step events you find distasteful, and become indecisive and even deceitful in the process. Yet you are so honest at other times. Your tendency to slip into seemingly shallow behaviour is a kind of last-resort pattern, and one that does not serve your purpose. It is merely a detour, even if it may seem a useful response to intense situations you dislike.

As a friend you're loyal and true. As a worker you're honest and straightforward. As a partner you're adventurous and sincere. You're one of life's stalwarts partly because you have an understanding of fairness and justice, and you'll always stand by the universal protocol of compassion and kindness.

Perspective

Positive, fair-minded, fun, flamboyant, direct, kind, diligent

Talents

Determination, pragmatism, dependability, honesty, inclusiveness

Interests

Sports, socialising, broadening horizons, adventure, wisdom, technology

Challenge

To focus, aim high and attain goals

Potential pitfalls

Indecision, selfishness, shallowness, insensitivity, ambivalence

Affirmation

I am true to myself.

Values and self-expression

You express yourself in a direct and immediate way. You can appear matter-of-fact, leading people to believe you're sure of yourself. And yet your directness comes from uncertainty, especially as a youngster, and from your need to sort the truth from the lies, to find the side of the story that is correct.

Your frank mannerisms indicate your wish to be sure that what you're saying is in fact correct. As you mature you'll assert yourself with yet more conviction, being one hundred per cent sure of the validity of what you're saying and doing.

You're on a mission to stay on top of life's changing scenarios, to know about the latest inventions, gadgets, food stuffs, scientific insights, gossip, facts, shared knowledge—in fact anything that will give you a foothold in life or help you search for the truth.

Your search is for meaning—anything to provide a safe platform from which to launch yourself and your high aims into the world. And you'll express yourself enthusiastically and engage with many people in your quest for knowledge because you know you need to ask the right questions to get the right answers.

In the process you'll want to stand out, be open-minded, learn from mistakes or from history at large, forge ahead and make a stand about codes of conduct and morals. You'll also want to set a positive example to others, and investigate new territories literally or figuratively. You'll enjoy expressing your dynamic nature through sports and physical activity, being gifted or at least attracted to competition.

You're an adventurer at heart and if you ignore this you risk obscuring the very impulse in your life that spurs you on to create and achieve great things. Some with a Sagittarius north node will accrue financial and material possessions to the exclusion of all else, but you are a generous soul and will feel happy sharing your bounty.

Some will uphold morals or pursue particular values to the exclusion of all else as you're flamboyantly invested in your every action. Whatever you put your mind to, you'll do with one hundred per cent application and may be tempted to become fanatical—once you hitch yourself to a cause or a new activity you'll pursue it fervently. That is, until you discover it wasn't for you after all or else you've already jumped to the next good thing.

A tendency towards being changeable to the degree of being directionless will generally subside as you mature, when you discover what you've been looking for all along: your own ability to embrace the enormity and vastness of the life experience. This ability comes from you yourself, and in the way you react to the world in your own unique, inclusive and adventurous way.

You'll feel fulfilled by balancing your eccentricities and keen sense of adventure with a healthy respect for all that is time-honoured and universal within your existence. You will balance your ambition and thirst for knowledge with respect for others, yourself and your wisdom.

The basic pillars of human happiness—compassion, kindness and respect—are the time-honoured values that you'll be happy to uphold during the adventure that is your lifetime. Your search for the truth will eventually simmer down into a search for the meaning of life, which you'll find comes from deep inside you. Deeper values rise above the difference between truth and lies, right and wrong. You'll find that commitment, love, wisdom and loyalty are absolute values—there is no uncertainty, debate or compromise in their terms.

Perspective

Ambitious, materialistic, generous, jovial, well-meaning, risk-taking, progressive, adaptable, honest, blunt, conscientious

Talents

Communications, initiating projects, strategy, clear-sightedness, kindness, self-motivation

Challenge

To value yourself and others

Potential pitfalls

Superficiality, changeability, fanaticism, restlessness

Affirmation

I value kindness and love.

Communication

Communication is the ideal vehicle to find meaning, truth and freedom in life. You will actively pursue ways to be an accomplished communicator. You have a natural learning and teaching ability because you have a grassroots understanding that borders on street smarts of the girl/boy next door variety. You're able to implement knowledge in a practical way through teaching, research and strategic planning.

During periods of your life you may be more interested in disseminating information than gathering knowledge, and this may well prove to be a fun activity or job, but it's unlikely to satisfy the adventurous, explorative side of your personality.

You're goal-orientated, and you must know that you'll attain end results before you even commence a project. Your excitement comes from not necessarily knowing *what* the end result will be. This is what contributes to your seeking self: you will not limit your activities to a set, expected outcome.

The knowledge you gain during your lifetime will help you attain your goals, which are self-perpetuating. You'll pool knowledge, then spread knowledge, then pool it once more to gain further insight and on the cycle goes. You know that discussion and sharing of knowledge is the only reward you need and this itself exemplifies the power you display throughout your life. Your rewards are instant because you're engaged in the pursuit of the thing you love most—knowledge—which as you already know is, in itself, powerful.

It's for this reason that gossip and discussion for the sake of interaction alone will leave you cold. You enjoy knowing that all the information and discussions you're involved with will lead to something, that there will be a beneficial outcome.

Travel, research, trade, communications and learning will attract you but your true reward will come from sharing your insight on a grassroots level and to sow the seeds of your knowledge and enjoy seeing them sprout into blossoming trees of knowledge for everyone.

Your close relationships will also be your platform for a happy life: the enthusiastic way you interact and communicate with your siblings, your closest family members and your neighbourhood will all provide you with a strong source of contentment and joy.

Perspective

Inquisitive, larger-than-life, fun, talkative, fair-minded, knowledgeable

Talents

Research, writing, teaching, communications, negotiation, languages

Challenge

To use knowledge constructively

Potential pitfalls
Distractions, shallowness, aimlessness

Affirmation
Knowledge is empowering.

Home and family

You're an extremely adaptable person, and almost chameleon-like in your ability to adjust to and excel in new environments. You're likely to move home frequently, especially in your childhood, and probably in connection with your parents moving due to work demands or simply because they're bohemian, restless or perennial globetrotters.

Your own family may blaze trails within the domestic arena in some way and you may not even realise that by normal or everyday standards you are an exception in some way at home. Perhaps you have a blended family with overseas connections or you travel a great deal to different countries with drastically contrasting economic models. Being uprooted or pioneering in some way domestically could be a feature of your youth. One or both of your parents or a family member is likely to be overtly ambitious.

As an adult your domestic circumstances will mirror the pioneering spirit. Being able to expand your experience in personal terms will appeal to you, and family will be an area where you learn some of your most empowering lessons.

Your home decor will reflect your multicultural or well-travelled background through a plethora of different design styles and furniture from various countries or cultures. Your home is also likely to reflect your need for open space and movement by being close to or including large outdoor spaces, and by including activity rooms as opposed to simply living rooms.

Through your varied upbringing you'll attain a great deal of insight into human relationships, but as a child you may feel unsettled or restless. This can contribute to a lack of commitment to people or to situations as a youngster as you may wonder when it'll all change again.

Your extraordinary insight into the human condition will serve you well in your quest for meaning in life, and as you mature you may also develop a deeper sense of loyalty to those you love as they become your rod and staff in changing scenarios.

Your unique insight into the human condition and the diversity of cultural creeds will help you not only to find direction in life, but also to develop a deep tolerance of other people's ideas, feelings and cultures.

Although your life may begin as unsettled, restless, troubled or simply larger than life, this very situation will help you to value and honour the true rewards in life that are closer to home: your family, property and personal life. And even while you'll find career moves and attaining status relatively straightforward, your mature, adventurous, goal-oriented, free-spirited personality will measure success in personal terms—not in worldly, financial or professional terms. The liberty you're looking for comes from a happy heart.

Perspective

Adaptable, chameleon-like, communicative, big-hearted, prime mover, tolerant

Talents

Imagination, protectiveness, caring, progressivity, generosity, loyalty

Challenge

To find stability within a restless life

Potential pitfalls

Being unsettled or displaying a lack of commitment

Affirmation

I am committed to a wonderful life.

Creativity and life force

You're the ultimate networker, and you're able to pull a rabbit out of a hat at, well, the drop of a hat. You're the maverick and joker at get-togethers especially as a child and youth. As you mature you'll facilitate many events and gatherings, be the taxi for the kids, the cook, the breadwinner, the organiser and general master/mistress of ceremonies within family life and community.

You're also forward-looking and progressive, able to plan and gauge what your nearest and dearest will need next. Largely because you're deeply invested in people, you want to know what makes them tick, how they fit into your circumstances and what their contribution to life is.

And yet your intensity and the full attention you pay to others may seem out of keeping with your general free spirit. Especially as a youngster, you may seem two-faced or even superficial as you're able to flit from one person and one situation to another milieu in the blink of an eye. As you mature your loyalty and steadfastness will develop in line with your discovery of what—and who—holds true value for you.

Your sense of adventure will expand into your sexual activities. You may even push forwards the boundaries of acceptable relationships, preferring to keep a degree of freedom within your liaisons despite the ability to be committed to family and the concept of family at least.

Your independence may be a bugbear for those close to you— and it may become a bugbear for you too. Yet fulfilment will come from maintaining your own individuality while being completely loyal to those you love and respect, which is no easy task. But if anyone can maintain a carefree sense of independence while being wholly committed to a relationship, a job or a cause, you can, and you'll be admired for it, too.

Perspective

Kind, generous, fun-loving, dynamic, creative, family oriented, creative, lucky, independent, free-spirited

Talents

Organisational skills, networking, socialising, mediating, trend setting, open-mindedness

Creative career

Entertainment, nightclubs, theatre, event facilitator, PR, marketing, religious, spiritual, travel, advertising, equestrianism, esoteric

Challenge

To balance your free spirit with commitment

Potential pitfalls

Inability to commit, directionless, impartiality, aloofness

Affirmation

I am loyal.

Work and daily life

You're unlikely to settle for a drab nine-to-five existence. You will want to move, like a butterfly, from one experience to another, especially as a youngster. You're ambitious and self-motivated preferring to be self-employed or freelance, and to have the freedom to dictate your own routine and timetable.

As a child at school you'll flit from one friend to another reluctant to commit to one opinion or group until you've fully experienced your options and calculated their likely trajectory. You're adaptable and can apply yourself to your work one hundred per cent. You'll want to experience circumstances as deeply as you can because you know you will potentially move on in due course.

Your work will push you forwards into new territories as you investigate new horizons and you'll extend your knowledge as you learn. Being a fairly lucky and joyful person you're drawn to spreading your luck around through your work. You're drawn to humanitarian activities including voluntary, educational, legal and travel-related work. The gambling industry may also appeal.

You enjoy the outdoors and large open spaces where you can roam around. You will be attracted to work outdoors including equestrianism and agriculture.

You will excel in activities where you must research, calculate or progress onto another level at every turn as opposed to repetitive work.

Your natural understanding of fair play will make the legal system appealing as a working environment. You also have a natural ability for publishing and languages.

Your big-hearted, upbeat and optimistic approach to life will keep you fairly protected from life's darker moments, and you'll enjoy the rituals of daily religious or spiritual activities.

Perspective

Ambitious, curious, jocular, light-hearted, hardworking, inspired, capable, optimistic, magnanimous

Talents

Analysis, calculation, strategy, independent research, motivation, precision

Type of work

Teaching, academia, health, performance, sports, archaeology, space science, journalism, media, finances, catering, art, inventor, veterinary, equestrian, agriculture, legal, transport, admin, gambling industry, travel

Challenge

To commit to one task at a time

Potential pitfalls

Changeability, aloofness, lack of interest, boredom, dissipation, inconsistency

Affirmation

I have a valuable contribution to make and I love to do so.

Relationships

You'll gain a sense of purpose through relationships that are both empowering and liberating. You'll also gain a sense of satisfaction and self-knowledge through a detailed understanding of both your family history and your socio-cultural background.

As a youngster you may be promiscuous or sexually experimental as this is your way to learn more about the intricacies not only of relationships, but also of yourself. You're emotionally invested in understanding sexual roles.

As you mature your tendency to learn about life and yourself through relationships will extend to all relationships, not just those in your personal life. You will look for answers of some sort through your relationships at work.

You will feel dismayed if truth or trust is betrayed within a relationship. As a youngster you risk having double standards as you demand honesty and sincerity, and yet you'll flit from relationship to relationship without a second thought as you prefer to be independent. Lack of commitment in relationships as a youngster may be due to a restless childhood or parents who were lacking in commitment themselves.

Your blunt insistence on being truthful can be hurtful to sensitive souls. Your indiscriminate pursuit of physical and sexual gratification with no remorse can also lead to intrigue and gossip—a far cry from the high ideals of truth and dignity upon which you base your actions.

As you mature your willingness to understand the profound dynamics of true commitment will encourage you to trust, form partnerships and love in return. Your sense of fulfilment and independence will come from understanding the wonders of relationships, and knowing that a truly independent spirit arises from being able to give and receive love equally from the heart, not the mind. You'll discover that to be independent and in a loving relationship is not a paradox: it's a pleasure and a powerful delight.

Perspective

Life and soul of the party, adventurous, outgoing, experimental, can be blunt, honest, can seem superficial, independent, free spirit

Talents

Understanding, compassion, productivity, attentiveness, diligent

Challenge

Commitment

Potential pitfalls

Lacking in trust, brutal honesty, immersion in intrigue

Affirmation

I give and receive true love.

Motivation

Even though you're motivated by your search for the truth, and for meaning in your life, what compels you is finding out what rises above meaning and truth—if anything at all.

This lofty compulsion could prove distracting, and the plethora of information you discover on your travels through life may be confusing and beguiling too. What is true? Is there an ultimate right and wrong? What is more important than truth and meaning?

You'll come to realise that your connections with people, your intimate relationships and also your work have more value than abstract concepts because, for you, truth and meaning must be applied in a practical way. You must sense that the application of your values results in some form of accomplishment.

Your investment in other people and in your self will naturally cry out for expression within society as a whole, beginning with your local community and then expanding into society at large. Legal and civic responsibilities such as government work could increasingly appeal to you as you mature, as will the education system. Publishing in some format will be a useful medium that will appeal to you.

The risk in your lifetime is that, as you have such lust for learning and life, you leave many of your tasks and projects—even your relationships—incomplete, deeming the magnitude of a thorough job or a successful relationship to be nigh on impossible. A mountain simply too high to climb. But if you set yourself clear goals and exercise your capacity to be discerning and avoid being misled by irrelevant distractions, you'll blaze a trail.

You'll enjoy expressing your discerning nature through activities connected with human rights and the justice system or, closer to home, within your neighbourhood, becoming a respected member both of society and of your extended family. In this way you'll gain a sense of freedom and belonging.

Perspective

Inquisitive, innocent, straightforward, sincere, knowledgeable

Talents

Communications, sharing information and resources, research

Challenge

To be discerning

Potential pitfalls

Being easily distracted, indecisive, confused, leaving unfinished business

Affirmation

I am guided by truth and justice.

Seeking . . .

You'll feel fulfilled when you embrace the vast horizons of the universe, and explore the various corners of the earth and all its potential. In so doing you'll enjoy exploring your own potential, and that of others.

You have natural communication skills and will simply know how to get along with people from a young age. You may be chatty to the extreme or reticent until you discover your mojo. Once you do there's no holding you back as you'll enjoy getting along with everyone in your own inimitable way: fun-loving with a jovial, attractive and easy-going manner.

As an adult your frontiers-man type personality could take you into uncharted territory, but it is the very call of the wild that attracts you and helps you feel that you're doing something worthwhile.

As you investigate and explore human potential you'll manage to clear a path for less gregarious people, opening up new frontiers for them too. Searching for meaning and knowledge is useless if the fruits of your labour are not shared with others. For this reason you'll value the practical and applied methodologies of religious or spiritual organisations, and their charitable work.

You are a progressive seeker of the truth because you always want to take things to the next level. You will not stop at one answer to a question; you will want all the answers. You are able to understand that there are many facets to the truth, and that everyone will find their own truth deep inside their soul. You'll also find that when you align your actions, thoughts and beliefs with your conscience, you will find the ultimate truth.

Perspective

Enthusiastic, sporty, inquisitive, generous, gregarious, jovial, self-confident, spiritual

Talents

Research, physical activity, industry, accumulation of wisdom, street savvy

Interests

Exploration, spirituality/religions, travel, communications, equestrian, writing, sports, education

Challenge

To be guided by your conscience and intuition

Potential pitfalls

Holding back, not pushing yourself forwards, being a sheep

Affirmation

I align myself with my inner wisdom.

Career and direction

You're set to make your mark on the world! Whether you set a strong example for your children by creating ideal family dynamics, you work within a daring and ingenious field of research or you become a corporate tsar, you're going to lead the way in some format. And you won't be afraid to speak your mind. You'll personify and champion the idea of free speech in whichever area you work.

In your career as a youngster you'll be happy to learn the ropes of every new job that strikes you as appealing. You're a chameleon at heart so you'll adjust to many different work situations. But as you mature you'll wish to be self-employed or freelance as this satisfies your free spirit.

You will find career progress and attaining status relatively straightforward, but your choice of occupation and general life direction may pose more challenges as your vast interests and array of talents will present you with a smorgasbord of options that will be hard to choose from. Because you're so adaptable you'll succeed in just about any profession so play to your strengths and decide which qualities and beliefs in life you'd like to promote. To play to your strengths means you'll not only enjoy your days more, but you'll also find your work flows more easily, making it more enjoyable and making you more successful.

Your natural interests will revolve around some form of communication such as publishing, and around the group dynamic as you're a people person. You may find a natural empathy with animals, and will enjoy caring for them. You'll also be drawn to legal work or any job that involves fair play, justice and a social conscience.

You'll fulfil your potential by setting yourself goals. You will attain them. Always aim for the top, and you'll get there. Especially if you avoid being sidetracked by distractions or petty issues that will only dissipate your focus and energy.

Your tendency to get embroiled in minor disputes could hinder your progress, causing frustration and petty mindedness. And yet you have an in-built understanding of human dynamics, which will help you to generate a positive attitude. Your understanding of human nature and communication skills is the key to your progress, especially when you employ tact and diplomacy. You'll find championing other people's causes straightforward.

You have natural flair and intellect. Combined with your get-up-and-go you'll aim for the bullseye in life and hit it every time.

Characteristics

Motivated, talkative, goal-oriented, flamboyant, fortunate, intellectual, wise

Talents

Communications, natural empathy, conscientiousness, flair, poise, social adeptness

Type of career

Politics, corporate, travel, sportsperson, explorer, scientist, communications, publishing, research, investigative work such as police work, equestrian, administration, government/civic duties, finances, law, human–rights law, religious, spiritual

Challenge

To aim for the bigger picture

Potential pitfalls

Minor disputes, being aimless, without goals, can seem shallow

Affirmation

I love the world and I express this in my daily actions.

Goals, groups and humanitarianism

You're a humanitarian, and you'll find that at some juncture in your life you'll fight for a cause, either your own or someone else's. Throughout your life your research and investigations are likely to lead to a great deal of involvement with groups, organisations, association and clubs, and you're likely to be particularly creative within the group dynamic.

You have a strong social conscience. This can be the result of having begun your life in a family with a strong social conscience or because you were raised by a family who lacked a moral code or slipped through the social safety net in some way. In turn, you will wish to support people who have slipped through this net themselves.

As you mature your deep understanding of the rights and wrongs in life will help people see how committed you are to social reform and the necessity that people be free, valued and respected on an individual level, and in society as a whole.

Above all you're fun loving, sociable and gregarious in the group dynamic, enjoying lively get-togethers and the party atmosphere. You thrive in this arena and your aims and goals, especially to do with work and your social conscience, will take seed here more than in any other environment.

Perspective

Frank, open, blunt, kind, jovial, gregarious, optimistic, honest, extrovert, helpful

Talents

Mentoring, good team player, public speaking, social conscience

Interests

Social reform, government, the arts, politics, charity, social services

Challenge

To fight for a cause

Potential pitfalls

Unreliability, bluntness, insincerity, fanaticism

Affirmation

I make the world a better place.

The secret you

You'll leave no stone unturned once you have sunk your teeth into a project or a line of inquiry. You're determined, an excellent researcher and would do well in investigative and criminal forensic science. You're likely to be drawn to exploration of the human psyche or biology, in your spare time at least.

During your lifetime you will be presented with a large array of options, and this may be daunting because you know how important it is to make the right choice. This in itself could cause you to be indecisive (and consequently directionless or aimless), or at least living in fear that you will make the wrong choice.

At the bottom of your indecision lies doubt in your own abilities and fear that there is nothing at the end of the rainbow. As a youngster especially you may be wracked with self-doubt and restlessness, especially if your background was particularly unstable, unsettled or changeable.

You are likely to be followed—and influenced—by a lucky star wherever you go, as your ultimate search is for the manifest truth, and your destiny is to learn what is real. Your frank sincerity is so endearing you'll attract bright people who will help keep your feet on the ground and your heart reaching for the stars. As you mature you'll feel more able to express yourself clearly and your predisposition towards uncertainty and indecision will wane.

You project such a jovial personality that you don't appear to be a deep-thinker, and yet you are nevertheless on a mission. You may enjoy the ritual and higher ground of religious traditions, and as you mature spiritual texts from various cultures and traditions will feed your search for meaning in life.

As you can see the many sides of a story, you can spend many of your quiet moments debating the relative merit of ideas, methods and even people. You may secretly fear that there is no ultimate truth in life, that you will be lost in the banalities and complexities of life. But once you develop a strong sense of the fairness of life—of karma, equality, respect and cooperation—this tendency to deliberate and your fear of a fundamental lack of significance and order will give way to a more trusting understanding. One in which your sense of adventure and confidence that all will be well, plus your belief in your own abilities, will help you attain a deeper delight in life and everyone in it.

Yours is a narrow path to tread despite appearances to the contrary. Walking the path of inner truth is challenging because you are your own guide. Ultimately you will realise that your life's path and all the actions you perform along the way are between you and your conscience, and that by aligning your actions and thoughts with your conscience and your soul, you attain your ultimate goals: the truth and significant meaning in life.

Characteristics

Intense, philosophical, thoughtful, sincere, candid, honest, private, clever

Talents
Investigation, research, exploration, helpful, understanding

Interests
Research, forensics, social services, mining, space exploration

Challenge
To believe in yourself

Potential pitfalls
Self-doubt, procrastination, indecision, distractions, lack of conscience

Affirmation
I am guided by my conscience.

Capricorn

The nurturing guide

SITUATION

You are on a quest to develop a sense of responsibility, self-reliance and stability. To do this you may have learned lessons in these areas during childhood. For example you may have been required to stand on your own two feet at a very young age due to your particular family circumstances. You may have been asked to become responsible for someone else's wellbeing at a young age or become a carer within your own family. Concerns surrounding nurturing may be a focus for you as an adult due to an abundance or a marked lack of nurturing from one or both of your parents.

You'll also feel the need to learn about and understand the boundaries, limitations and restrictions of everyday life such as what is and isn't permissible in your society, neighbourhood and culture. To do so, you may push against boundaries, restrictions and limits when you are young, appearing disrespectful until such time as you learn to understand the value of limitations and why they are much more important than they seem at first.

Respect is another quality you'll learn because out of respect comes the talent for true nurturing, which is a skill you'll embrace. Issues of nurturing are bound to follow you wherever you go. You'll become the nurturing guide—someone who, by understanding their responsibility to look after those who are dependent on them, also understands that they must look after themselves first.

Throughout your life you'll be accompanied by someone who has a strong influence over you—perhaps within your own family as you grow up, an employer as an adult or an iconic religious figure. You'll enjoy having idols to look up to and, in turn, as you mature you will provide inspiration for your own family or youth around you.

You're likely to gain positions of authority and responsibility that will challenge you to attain your highest possible potential. In so doing you'll learn how to activate your nurturing side as opposed to becoming an authoritarian figure for the sake of it or, worse, a despot or tyrant. Your life circumstances will clearly depict the difference between these two models—the tyrant and the nurturer—and it's your task to decide which icon you'll represent in your life.

PURPOSE

You'll gain a sense of purpose by recognising that you must look after your own interests first *so that* you're able to care for others. If not, care-giving can become a problem rather than a fulfilment of your purpose as you may often be besieged by people who need your help or care. This can lead to burnout.

A degree of sentimentality will accompany you through various phases of your life. This could distract you from your practical duties as you risk being swept up by emotions and melancholia rather than focusing on being practical and hands-on. Taking responsibility for your own happy future as a mature person who is able to set boundaries must come first. In turn, you can then care all for others by having the energy to do so and setting a stable, authoritative, mature example.

Feelings of having been smothered, or conversely under-parented, will lead you to examine the role of parenthood both in the way it has affected you and in turn how your behaviour will affect your own children and generations to come.

Your purpose is to understand how important self-nurturing is rather than merely to understand how you are a product of your parents' nurturing. Your purpose is to become empowered by your own self-nurturing because you have a role to fulfil as a nurturer of others.

You have a practical approach to life's dramas even if your life is backlit by tales of romance and ideals. Your approach to nurturing will be realistic and straightforward: nurturing requires love, and love is an intelligence, a concept that can be applied in a practical way in everyday life. Your approach to love is that it's a learned skill, and you'll excel at implementing it. You're a hands-on leader with a glint of romance.

Affirmation

I am a guiding light.

Famous people

Woody Allen, Roy Orbison, Glenda Jackson, Kevin Costner, John Travolta, Oprah Winfrey, Luciano Pavarotti, Robert Redford, Burt Reynolds, Dalai Lama XIV

Your unique approach

You were born with the strong need to be loved. Once you feel you are loved you become a wonderfully loving, protective and caring person in turn, but your search for love can cause you to appear needy, clingy or even co-dependent. You can be overly emotional, melancholic and discontented, especially as a child.

The paradox is that you'll derive the greatest sense of love by acknowledging that you have a never-ending pool of love yourself. Acknowledging this will prepare you for healthy relationships because once you've mastered a degree of self-sufficiency through self-love and self-reliance you'll experience a free-flow of love within your relationships, both personal and business.

You'll no longer feel the *need* to be loved by others, so that when you are loved, you're able to accept this graciously and return the emotion, purely and without displays of clinginess or unrealistic demands on your loved ones.

As you are essentially a practical person you're likely to pursue applied knowledge of self-love, care-giving and life skills at various stages in your life. The idea of love being an intelligence will appeal to you.

Learning how to apply love in life in useful ways will present you with the joyful task of spreading love in practical terms and displaying your own nurturing abilities. For this reason you will reveal a maturity beyond your years at a young age.

Your position as a valuable nurturer and respected member of society will blossom as you accept responsibility for your own feelings and destiny.

Perspective

Caring, shy when young, self-disciplined, authoritarian, mature beyond your years

Talents

Accountability, responsibility when mature, ability to focus, hard working

Interests

Self-help, self-improvement, philosophy, social responsibilities, reading, healing

Challenge

To learn self-love

Potential pitfalls

To become clingy, over-emotional, co-dependent, sentimental, needy

Affirmation

Love is abundant. It's inside me.

Values and self-expression

Your self-esteem and self-worth stem from your compassionate, sensitive and caring approach to setting boundaries of acceptable behaviour both for yourself and those close to you. You will learn to recognise when someone's faults are their own issue and not yours, especially as you have a tendency to mirror other people's feelings, values and ideas.

You can be vulnerable and hypersensitive to others' deficiencies, potentially even believing their deficiencies are your own. You have a need to identify with people on an intimate and emotional level as well as a financial and materialistic level. This impulse will leave you vulnerable both to financial loss and emotional intrigue because, as a compassionate soul, you assume others are the same. When respect and compassion are not reciprocated (through no fault of your own), you may feel truly hurt and retreat into your shell.

Knowing your own vulnerabilities as an adult you will guard against personal hurt or damage by becoming extremely methodical. The risk is that this extends to controlling behaviour, which is to be avoided as you will bypass your more nurturing purpose as a result.

You'll gain self-respect and fulfilment by celebrating the place material objects and moral boundaries have in your life. You recognise that you are flesh and blood and require practicalities (such as a roof over your head and food in your mouth), as well as boundaries to safeguard basic values such as respect. You have a strong value system, which will be regarded by others as traditional at best and outdated at worst. To you, though, your strong sense of values and principles are simply practical.

In your search for self-esteem, status and self-worth you may during various phases in your life pursue material status through luxury goods and status symbols, especially as a young person. Much of your materialism will come from a practical sense of wishing to create the best future you can in the sense that the best products will last longer or the best car is safer. You will value wealth because it is often seen as the best goal or outcome in our materialistic society.

The idea 'get real' will follow you around. Being realistic and keeping up with the times is something you will learn, and you'll encourage others to be the same. But in your mission to fit in with other people, and to be an important force in society, you're liable to forget your own worth and even potentially give your power away, thereby being anything but real.

You will learn that by accepting and remembering to honour your own worth and capabilities you're more able to contribute to positive relationships and to society as a whole. And, in turn, you'll more easily accept and honour other people's worth and abilities.

You'll become increasingly grounded and productive as you mature. As a result you'll be seen as a true authority in many areas of life.

In this unique way you'll express an important aspect of your nurturing abilities: to lead and guide by example.

Perspective

Cautious but practical when mature, sympathetic, materialistic and status-oriented when young, grounded, sense of authority, traditional values, respectful

Talents

Organisational skills when mature, achievement, empathy

Challenge

To realise your own self-worth

Potential pitfalls

Materialism, domination, hypersensitivity, vulnerability

Affirmation

I am practical and realistic.

Communication

You communicate in a practical, factual manner, and prefer to rely on information and facts rather than on mere supposition or emotional innuendo. Yet your ideas and interests—and the way you indulge in them—may be quite the opposite. You can appear to be idealistic and imaginative, enjoying storytelling, myths and legends, and you may even be fanatical and dramatically sentimental on occasion.

As such you can present a fairly complex character: at once imaginative, sensitive and even other-worldly while at other times no-nonsense and practical. This unique combination presents one of your true talents: to be inspired and sensitive while being incredibly well organised and methodical.

As a result your talents include being able to visualise the bigger picture and the connotations of inspired ideas, and being able to act on notions, sentiments and impressions that seem impractical and unlikely. You have an inventive, inspired mind and you can build bridges between opposing ideas and values. You have good negotiating skills and will find teaching straightforward.

When you learned to communicate and to interact as a child you were actually in the process of working out how your thoughts, feelings and ideas can be expressed tangibly in the world around you. You were also learning how to communicate those impressions and ideas so that they were acted upon or so that they could become real.

Yours is a particularly inspired learning and communication process as you're practising how to build structure in life through your sentiments, impressions and experiences. On top of this you're not simply learning how to navigate through life, and how to communicate your impressions, intuition and desires, but also how to navigate traditional structures and belief systems and then add the cherry on top—your own additional insight and some form of practical application of the knowledge you've gained.

In this lifetime you have the very real opportunity to anchor your intuition, dreams and ideas in reality; to build a life that is practical even if it is based on your emotions or on a fairytale you once read. You're engaged in a kind of applied experimentation, attempting to build a bridge between fantasy and reality, between intuition and deed, and making something out of nothing by being practical and methodical.

Your starting point is the way you process and administer your fine sensory perceptions. Being personal, physical and up-front in your communications will appeal to you throughout your life as it's the best way to anchor yourself in the physical world. As such you may communicate with gestures, deeds, actions and even possessions far more than with words. And when you do, you're putting substance to form. Eventually you'll also be adept at making other people's dreams come true too.

Perspective

Practical, idealistic, far-sighted, whimsical, irrational, dreamer, sensible, methodical

Talents

Negotiation, diplomacy, empathy, teaching

Challenge

To turn intuition and ideas into reality

Potential pitfalls

Living in a dream world, impractical

Affirmation

I turn my impressions into reality.

Home and family

Family and your role within it are some of the most important areas of your life because so much of your nurturing and caring personality is formed within the confines of your home.

As a child a strong parental figure (for many a father figure), will have a firm influence either due to their absence or an overbearing presence. As a result you will look for a more stable outlook by seeking more balanced authority figures in your life.

Paradoxically you may be attracted to people—and potential partners—who mirror one of your parents' behaviours (or that of a father figure), so your family dynamics risk continuing within the family you create yourself.

Your desire as an adult is to provide a stable, secure home life for yourself and your family. It's something you can achieve as you have the benefit of hindsight due to your upbringing.

The risk is that your desire to provide security and stability in your life causes the qualities of love and nurturing to take second place. The restrictions and ground rules you construct, especially around your home, could paradoxically cause love to take second place to stability and security. You eventually risk becoming the benevolent despot as opposed to the wise nurturer you truly are.

By large, providing boundaries and checking that traditions are upheld both in your personal life and at work makes you a dependable and stable member of society and your family. You may wish to add your own take on tradition and values as you learn to decipher which social models are nurturing, and which are simply controlling.

It's within the four walls of your home that your template as a wise nurturer and a nurturing guide is formed. If you believe this template leaves much to be desired, you'll find that these deficiencies themselves will teach you how to be the role model for your own children and the family you create yourself.

For some, the desire to have your own family will not arise and you will take your nurturing role out into society, becoming a role model for those you will eventually admire.

You appreciate traditional architecture as well as the stability and structure a home and family can provide. You enjoy learning the history of buildings, homes and family trees. Your home, above all, will represent the backbone of your life. As such it will serve you well as a haven of nourishment and support.

Perspective

Authoritarian, motherly/fatherly, patriotic, traditional, dependable, caring

Talents

Being methodical, systematic, rational, a provider and nurturer

Challenge

To be a strong and loving family member

Potential pitfalls

Rigidity, unwillingness to learn, overtly disciplinarian, despotic

Affirmation

I build my castle with love.

Creativity and life force

Your creativity will surprise even you because you may consider yourself to be anything but creative, especially as a young adult. As a child you'll learn slowly but surely and with a serious, methodical attitude. You'll want to know the bricks and mortar of every subject you learn. If you're lucky and have perceptive teachers they'll see you as a meticulous student with a vivid imagination and love of storytelling.

As a youngster your need to be exacting and to deliberate over each step of the learning process may cause you to see yourself as slow or as less gifted than other children. And yet your rich, creative soul nurtures your learning process that will, in time, blossom to reveal your unique abilities.

As you mature, you (and those around you) will see that you're truly brilliant and ingenious. You have the rare talent to be able to turn the normal into the inspired. It's as if you're fed from a never-ending stream of inventiveness that enables you to create form and function out of mere supposition or whimsy. You'll enjoy playing the role of the true inventor, turning ideas and notions into reality. You have a direct line to inspiration, the strength of which even you may not recognise at first.

Your sense of purpose will thrive by striving to make something extraordinary out of yourself as opposed to losing your identity in the group dynamic. You'll be prone to being easily influenced as a youngster, becoming awash with other people's wishes and dreams, identifying with their deficiencies as if they are your own. And yet your own ideas and wishes are so much more practical and easy to manifest. This is something you'll come to appreciate as you mature. Not only that you are a capable and productive person, but also that you have a strength of character that few possess. It's by taking responsibility for your own actions and harnessing your true talents so that they may be put to good use that you'll express your creativity the most.

When you realise that you are an individual with authority and natural poise, you'll begin to believe in your own abilities—and excel— as only you know how. You have the magic of creation brick by brick, and step by step, at your fingertips.

Perspective

Imaginative, inventive, hands-on, organised, masterly, poised

Talents

Synthesis of art with science and inspiration with practicalities, diligence, ingenuity

Creative career

Inventor, artist, writer, film, theatre, architect, homemaking, interior designer, charity, nourishment

Challenge

To trust your inspiration

Potential pitfalls

Deliberation, self-doubt, lack of confidence, over-exacting

Affirmation

I harness and apply my talents.

Work and daily life

You're an excellent employee. You will work hard and enjoy the structure and order of everyday working life. You're able to work diligently and methodically to the top of your particular ladder in any work that requires a disciplined, practical approach such as finances and agriculture.

Your organisational skills, self-discipline and administrative abilities are outstanding. You'll enjoy a well-planned fitness and diet schedule. You'll also enjoy working within a caring profession such as the medical or charitable fields, and with animals.

You're more likely to enjoy being self-employed as you mature, as responsibility will not faze you. You'll relish being in control of your own income and accountable for your actions and products, in all likelihood within a caring capacity as an advisor, care-giver, guide or in a supportive role.

As a youngster your self-assured demeanour may take employers by surprise. You may even appear a little cool or confident beyond your years. A wise employer will promote you because you're evidently dependable and capable.

Some may find your natural reserve cold or unfeeling, and yet you have a fountain of emotions and good intentions behind that calm façade. Just scratch the surface and it's plain to see. It's worth your while to show your sensitive side more often especially in the workplace as otherwise you can risk falling under the radar and miss opportunities.

But your talents may go undiscovered because of your apparent reticence. Your reluctance to show your true feelings may result from your fear of revealing your softer, giving side and yet, when you do, your depth of character will be admired.

Being respected and admired puts the cherry on the cake for you. You'll gain respect in life without the need to put yourself on a pedestal, and your humility and understated charm is part of what makes people value you, especially in your everyday life and at work.

Perspective
Self-assured, supportive, respectable, responsible, reserved, humble, cool, detached

Talents
Organisational skills, meticulousness, precision, dependability, hardwork

Type of work
Medicine, hospitality, charity, veterinary, sports, admin, financial, agriculture, homemaking, building, food industry, insurance, locksmith, security business, technology, motivational, self-help, film, acting, marketing

Challenge
To reveal your softer side

Potential pitfalls
Talents remain undiscovered, depression, missed opportunities

Affirmation
I attain my goals because I care.

Relationships
You'll enjoy indulging the people you love, and taking a parental role at home. For some, though, parenting can extend to parenting a partner where you or your partner provides quasi-parental support for the other. You may be attracted to significantly older partners or, conversely, you may be the older partner yourself.

In adulthood you're sure of yourself and your abilities, and you're a born authority figure who is self-confident, especially within relationships. You're likely to want your relationships to be long-standing. For this reason you're a loyal friend, partner and lover, but you tend to cling to a relationship even when it is clearly no longer functional. This can be due to overt sensitivity and sentimentality that could, long-term, lead to heartache.

As a child you may have people in your environment who require additional care. You can feel particularly sensitive to other people's pain as well as your own, and you have a tendency to mirror other people's emotions, believing them to be your own. You are aware of your powerhouse of emotions that you know will, if left to their own device, overcome your rationality. Learning to express your strong emotions and intuition in a healthy, practical and nurturing way will help you to feel balanced.

You can appear aloof, and retreat inside a comfortable shell of inscrutability when you're under pressure. This helps you project the impression that you're in control and safe from harm.

Money and possessions will appeal to your sense of self-worth. You may pursue relationships for financial gain and may even marry for money. You risk devoting your energy to the acquisition of money and possessions to the detriment of all else only to find, later in life, that the pursuit of fool's gold has led you to miss much of value such as companionship.

You are also tempted to pursue particular relationships to gain social status. You like to communicate emotionally through expensive gifts, and you may subconsciously want to buy your partner's affections. As such you can be seen as patronising and potentially even controlling. You may be inclined to measure a relationship by the size of the engagement ring rather than by long-term and emotional compatibility.

As you mature you'll understand that love and nurturing have the greatest worth and reward for you, and you'll feel all the more successful and happy in life when you attain happy relationships. You're fundamentally a natural in the field of love and care.

Your cool exterior can lead to misunderstandings as it belies your sensitive and caring nature beneath. Once you're comfortable balancing your practical needs with your strong emotions, you will succeed in giving and receiving love in an easy-going, natural way.

You'll gain a sense of purpose, stability and happiness through your relationships by being sincere, showing mutual respect and taking responsibility for your own actions. And then your more sensitive, playful, imaginative and vulnerable side will surface in the most endearing way. At work you'll display your more inventive, imaginative talents, and at home your sensuality and playfulness will increasingly appeal to those who love you.

Perspective

Natural leader, sensitive, giving, protective, responsible, dependable, pragmatic

Talents

Caring, organisation, giving support, loyalty, sensuality, respect

Challenge

To avoid mirroring others' emotions

Potential pitfalls

Buying affections, being rigid, domineering, demanding, aloof, cold

Affirmation

I express my emotions in a nurturing way.

Motivation

You'll enjoy being a provider and sharing the many assets, possessions, finances and insights you attain throughout your lifetime in your family role, via the strong role model you set in society or by leading others to a new understanding in some way. As such you're motivated by your abilities and talents to create structures and amenities that enable you to be a strong example and a provider for others.

In turn, as you mature, you'll appreciate the rewards your role as provider gives you personally, so that your ability to share comes back to you tenfold in a reciprocally advantageous cycle of mutual benefit and support. For this reason you'll enjoy being a strong parental figure, a guide or mentor to younger people, and the rewards you feel when you see the positive results of your hard work will motivate you further to continue with your influential work.

You'll find accruing possessions and finances fairly straightforward and your purpose lies in directing your energy into productive pursuits for the benefit not only of family and those close to you, but also of society as a whole. When you discern that possessions are merely expressions of your own unique and powerful energy, you'll realise your talents as a provider are far more valuable than objects or money alone.

You'll become truly valued for your wisdom, and the attainment of wisdom will increasingly motivate you as you mature, as will a strong value system. You'll take great joy in sharing the knowledge and wisdom that age brings. You'll be admired for your wealth of knowledge, especially if you follow your heart as a youngster, your intuition and your higher purpose. In this way you'll come to understand that the true meaning of your life—and therefore your true motivation—comes from providing love, not objects and money.

Perspective

Masterful, confident, nurturing, kind, sympathetic, materialistic

Talents

Accumulating and expressing wisdom, developing a strong character

Challenge

To value your inner wisdom

Potential pitfalls

Can be overbearing, controlling, materialistic

Affirmation

To give is to receive. To nurture is to love. To be loved is to be rich.

Seeking . . .

You're seeking status. For you success comes from having status and a valuable, prominent or respectable position in life. You'll prefer to be acknowledged as an expert, an authority in a field of your choice or as a competent role model. As a youngster you're likely to seek status through finances and possessions unless your parents are particularly non-materialistic and instilled this concept within you at a young age. For you the status you seek is not bound up with ego and pride, but rather with the need to be looked up to and to be an influential and caring figure. As you mature you'll seek status through knowledge, communication, exploration and understanding.

To gain this position you'll follow the company and advice of experts and teachers, and you'll pursue spiritual or religious wisdom. You may attempt to gain social status by networking with people in higher social echelons and, for this reason, at various times in your life you may be seen as a social climber.

If you pursue your status with little regard for other people's feelings you can become cut-throat, something that clearly contradicts your life purpose of being a wise guide and nurturer. For this reason attaining status without regard for your values and conscience is the quickest route to unhappiness.

You'll seek to gain status by becoming a go-to authoritative source of reliable information. You're a natural-born storyteller, and you're likely to have communication skills beyond the norm. By extending these into a broader platform through research and commercial inquiry you also have a natural flair for commerce and trade, making you a competent businessperson and negotiator.

While your work and interests will take you into new fields outside your comfort zone you'll seek a supportive environment at home. Once you've accomplished your tasks and learned what you must, you'll return to familiar territory, either the family fold or your community, with new information and skills that you'll enjoy sharing with those you care for, much like a bird feeds her chicks in the nest.

Ultimately you're seeking to obtain a reputable and responsible position in life, one in which you will be respected. You don't necessarily require admiration, as yours is not an egotistical quest, but clearly being admired for your success will be a bonus. As such, you're one of life's rocks, and your desire is to provide stability, reliability and structure for those you love, whether this is your family or society at large.

Perspective

Inquisitive, broad-minded, adventurous, encompassing, wise, dependable

Talents

Research, study, writing, storytelling, being an expert, sports—especially climbing

Interests

Academia, blogging, languages, mediation, mountaineering, teaching, hospitality, mentoring

Challenge

To achieve status through good deeds

Potential pitfalls

One-upmanship, competitiveness, cutthroat activities

Affirmation

I am a source of wisdom.

Career and direction

You'll strive to attain great kudos. You're the ultimate achiever because you'll reach your goals no matter what. In the realm of career and life direction you'll feel that happiness stems from material success, from having a skilled profession or by social means.

You'll try many different avenues to achieve success. You're a hard worker, and able to work methodically to the top of your field. You may marry for money or status, or you may choose a career because it pays well. And if you have a successful family business you're likely to follow in the family footsteps.

You're likely to have authoritarian or unusually successful working parents, and may become very successful yourself. You'll strive to establish the kind of feelings true family values can bring: togetherness, love and nurturing within your career and general life direction.

You're rational and practical, and you are able to plan ahead with incredible diligence and attention to detail. You are then able to execute your plans methodically and relentlessly despite all the odds. Clear goals are very important to you as without them you risk working toward a goal for an entire lifetime only to discover it wasn't what you were looking for after all. This can clearly lead to disappointment. You tend to mirror and reflect your environment, and therefore you can risk mistaking other people's goals and opinions for your own.

You'll learn that nurturing has a place not only in society and culture, but in the workplace too. This will lead you to a greater awareness of what success really is: feeling supported, valued and loved. In turn you'll appreciate and encourage a hands-on approach to provide supportive, ergonomic and nurturing infrastructures in society, within daily activities and in the work environment too.

Characteristics

Organised, practical, logical, authoritative, diligent, determined, structured, industrious

Talents

Leadership qualities, dependable, practical, self-motivated, a good example

Type of career

Business, finance, care-giving, hospitality, medicine, family support, military, promotions, management, corporate, construction, home-making, teaching, police force, trade, commerce

Challenge

To promote love, comfort and nurturing in the workplace

Potential pitfalls

Social climbing, veering off your own path, easily influenced

Affirmation

I am a positive role model.

Goals, groups and humanitarianism

You'll feel fulfilled when you're with your peer group whether this is a group with similar interests or a society or club where you take a proactive role. You're attracted to certain clubs that bestow prestige upon their members or that are hard to get into as they will provide the status you appreciate.

You'll enjoy being the leader of the pack as a teenager, and are unlikely to be a wallflower or a follower within a group or a club even if you do feel sensitive or must mask your vulnerabilities with bravado. The challenge will arise when you realise you will need to work from the bottom of the ladder up to gain status and recognition, and there will always be someone with a higher status than you.

You will learn to be patient and compassionate at a young age, and your creative and artistic abilities, combined with your organisational skills, will ideally be honed in the group environment and through clubs and guilds with master teachers and expert instructors. As an adult you'll enjoy bringing together groups of people with similar interests, and taking the role of guide or mentor yourself.

You have a strong need to fulfil your goals, to be a success and/or to follow family tradition. You'll feel fulfilled by bringing creative projects to life, finding meaning and purpose in creativity rather than art or creative endeavours for their own sake. You'll enjoy applied art such as design, as it anchors ideas and dreams in reality.

You enjoy being the motivator behind theatre productions, plays and dance troupes. You enjoy cultivating seeds of ideas so that they can grow into something manageable, productive and real, and finding a practical use for mere whimsy and inspiration.

This talent makes you the ultimate craftsperson and inventor as you can turn design and ideas into something tangible. You're not to be underestimated. Your calm, organised demeanour (especially at work) belies a hugely sensitive and imaginative being inside.

You're the quintessential humanitarian, but your brand of humanitarianism differs from the popular 21st century brand that seeks to spur the masses into charitable action through shock-and-jolt images of poverty and need. Your version of humanitarianism is, in contrast, a slow, well-planned, grassroots, long-term manoeuvre to mobilise and improve the lives of those around you, both at home and in society at large. This cool, well-oiled approach belies your underbelly, which is fuelled with emotion, compassion and love.

Perspective

Hands-on, inspired, purposeful, organised, methodical, team-player, considered, well-planned, helpful, calm

Talents

Cooperation, consultation, mentoring, able to instigate and inspire, has creative and constructive abilities

Interests

Arts, crafts, carpentry, toastmaster, theatre, music, construction, quality goods, status symbols, authority

Challenge

To apply the nurturing principle

Potential pitfalls

Impatience, remoteness, coolness, stand-offish

Affirmation

I inspire and teach others how to be successful collaboratively and compassionately.

The secret you

You'll enjoy the feeling that like-minded people respect you. As a child your talents may go unnoticed as you're happy to work quietly or down-play your achievements, but when your moment in the spotlight does finally come you'll play your cards right.

As an adult you're equally happy working under the radar even though you'll enjoy upholding certain traditions and customs, boundaries, rules and regulations for the benefit of all. This is because you have a strong appreciation of society and its traditions.

If you decide to disregard your strong value system you may be tempted to veer foul of society's values and guidelines and engage in underhand or even illegal endeavours and work. The greatest temptation, which could potentially derail your moral compass, is pursuit of money, possessions and status for their own sake and above all else.

Luckily, for the most part, you're motivated by your need to look after other people, and to guide them. This will underpin your actions in the final analysis, but you can be tempted to forego your own wellbeing in favour of looking after everyone else. You may be a carer within your own family, for example, and although you'll gladly undertake the task, you may secretly identify with the plight of those you look after, seeing yourself as weak or incapacitated in some sense.

Your secret fear is that you are ineffective, and that you will not be able to scale the heights of the challenges you set yourself. A fear of failure will lead you to never really learn how to express your true magnificence in your own individual way, and your unique talents could remain hidden.

Your fear of being weak and ineffectual can also be due to a lack of respect or regard for your own nurturing side. The patriarchal society dictates that you be strong and successful, and places less emphasis on the caring, nurturing roles of human beings. Yet nurturing and love are the qualities that truly underpin a productive, enduring and progressive society.

Ironically, your strength lies in expressing your softer, weaker, nurturing side. Masking your vulnerabilities with bravado or ignoring your caring personality will lead you to a position of weakness.

You'll enjoy being of service to others, and you're likely to be charitable. You're unlikely to blow your own trumpet, and you may choose to keep your philanthropic side a secret. You realise that you cannot take the money and possessions you accrue into the afterlife, and will develop your ability to be a benefactor, philanthropist and all-round good character at a relatively young age.

You'll gain fulfilment from understanding the value of your own self and your contribution to life by avoiding being a martyr or down-playing your role in life, as well as by celebrating life in all its complexities and wonder. You'll live life to the fullest by understanding that you are the creator of your own destiny, and by living life for your own benefit as well as for others.

The way you live your life will be a source of inspiration for generations to come, in your own family and society itself, and you'll enjoy honouring and gaining strength from your role as the nurturing guide.

Characteristics

Self-effacing, dependable, traditional, helpful, kind, tender, gentle

Talents

Organisation, resourcefulness, diligence, persistence, a go-getter, understanding

Interests

Charity work, philanthropy, institutional work such as hospitals, respite care

Challenge

To indulge your own wisdom

Potential pitfalls

Identifying with everyone else, lost at sea, keeping your light under a bush, materialistic, lack of morals, afraid to show your nurturing side, fear of failure

Affirmation

I am strong. I am a nurturing guide.

Aquarius

The awakening spirit

SITUATION

You have a profound understanding of life. You comprehend the dance between what's possible and what is simply a law of the universe, between what is being created and what is a product of our own minds. As such you hold the key to your own, constantly evolving future. You are aware that you are the centre of your own universe and the creator of your own destiny even within the boundaries and finiteness of your human life.

As a child this understanding can manifest as a hugely artistic, eccentric, colourful personality. You will have an original and extraordinary take on life, and may even display rebellious behaviour. Whatever the circumstances of your youth you deserve careful nurturing as you hold the key to a greater awareness of the capabilities of the human mind and spirit, of how we can fulfil our destinies as creative, happy human beings.

You are ahead of your time, and will constantly push the boundaries of perception, possibility and human understanding. But because you're unique you can appear oddball, non-conformist, quirky and alienated.

Your deep understanding of life springs from your belief that you can initiate change. With this belief comes a great advantage that many people do not possess. Your sense of purpose will strengthen when you exercise and communicate your insights and abilities, when you ask people you encounter to wake up to a new paradigm, a new way of thinking, and therefore a new future.

PURPOSE

Your purpose is to understand and communicate that you are part of a much greater paradigm and pattern in life than first meets the eye. You desire to understand that you are a part of the greater potential human beings possess, and to express your inner power, which when used productively can manifest wonderful results.

The risk is that this understanding leads to great pride and potentially misuse of power and the feeling that you must somehow reign by using this power. This will merely perpetuate a counterproductive hierarchical archetype and a massive ego that your soul will fundamentally reject. This will cause you inner tension and conflict because you know that it's time to understand the bigger picture that ties every single human being together, which leaves no place for ego, pride or power struggles.

You encompass the paradox that no-one works alone and no-one is alone, while everyone has their unique life, is independent and has a unique ability to create and initiate change. Part of your quest is to find the right medium to convey your particular message, which is that this needn't be a paradox. You want to find a way that people can understand your take on life, and a modality that is acceptable within current social infrastructures and paradigms.

The alternative is to cut loose, blaze your own trail, and potentially ostracise yourself from the mainstream, which creates another paradox: that in trying to communicate your—and everyone else's—connectedness, you ironically disconnect yourself from the world.

Ultimately you recognise that everyone's spark of life is infused by love, and that love is the tie that binds every human being together. You will highlight this spark of creation, this cosmic dust that enables each and every person to create a wonderful future as individuals, in society and the world. The sense of purpose you gain from this will in turn radiate from you as a unifying force.

Affirmation

I make my own future.

Famous people

Brigitte Bardot, Sophia Loren, Edith Piaf, Elvis, Frank Sinatra, Barry Humphries, Shirley MacLaine, Roseanne, Tony Blair, Albert Einstein, Billie Holiday, Julian Assange

Your unique approach

If you can create your own destiny, doesn't that make you all-powerful? Doesn't that make you the centre of the universe? And so within your everyday interactions such as your relationships, doesn't that make you the one who's going to wear the trousers—at the very least?

Certainly if you'd like to subscribe to the traditional idea of power. But if you're true to yourself, and to the new understanding of the Aquarian age—namely that we are all one and connected under the power of love (or God, Buddha, divine consciousness)—then the traditional power structure no longer fits the new paradigm and won't sit comfortably with you either. Ultimately you're unlikely to put yourself first in an egotistical sense—you're a humanitarian at heart, or at least learning to be one.

You understand that you are uniquely special and at one with everyone else at the same time. This will be played out within your life again and again, causing conflicting notions and impressions about how best to interact with those close to you, especially family and marriage partners. At times you'll feel special, and your ego will cause you to appear self-centred or act out of pride. Then, at other times, you'll feel ready to connect with someone, but fear losing your independence. Both these scenarios can cause you inner strife.

While you decide for yourself what power really is, power struggles will arise in your relationships and you may alternate between being the dominant partner and the submissive partner, between playing a traditional role and a progressive one both at home and in society. Relationships, and your approach to people in general, will be the area in which your inner debate between traditional power structures and progressive ideals will rage.

You understand the value of being an aware and conscious modern-day citizen, and you can bridge the gap between people's beliefs. You can be traditional and forward thinking at the same time, mix power with acceptance, orthodoxy with open-mindedness. By bridging these seemingly disparate ideas you can work for the benefit of everyone in your own unique, supremely broad-minded way—and find true fulfilment.

As an insightful, proactive and progressive character you will dabble with many different approaches to life. This will cause you to appear at once eccentric, quirky, unusual and inconsistent. But these aspects of your personality are how you express the new paradigm. Can you not be multi-faceted? Can you not express yourself diversely and in unexpected ways?

Your understanding of the basic tenet that every action has an equal reaction leads you to believe that we as individuals and en masse can change what comes next. You're a bright spark, and your approach is idiosyncratic and enlightening. You have authority beyond your years at a young age, and this in part is what will get people to sit up and take notice of you.

Perspective

Inconsistent, unorthodox, traditional values, honest, quirky, unusual, can be egotistical, rebellious as a child, proud

Talents

Perceptivity, self-awareness, good communications, inventiveness, creativity, motivation

Interests

New age, health, surgery, religion, humanitarian, aviation, technology, mindfulness, social reform

Challenge

To allow the spirit of cooperation to work through you

Potential pitfalls

To become alienated, egotistical, greedy, self-centred

Affirmation

Let's build a new paradigm.

Values and self-expression

Your unconventional desires and values may become evident early in childhood. As a child you may also have unusual nutritional demands and be a picky eater.

> NOTE TO PARENTS: *preparing fresh fruit and vegetables in unique combinations will help ensure your child receives a nutritious diet. S/he'll love funny shapes and colour combinations.*

You may come from a large family or were the first-born, and hold a position either of more influence than the other children in your family or, if from a large family, markedly less influence.

As an adult you'll be attracted to unusually egocentric and successful people, and unconventional groups or societies will admire your individuality. You may be attracted to other people's wealth, and accrue debt easily. Your natural grace and social skills make you appear friendly and adaptable. You're likely to express your values up-front, and won't hide who you truly are. For this reason you may appear unusually direct, especially in cultures that value social niceties and manners above all.

You will feel fulfilled from understanding your unique position within the whole, and knowing that while you're in a closely interconnected web of humankind you're a unique person and your wishes and values are as important as anyone else's. Your greatest risk is that you become a victim of your own pride, which stems from being aware of how unique you are.

Your insight and ideas will seem almost futuristic. And yet your insight is unparalleled, especially when paired with the desire to provide benefits for all—and not just yourself.

You'll often strive for success in avant-garde ways. And succeed you will, as you're not only original and motivated but you also have a powerhouse of energy to keep you on top.

Perspective

Quirky, individualistic, affectionate, generous, giving, progressive, unconventional, rebellious, friendly, direct

Talents

Industriousness, ingenuity, inventiveness, inspirational, originality

Challenge

To use your gifts for good

Potential pitfalls

Pride, to be self-serving

Affirmation

I love life and life loves me!

Communication

Your curiosity knows no bounds. Your learning curve will take you to new pastures and you're able to add inventive and unique information to existing ideas, traditions and knowledge. You love discussing new notions with friends, family and experts alike, and you enjoy mixing with many different people from diverse social groups and cultural backgrounds. Your networking skills are impressive.

You may appear oddball in your communications at various points in your life largely because you're ahead of your time. You have distinctive traits or a turn of phrase that sets you apart from others. At various times in your life you will be the quintessential computer geek, preferring to communicate via technology rather than in person because technology has broader scope and suits your vision. Your fascination for IT risks alienating you from everyday life, though, so keeping your feet on the ground will become key to maintaining a balanced life.

You're a natural-born scientist and investigator and will set up experiments, even social situations, just to see how they pan out, taking mental notes that you can carry over to your next experiment. You have an incisive mind and are able to discern what's true and what's not at a hundred paces, which some people may find disconcerting especially when you are a child.

NOTE TO PARENTS: *encourage your child's insight; it really is illuminating.*

It's important to remember that you're a part of your experiments, too, and have a vital part to play in life. Guard against becoming detached and aloof, especially as this could adversely influence your closest relationships. Communicating your bright-spark ideas may take extra effort and diligence, but you do have an analytical mind and with practical application you'll manage to communicate complex issues.

You have a distant or lingering sense that you come from a position of authority and grandeur, and striving to recreate this may distract you from achieving a deeper sense of purpose. Remember that you already have it all.

Your particular holy grail is your ability to create your own destiny in new and groundbreaking ways, and this is what provides you with a truly fascinating life. In turn it's your ability to communicate this faculty that everyone has, which truly sets you apart.

Perspective

Detached, discerning, incisive, humorous, outgoing, inquisitive, enthusiastic, quirky, technologically minded, enterprising

Talents

Communications, simultaneously practical, reasonable and inventive, astute

Challenge

To communicate abstract ideas

Potential pitfalls

Becoming isolated, marginalised, excessively oddball

Affirmation

I communicate for positive ends.

Home and family

You'll enjoy demonstrating your skills from a very young age, beginning at home. As a child you'll question just about everything. Your curiosity could get you into scrapes, and nooks and crannies you didn't even know existed!

NOTE TO PARENTS: *your child's mind is exceptional. Spontaneous deductions and ideas will surprise and, with a little application, can be practical, too.*

As you mature and leave home you will stand out in a crowd, just as you stood out in your family as a child. (Even if you did have to misbehave to make people notice you!)

Your family background is unique in some way. In the same way you like to push forward the boundaries of human understanding your family or home life will be unusually progressive or forward thinking.

As an adult your extraordinary style is hard to ignore, and this will be reflected in your choice of home too. You enjoy innovation in design, appreciate architecturally stunning buildings and will ideally create a living space that is ahead of its time or at the cutting edge of eco-friendly design or smart technology.

You have a quiet, authoritative bearing at home. You are aware after all, that you are the creator of your own particular circumstances, and as such you'll command respect in the home as a parent too. You can at times appear aloof, largely because you're immersed in your own world of inventiveness and ingenuity.

You will not command respect without having the substance to back it up. Being the enormously innovative person you are you will demonstrate, in the nicest possible way, just how special and unique you are—often in unexpected ways. Small gifts, spontaneous meetings or sudden changes of schedule will keep the spirit and spark of creativity alive in your household.

In the process you'll demonstrate just what being ingenious is—indeed how you came to be so great, and such a special being by following your heart and believing you could make a difference. In this way you'll discover the part of your unique calling that is to show people exactly what their contribution to life is by setting a good example yourself. In so doing you complete the cycle of awakening the spirit—yours, and others' too.

Perspective

Unusual, bright, unique, self-confident, team-leader, gregarious, individualistic, eccentric, curious

Talents

Innovation, invention, motivation, nurturance

Challenge

To demonstrate your unique talents.

Potential pitfalls

Arrogance, aloofness, disconnected

Affirmation

I am unique and so are you.

Creativity and life force

You're a live wire. Harnessing this vital energy and channeling it into upbeat activities will give purpose and structure in your life. If you allow yourself to become too distracted by your many diverse interests you risk running around in ever decreasing (even if colourful) circles, accomplishing little. You're attracted to extreme new ideas and radical and progressive design, and you may risk on occasion being impractical, becoming eccentric and operating in the margins of society as a result.

Your imagination knows no bounds, and investigation, innovation and discovery will appeal—anything from the realms of the occult (anything hidden), to scientific research such as applied physics or alternative energy resources. You'll enjoy being at the forefront of social advance and immersing yourself in groups, clubs and discussion panels to be an active part of your generation's zeitgeist.

You'll take an interest in many different fields—psychology because you want to understand how people tick; architecture and construction as you will want to understand the structure of buildings and how they function and relate to humans; and healing and medicine because you want to see how people can work at optimum capacity.

Essentially, you'll enjoy working with the nuts and bolts of many different areas of life to form a whole picture. You'll also enjoy bringing opposites and conflicting ideas together, if need be by researching opposite opinions, discussing them with experts and friends alike to reach an informed decision yourself.

You do this because you understand the spark that initiates everything, the creative process, inventiveness, relationships, understanding, action. And being able to understand how this spark is expressed in so many different ways helps you to be the original person you are, bringing value to your own work of art that is your life.

Perspective

Curious, vivacious, helpful, inventive, imaginative, inquisitive, progressive

Talents

Insight, originality, creativity

Creative career

Design, architecture, philosophy, art, performance, lifestyle, ecological inventions, new-age activities, horticulture, media

Challenge

To channel your energy into positive pursuits

Potential pitfalls

Distractions, delusions, over-stimulated imagination, extreme eccentricity, disaffection

Affirmation

I understand the spark of life.

Work and daily life

All the latest types of activities and interests will appeal to you as you wish to be at the cutting edge of life and the forefront of developments. At a young age you'll begin to immerse yourself in technology and research.

You know you'll need to start at the bottom and work your way up so an early start will give you an advantage. You're able to make your way to the position you wish to be in within any organisation, and your bright spark and quirky attitude belies your methodical and diligent abilities.

A pitfall is professing to know more than someone who has more experience than you—even if you do! After all, experience is as valuable as knowledge itself, and a humble attitude will get you much further, and much more quickly, too, than an arrogant, know-it-all approach that will only ruffle feathers.

You will, at least at some point, flirt with an interest in film and media. You'll succeed in advertising, especially film and TV advertising, as you have a talent for communicating through images.

Above all, your gift is your ability to combine your extraordinary take on life with reality and the people who it will benefit. You're able to apply your knowledge and experience methodically and diligently, making you an accomplished and valued employee and, later in life, an inspired employer too.

Perspective

Original, bright, optimistic, diligent, methodical, quick, smart

Talents

Quick wit, practical yet inventive, forward-thinking

Type of work

Film, technology, computers, exploration, invention, law, health, humanitarian causes, voluntary work, academia, science, teaching, travel, aviation, engineering

Challenge

To know when to be humble

Potential pitfalls

Dispersed energy, arrogance, pride, laziness

Affirmation

I help move things forward.

Relationships

You'll gain a profound sense of purpose and belief in yourself through your relationships because you'll learn how to resolve your own inner dilemmas through them.

You may be attracted to eccentric or unusual people such as those who come from radically different backgrounds. You may be perceived as non-conformist or unorthodox yourself due to the kinds of arrangements you make in your personal life. You may be drawn toward pushing forward the boundaries of acceptable relationships.

You will have a strong pull towards humanitarian values, which will help you promote a broader view of what is acceptable in love and life.

At work you're likely to be seen as fairly cool, remote even, and in your personal life you can appear equivocal or detached, especially if you feel you're under pressure to conform. You appear to be a free spirit, and yet if you scratch the surface deep loyalty lies beneath, which is radically different to your equivocal demeanour. This may be a source of confusion as people get to know you, and may even be a source of confusion for you too. It's as if you're constantly in two minds about freedom and aloofness versus commitment, and the ability to be yourself versus the wish to be a family/couple/friend.

Your relationships are a key area in which your own inner paradox will be played out, and will exacerbate the conflict you feel between being unique and independent while still being able to form a union, and between being a free spirit while still being able to commit. As a result an endless inner debate could rage under your free-spirited demeanour.

In the process you may be accused of being inconsistent, selfish or egotistical. You may even be suspected of having tunnel vision and being unable to see anyone else's point of view because, when you're under pressure, you can allow your ego and pride to dominate and overshadow your better self.

You may suffer from misunderstandings in your relationships. A part of your journey is to understand other people's point of view as well as your own, to demonstrate to those you love, and to those who care, that it is possible to be both independent and committed, to be both a free spirit and loyal, and also to have healthy self-interest while still being interested in other people too.

When you learn to understand and accept the paradoxes of your true nature you will enjoy the fulfilment of your deep desires, and further the causes of many other people who have similar attitudes to yours.

As someone who is searching for a new way to live their life, and interested in alternatives and new paradigms, you'll learn that there is a quality that connects your inner complexities, that rises above and beyond the paradoxes of your personality. And this, as you'll learn through your relationships, is love itself. Love is the highest denominator that rises above paradoxes and inconsistencies and it is this power that you'll embrace as it unites and binds people together in their common aims.

Perspective

Lively, idiosyncratic, theatrical, independent, generous, equivocal, individualistic

Talents

Lateral thinking, analysis, loyalty, kindness

Challenge

To accept your inner paradox

Possible pitfalls

Inconsistency, detachment, egoism, rebellion, ambivalence, drama

Affirmation

Love is an expression of my higher spirit.

Motivation

Your motivation comes from the heart. You are a true lover of life, and in connection with your search for a new paradigm through which to live your life you also want to be heard. This is partly due to the fact that your motivation in life is for the greater good, seeing yourself as a vanguard of new ideas and enlightened social mores.

Your values and principles can stretch outside the norm, and you can feel alienated. You are also likely to undergo a form of struggle or have to fight for your rights at some point in your life so that you feel included in society, and so that you have a voice.

Once you've gained your right to be heard you'll be in a position to teach new standards and open the gates to a new understanding of each individual's role in the bigger picture. In the process of finding your voice you may veer from quiet to overbearing, but once you've found it your ideas will flow so much more effectively—and you'll see positive progress in your life so much more quickly.

You can be motivated by a strong ego as a youngster, and this will help you develop your voice and implement your unique insights in practical ways. As you mature you'll know that even though your ego has a part to play in your life, a higher calling will take the place of it— especially if, as you believe, the human species really is to evolve collectively.

Your quest is to see yourself—and society at large—as a more awakened and spiritually conscious organism. As such, you are motivated to share your insights, and to push forward on your pathway to new possibilities, taking with you anyone who wishes to accompany you.

Your life path may put you in new environments, perhaps through travel with your parents while you were young, and your circumstances will show you to be different in some way within your own environment. You'll be motivated to establish some form of stability both psychologically and physically amidst the rollercoaster ride that is your life.

Your possessions and values may be different to the norm. You may come from a markedly wealthy family or from a remarkably poor family, and your own financial fortunes may depend on someone else's fortunes. The boom and bust cycle may be significant in your family as your financial fortunes escalate then dip before escalating again.

To help negotiate life's rollercoaster ride you'll discover tenacity and the ability to create stability while simultaneously maintaining the spark that fuels your lust for life. Your difference and uniqueness will be a point of discussion, and a blessing and vindication of your life force as you experience life's marvels so much more profoundly than many.

You'll shine a light on alternative approaches and solutions, and this will increase not only your own appreciation of life, but also others'. This is your true motivation: to be a light bearer of sorts, and show the way forward.

Perspective
Bright, intuitive, zany, different, rebellious, progressive, searching for a voice

Talents
Trouble-shooting, strategy, social conscience, tenacity, being unique

Challenge
To be heard

Potential pitfalls
Being distracted by the fight rather than keeping your eye on the goal

Affirmation
I shine a new light.

Seeking . . .
You're a bright spark, there's no denying it. You'll enjoy maintaining an active search for a better way forward, and value clear insight and understanding. Unusual or uncharted waters will appeal to you, and you'll enjoy discovering new information.

Communicating your insights will bring you a great deal of pleasure. Higher education will appeal, and you'll also enjoy teaching what you learn. Your travels may take you into new territory for the purpose of research, negotiation and trade, and you'll actively enjoy bartering and commerce.

You'll also seek out spiritual activities such as prayer and meditation. New-age ideals will appeal and you'll become actively involved in some form of humanitarian endeavour. You're naturally talented at public speaking and creative expression, with acting roles and performance appealing to you.

You're one of life's true adventurers and explorers. You'll take life's bigger picture and give it a makeover, and put life's details under a microscope to discover new worlds within. You'll understand that the freedom gained through knowledge is invaluable, and that the undertaking of true enlightenment will unite the world.

Ultimately you're seeking to identify and promote a new paradigm that will at once satisfy each individual's calling including your own, and simultaneously promote the greater social good. This is a vast task, and one that is best managed in small steps. The giant leap is, after all, fuelled by your belief in the power of the awakened consciousness, which is a collective power much greater than yours alone. Through your life experiences you will learn that the final job of awakening the collective consciousness ultimately rests with each individual and your job is merely to highlight this.

Perspective

Gregarious, adventurous, upbeat, humanitarian, good communicator

Talents

Research, study of progressive subjects, being ahead of your time

Interests

Science, research, academia, progressive, religious, spiritual studies, human-rights, technology, IT, law, nutrition, horticulture

Challenge

To focus on one area of expertise at a time

Potential pitfalls

Being distracted by so many interests

Affirmation

I believe in the collective consciousness.

Career and direction

You're powerful and will never lose steam. It's as if you have an internal generator that simply keeps you running. And yet this is something you may forget early in life as you'll be under a spotlight in a way that will accentuate your uniqueness, and which can feel draining.

You're predisposed to strive for success in unconventional ways, and you will succeed because you're original and motivated. Your sincere heart and profound tie to family, friends, a partner or your home puts you firmly in loving hands that will support your every move—this is something never to be underestimated.

You will frequently find that you have the support you need even if your situation appears stressful. This strong feeling of being supported is a benefit you'll appreciate, but if you become self-involved your lack of discretion will compromise your ability to be the bright person you are, and then you risk losing support from the people you count on.

Your unique take on life will put you in many controversial or challenging situations. Yet your sense of being supported by the very life force you come from will always bring you back to reality and to a sense of being connected to everyone else, even when you must stand out in your inimitable way.

Due to your unique take on life you will have many opportunities to make positive changes to the world you live in, especially through your work or your status in life. Working for government, in advertising, film, IT or voluntary organisations will put you in an influential position.

It is your destiny to celebrate your individuality. You will be in a powerful position to encourage others to assert their own particular life spark, and to unite and celebrate the diversity of nature's creations together.

Characteristics

Extrovert, unique, unpredictable, loyal, ambitious, controversial, motivated, unconventional

Talents

Inclusivity, compassion, motivation, influence, charm, trail-blazing

Type of career

Progressive arts, advertising, film, technology, psychic, spiritual, religious, aviation, oceanography, eco activism, human-rights, law, government, IT, medicine and surgery in particular

Challenge

To assume your place in the world, and recognise that you are supported

Potential pitfalls

Feeling like an outcast, opinionated, lack of discretion

Affirmation

I'm unique and so are you!

Goals, groups and humanitarianism

You're a rebel rouser and will enjoy cutting through red tape and rewriting the law. Bureaucracy will tire you out, and you may even envisage new social structures and routines that could maximise productivity within established social institutions.

You have the ability to embrace the big picture. You have vision and can see how various social strata can operate at optimum capacity. Principally, you understand the flow of energy at a fundamental level, and how this can best be utilised.

You are foremost a people person. Walk into a crowded room and you're the standout, the eccentric, and the spotlight will be on you for some reason. You'll be wearing bright clothes or you'll have the loudest voice or quirkiest mannerisms. You'll be gesticulating and laughing, but get you alone and you'll cry the tears of a clown.

Life's a stage for you in many respects. You're a born performer, happy to mingle and stand out in the process, but make no mistake, you're no-one's clown. You're not just the life and soul of the party; you're much bigger than that. You're the life and soul of the whole show—your's, other people's and your entire environment.

You add sparkle wherever you go, and yet a serious message underlies your approach. You're a humanitarian, an artist underneath all that pizzazz and quirkiness. You have a serious message not only about how important it is to have fun in life, but also about how important laughter, joy and the spark of life are. If you're a rare wallflower, then look a little closer: you know you're a rebel at heart, you may just keep it to yourself a little more.

You'll back the latest craze, cause, friend's project, in fact the latest and greatest anything. But underneath you know it's all in the spirit of connectedness because the very spark that created each individual, the common thread shared by all life will continue making all great things great. Follow the spark, which you're happy to do, and you'll cause a few fireworks yourself!

Perspective

Bubbly, uplifting, clever, sociable, bright-spark, eccentric

Talents

Social conscience, innovation, enthusiasm

Interests

Humanitarian causes, social concerns, activism, showbusiness, performance, socialising

Challenge

To stay ahead of your time

Potential pitfalls

To lose your way, burn out, melancholia, taking on the world's woes

Affirmation

I keep the spark alive.

The secret you

You're a markedly different person in your quieter moments at home than in the broader social context. You'll enjoy resting, reading and other quiet pursuits that recharge your energy reserves. You know that your inner life must be nurtured so that your eccentric self can flourish, and that you must support your inner light so your good work can continue else you risk burnout.

Work, research and devotion will keep your particular spark alive. You're a live wire and you love to be physically, emotionally and mentally engaged in your activities. You'll enjoy getting down to the bottom of research, up to the heights of spirituality and devotion, and you'll simultaneously enjoy reaching the zenith of your profession. If you don't have to work you'll derive a great deal of satisfaction from supporting others in their own particular endeavours, happily sacrificing your time and energy for a good cause.

Your interest in health will see you determinedly pursue diet and fitness fads that some may consider unusual. Psychiatry and other modalities that plumb the workings of the mind will appeal to you as you attempt to understand what makes you, and everyone else, tick. Science and experimentation will appeal for this reason too.

In truly private moments you cry the tears of compassion and hope for those less fortunate than you. You are a true humanitarian because your kindness comes from your heart, not your mind. You truly feel the pain of others, and can be tempted to take on the world's woes single-handedly.

Your secret fears are that your avant-garde ideas will not be accepted, that you will be spurned for being different and that, secretly, you are weak or even an imposter. For this reason you can strive harder to make yourself understood and heard, and you risk mental exhaustion.

You have a fear of being stuck and alone on the edge of life rather than being in the vortex of creativity and the centre of attention. You have a faint memory of being vitally important, and simply know that the actions and messages you must deliver are of great importance in your lifetime, so you are passionate about your role as a prime mover.

A degree of detachment from society will enable you to act on your bright ideas without taking on the world's woes all by yourself. But being detached can, clearly, further contribute to your fear of being alone. You're all too aware of this catch-22, and it can tug at your heartstrings in quieter moments.

Your ability to believe that people will awake spiritually is what truly sets you apart. The awakening consciousness that we are all one made in the image of a great creator (God, Buddha, spirit, the one, creation), and that we all contain the seeds of our own salvation and fulfilment spurs you on. When you are able to tune in to this awakened consciousness directly your unique talent will help you rise above your fears and self-doubts. After all, you and your actions embody the awakening spirit of the new millennium.

Characteristics
Quiet, self-effacing, introspective, private, gentle

Talents
Research, persistence, experimentation, technology, diligence, self-belief, attunement to your higher purpose

Interests
Research, spirituality, health, psychology, reading, social science, IT, forensic science, archaeology, pets

Challenge
To self-nurture

Potential pitfalls
Burnout, lack of motivation, lack of energy, fear of being stuck or in a catch-22 situation, loneliness

Affirmation
I am awake. My higher purpose guides me.

Pisces

The realistic visionary

SITUATION

You will face many unexplained circumstances in your lifetime that will take you by the scruff of the neck and shake you until you understand their deeper meaning. You'll develop an understanding of the hidden depths and mysteries of life and will in turn take your life by the scruff of its neck and shake it until you wring out everything you need from it. This process may involve some form of self-sacrifice, either of your ideals, morals or dreams. If you sacrifice a dream this will be so that you may attain another.

If you fail in your tasks you'll become easily disheartened and even potentially misled by unscrupulous people or questionable circumstances. And yet you're a stickler for detail, so any research you undertake—either into the soul, or mathematics, or relationships, in fact any subject you choose—will leave no stone unturned. You'll have broad interests and the need to plumb their depths.

This dedication to understanding the essence and meaning of life makes you a devotee not just of spiritual matters, but of life itself. This level of devotion will lead you into many different areas—whether taboo or enlightened, beneficial to you or self-destructive.

Rest assured that you are a practical soul. You will always deduce the most reasonable, sensible and most useful conclusion, and you'll tend to take the most sensible action in the course of your life. This alone will help you avoid falling foul of haphazard circumstances as you take your place within the creative circle of life with flair and deep, visionary understanding.

PURPOSE

You'll feel fulfilled by deepening your understanding of the wonders of the universe, creation, existence and life. You'll enjoy passing your knowledge on to those around you through your role as some form of teacher or healer. You understand that your contribution in life is to help people gain similar insight into the deep, unseen mysteries and wonder of their own lives.

As you enter uncharted territory in your search for wisdom, you can risk immersing yourself in areas that may be challenging. It's important to be discerning and remember that when push comes to shove you have the means to be sensible, even if you are accused of having your head in the clouds as you immerse yourself totally in your interests and pursuits.

You already know that when you get in too deep it may be difficult to extricate yourself. Your natural wisdom and sense of realism will prevent serious damage as your soul enlightens itself on its journey to a new understanding not only of your own life, but of life itself.

Affirmation

I can reach for the stars, especially when I'm practical.

Famous people

Quincy Jones, Willie Nelson, Nina Simone, Elizabeth Taylor, Gene Wilder, Claudia Schiffer, Paul Cezanne, Michael Caine, Patsy Cline, Dr Phil McGraw, Edgar Cayce, Robin Williams

Your unique approach

People call you a dreamer, but you and those close to you know that you're anything but. In fact you're a realist. So much so that the wonders of the universe never cease to amaze you precisely because they're real, and being a realist you can see things exactly as they are! You're also well organised, should you put your mind to it. If anything, you tend to be your own worst critic because you are such a perfectionist at heart.

And yet it is true in a sense that you are a dreamer because you're looking for something above and beyond what you can see, feel and touch in your everyday life. You're looking for an ideal, a profound understanding of life.

Will you find it? That depends on how much you can let go of your preconceptions about how things are and how they should be. Will you let your mind wander to the extent that you discover alternate realities, or does this simply sound ridiculous to you? Yet suspending disbelief is what will help you to attain the ideals you're pursuing because when you stop placing limitations on what's possible everything becomes possible.

The key to your own happiness lies in the understanding that your hopes and ideals may begin in your mind, but they can exist in reality. If you want to make a project real, it's simply a case of making it real through disciplined and careful planning, logical application and a sprinkle of trust and belief!

You're prone to idealising your own situation, but then a little glamour and a hint of magic never hurt anyone. A careful balance between being idealistic and realistic will keep your feet on the ground and your vision in the clouds, which is, after all, how dreams come true.

Perspective

Imaginative, deep-thinking, practical, perfectionist, self-critical, dreamer, philosophical

Talents

Visionary, creative, sensuous, inventive

Interests

Reading, arts, finances, philosophy, literature, physics, fashion, swimming, meditation

Challenge

To methodically create your dreams

Potential pitfalls

Idealisation, martyr-like tendencies, naivety

Affirmation

I back up my great ideas with practical steps.

Values and self-expression

You see the good and the wonder in everything and everyone you encounter, largely because you value life and everything it has to offer. And so you'll wish to jump in at the deep end of whatever project, relationship or situation takes your fancy. You can be easily influenced so it's vital that you research activities, projects and people (when possible) first before you enter into close alliances or commitments.

But, you may ask, if you must beware, how will you live a fun, spontaneous life? You're actually one of the least impulsive individuals in the zodiacal kaleidoscope even if, to you, this may not seem to be the case. Your meticulous interest in life will encourage you to take things step by step, and research your options in depth. That is after the initial spark of interest has worn off—the one that could potentially see you take the big leap right into the deep end.

Your tendency to jump in feet first is partly because you'll enjoy reaching conclusions by your own means, and sometimes you simply need to dive in to do so. You know that to reach your potential you must let go of preconceived ideas and rigid expectations. So research has its part in your life's learning process as it will act as a kind of fail-safe mechanism, helping you avoid letting go and plunging into the unknown before you're ready.

Fortunately your intuition and gut feelings will give you the greatest indicator of the suitability of projects, people and activities to your own particular path before you even need to take that leap. Consulting your intuition before embarking on various projects will guide you, and your intuition will develop as you mature. You may sometimes find your intuition appears to be incorrect as a youngster until you learn to rely on it as you grow older.

Children with a Pisces north node may appear to be wise beyond their years, and your wisdom is gained principally by living your life through a delicate combination of acute instinct and hands-on experience. Adults will learn to trust that your values, principles, morals and standards will guide you accurately in life.

Financially you will see either remarkable growth or remarkable loss. Money is an area where you could be easily misled, and therefore sound advice is best sought from experts whose credentials you may wish to research first.

You see life as an expression of values and ideas and as such you already understand that what you think and express is vitally important. Through various phases of your life you'll enjoy passing on this knowledge in the form of guidance or mediation between people. You have a knack for getting to the bottom of issues quickly.

The value you place on life itself is immeasurable. You simply know and understand that it is supremely precious indeed. It's simply a case of diving in—once you've done basic safety checks!

Perspective

Compassionate, kind, easily led, pragmatic, imaginative, amiable, adventurous

Talents

Understanding others, mediation, meditation, guidance, intuition

Challenge

To use your intuition

Potential pitfalls

Being easily influenced, out of your depth, overtly trusting

Affirmation

Life is wonderful. Its value is beyond imagination.

Communication

You're a free thinker and you have an open mind. You're also self-disciplined, strive to be well informed and your intentions are good. This is the perfect recipe for success especially career-wise.

You're a source of interesting facts and fiction, delving so deeply into subjects that you'll become a true expert and your advice will often be sought. You will succeed in your chosen path in life, and your opinion is sought for that reason too.

From childhood on you may find that you're frequently misunderstood due to circumstances you find yourself in, and not because you're inarticulate. For instance, language barriers could create misunderstandings if you're brought up overseas. Being raised in a culture where the predominant customs are different from your parents' will cause misunderstandings, too, as you may express yourself differently to other people.

You may also be misunderstood because your insight is so much deeper than other people's. Avoid feeling disappointed if you are misunderstood as this could lead to feelings of victimhood, which could detract from your rich imagination and impressive communication skills.

You're inspired, and have wonderful ideas to communicate. You'll enjoy discussing philosophy and theology as well as finding new ways to convey your particularly brilliant views. You may prefer not to adhere precisely to traditional customs and practices in the process.

You're an innovator and an artist. Your head is in the clouds while your feet are still on the ground. You will express many new ideas and prove them to be valuable because you know your ideas are helpful to others too. In this respect you are learning new ways to express yourself and so if you ever feel you're only just learning to be heard or understood it's because you are learning how to apply reason and logic to the ephemeral, esoteric and the boundless. Quite a paradox, and quite a task!

Perspective

Open-minded, kind, sympathetic, dreamy, nostalgic, philosophical, innovative, free thinking

Talents

Art, creative writing, research, languages, self-discipline

Challenge

To articulate philosophical or deep ideas

Potential pitfalls

Being misunderstood, inarticulate, imprecise, vague, distracted

Affirmation

I'm articulate and inspired. I'm a success.

Home and family

You have wisdom beyond your years especially in connection with your home, family or property. You may even wonder where you get it from yourself.

You can make a house feel comfortable and welcoming. Your contribution in the home and with family is always appreciated because you're charming, inspired and hopeful. You have a sense of humour, and are a pleasure to be around.

Your artistic flair is evident in your home, in its swirls of colour at the very least. You're likely to choose gadgets and furniture for their clever combination of inspired aesthetics and functionality.

Your main pitfall is that during different phases in your life you may be asked to sacrifice your time and energy to your house, home and family, or conversely to sacrifice your career or work in favour of caring for your home or family. This will always be for a good cause, and you may find that you undergo enriching experiences as a result, but if you dwell on the negatives you risk falling into a victim–martyr role. This could lead you to lose yourself in discontentment and sentiment when your true calling is to provide quite the opposite: inspiration and insight for yourself and those you live with.

You'll see that you're not cut out for the role of victim or martyr because you have far more to offer than that. By taking a proactive stance in life your innovative ideas and way of doing things will take precedence over roles and circumstances, and you'll avoid being typecast. Unless of course that's what you want, and nothing can stop you once you've chosen a role!

Your desire for perfection can manifest in the shape of an immaculate home where every surface is scrubbed clean and every item of furniture matches. The worst-case scenario is that you develop obsessive-compulsive tendencies regarding cleanliness and positioning of furniture. This can manifest when you're under pressure, but when you accept that you are a realistic person you'll overcome the desire to demand perfection all around you—if only because it's simply unrealistic.

Your tendency to idealise your circumstances and effectively demand a perfect life can truly lead you astray, not least because of a constant, nagging feeling of disappointment and under-achievement. And this is where the important realisation arises once again: it's vital to be careful what you choose to do as it will become a deep, and lingering, concern. Above all you have a choice about how you respond to situations, and improving this ability will help you to remain always inspired, and never obsessive or disappointed.

Perspective

Progressive, determined, precise, detailed, wistful, imaginative, talkative, idealistic

Talents

Organisational skills, resourcefulness, creativity, practical sense

Interests

Property, home care, planning, entertainment, music, cleaning

Challenge

To remain inspired

Potential pitfalls

Falling into the victim–martyr role, indecision, obsession, lack of realism

Affirmation

I choose my responses to life.

Creativity and life force

You're a musical, creative, animated, joyful soul and you'll enjoy expressing yourself any which way you can! Your art has ephemeral qualities, and you'll enjoy inventing stories as a child. You'll be happy to indulge in the playground of your imagination, which is not to say you can't share or play with others as a child—you may simply not need to. You're happy with your imaginary friends, for a start. As an adult your imagination knows no bounds as you revel in the joyful life your imagination creates.

You have impressive networking skills and you're able to express yourself in corporate life and the world outside your own creative whirlpool. In fact you're a natural-born socialite, but you may just choose not to be. Yet you're a practical soul and unlikely to ostracise yourself completely because fun, games and imaginative play are augmented by interactions with your fellow human beings who increase your sense of joy and play.

You'll enjoy the company of children both as a child and as an adult because you enjoy surrounding yourself with similarly minded and playful people. The pitfall is that your admiration for the playful side of life prevents you from fully accepting your role as an adult, and you will grow up slowly. Consequently you will need to learn the lessons of duty and responsibility through the school of hard knocks, especially if you lose your more practical, sensible self in a giant swirl of play, imagination and creativity.

You'll enjoy losing yourself in music, theatre and dance as, at heart, you're a playful reveller in life's creative forces. And in the process you'll find your spirit and soul.

Yours is a vision that is so inspired that it allows the spirit of life and creation to flow through you unhindered. Even in moments of dire struggle your life will be enriched because you actively enter a new, deeper understanding and appreciation of life itself through the experiences you undergo.

Perspective
Musical, great timing, child-like, playful, inventive, fun, sociable

Talents

Art, music, dance, theatre, poetry, enjoying life

Creative career

Art, music, dance, drama, primary education, domestic god/goddess, psychic intuitive, telepath, horticulture

Challenge

To implement your deeper understanding

Potential pitfalls

Losing yourself, delusional, impractical, unrealistic expectations, remaining child-like, lacking in responsibility

Affirmation

I act on wonderful ideas.

Work and daily life

When is work no longer work? When you enjoy it? When it comes naturally? When you transform something that at first seems a drab chore and an uninviting prospect into something attractive and productive? Actually it's all of the above!

Work and duty are not chores or dull obligations when you absolutely love what you do. And you'll find out what this is through working in some field of service. You find great satisfaction in helping people less fortunate than you. And if you began life in difficult circumstances yourself you will rise through the ranks to help people who are still trapped in circumstances you came from yourself.

You have the tendency to idealise others' strengths, and you may undervalue your own, especially as a youngster. You also have a tendency to believe you are inferior, especially when you start at the bottom of the ladder in the workplace.

Feelings of inferiority are a pitfall for you, and your talents will remain undiscovered if you continue to believe this. You also risk never finding what truly makes you happy by simply making do. So at a young age it's in your interest to understand your own true values, your ability to succeed and to decide which line of work or activity truly resonates with you.

You understand the value of performing your duties and being committed to an employer, a job or a vocation. You'll always manage to turn a dull chore into a successful and enjoyable activity, and you'll enjoy putting your creative touch to just about any area of your life.

Your ability to find satisfaction in many of life's dull rituals will make you a valuable employee, but this ability may also prevent you from reaching your higher goals as you risk losing yourself in work, daily rituals and practices. It will be important to monitor your own activities, if only to double-check you're always following a satisfying path.

The 'life is beautiful' ethos is yours because how could life be any other way? You're an innovator within your field. You're following the yellow brick road, and understand many of life's mysteries, not least how to be happy. Life is essentially a healing journey for you in which you will enjoy transforming your talents into tangible results—and the workplace is one area you'll manage this best.

Perspective

Idealistic yet practical, helpful, bubbly, realistic, sensible yet creative, ambitious

Talents

Vision, sense of responsibility, good organisational skills

Type of work

Life coach, work in institutions such as gaols and hospitals, veterinary, chemistry, police force, career advice, film, advertising, design, writing, academia, science, horticulture, theatre

Challenge

To find out what you love to do early on

Potential pitfalls

Being without a goal, making do, being unfulfilled, inferiority complex

Affirmation

My work inspires me.

Relationships

You're prone to idealise partners, family and close friends. Yet you appear in many other respects to be such a practical, realistic person. So how could you misjudge people so often?

Idealising people is your Achilles heel, even to the extent that you exhibit alternately victim and then martyr-like tendencies when you discover who people truly are. You may lapse into criticism of others as you strive towards an ideal, and eventually you risk finally criticising yourself the most for having been so blind.

Your tendency to misjudge others puts you in a vulnerable position within close relationships. You can potentially lose your identity in someone else or in the dynamics of the relationship as you become utterly devoted once committed.

So your talent for research is a useful tool to employ before you commit to a long-term relationship. Naturally people change as do circumstances, so it's worth your while being particularly aware that your Achilles heel pertains to your own perception of others, and not to the actual person, and that you can grow out of your tendency to idealise people.

Your ability to plan and methodically execute various ideas will be useful in business relationships as you're able to combine your vision with practical strategies to see plans materialise. Your friendly demeanour and sense of compassion makes you a valuable co-worker and business partner.

But in a marriage partnership where spontaneity, fun and the ability to adapt to circumstances are just as important as the ability to plan, you may be perceived as rigid or stubborn. Your tendency to become obsessed with an idea can also be deemed inflexible, so by balancing your ability to plan and execute ideas with your sensitive, compassionate, visionary, romantic self, your relationships will flourish.

If you do find you cling to rigid structures, the cause may be self-doubt. You'll develop more flexibility by focusing on self-belief, your intuition and your faith in the greater good. Meditation, yoga and contemplation are particularly effective in helping tackle rigid, inflexible behaviour, allowing you to let go and take the plunge into the sea of love.

You'll find your relationships are some of the most imaginative, playful and creative areas of your life as you have the capacity for truly deep union and intimate understanding of another's soul. You'll discover that the most enduring and mystifying experience of life is love.

Perspective

Idealistic, romantic, poetic, affectionate, imaginative, devoted

Talents

Commitment, love, care, gentleness, deep sensuality

Challenge

To be real about relationships

Potential pitfalls

Gullibility, criticism, martyr tendencies, lack of self-belief, naivety

Affirmation

I see people for who they are.

Motivation

You are motivated by deep empathy for others. When you become committed to a person or a job you take this very seriously, but your depth of interest can lead you to lose perspective. If you gain a little detachment from your relationships and activities in general you'll find that your sense of self strengthens, and you're then in a better position to enjoy activities more profoundly.

What motivates you to immerse yourself so deeply in life is partly your sixth sense. You can simply know what is about to happen, and you'll have insight into other people's minds too. This could make you clairvoyant or mediumistic, although the latter ability may only surface after the passing of someone close to you who will serve as a kind of bridge to the afterlife.

Your overriding motivation is to discover something above and beyond what meets the eye, and your key to fulfilment lies in expanding your understanding of life, its mysteries and depths. The clear way to do this is to seek perspective, and to keep one foot on the ground while the other dips a toe into the lake of life's mysteries. And when you're happier going that little bit deeper you'll find your efforts are supported in mysterious ways.

Your need to be practical, methodical and analytical at all times will support your interest in life's mysteries, but you can become overtly pedantic or rigid especially with your approach to finances. You may be drawn to debt, either through your work in the field (as a tax collector for example) or conversely because you're unable to stay out of debt yourself.

By setting yourself boundaries and budgets you'll create a rosy financial picture and get yourself back into solvency. Conversely you can become penny-pinching if you exercise too much control.

You are fundamentally an idealist at heart and your every thought and action is fuelled by your hope for the best possible outcome. This can clearly lead to disappointment, and it is in moments when you're under dire pressure that you may resort to an obsessive attention to details that can degenerate into obsessive-compulsive tendencies if left unchecked.

You're essentially a sensible and reasonable person although flights of fantasy and the blurred lines between yourself and others—and between your own ideas and life itself—can lead to confusion. The delicate line you walk between being practical and methodical and being clear-sighted to the extent of being clairvoyant will ensure that you remain both realistic and matter-of-fact—and a true visionary as well.

Perspective
Deep thinking, amiable, easily influenced, well-meaning, critical, committed

Talents
Analysis, lateral thinking, understanding, logic, sixth sense, vision

Challenge

To seek perspective

Potential pitfalls

Inflexibility, dogmatism, perfectionism, losing touch with reality, forget-fulness, obsessions

Affirmation

I can balance my vision with practicalities.

Seeking . . .

You're seeking something above and beyond the everyday experience. You may not even be aware of it yet! Just like Dorothy starting out on the yellow brick road you do not know yet what you're seeking, and this can be confusing.

Every time you pause before making a decision, every time you're unsure of your next step, and every time you give in to someone else's agenda, it's because you haven't had the opportunity to find out what the low-down is. How can you possibly be expected to decide anything without having first studied it in great detail? You are motivated by simply having to know everything there is to know—including everything that isn't yet known—before making a decision let alone a judgment!

Luckily you have the ability and the self-discipline to collect data. Your search for information is not a mundane one. Your search is likely to relate to a spiritual need to retrieve soul-level information that you somehow know you must collect and disseminate on some level.

Your information-handling skills will help you to broaden your horizons. You'll be attracted to a wide range of subjects for this reason including the study of relationships. And you're ready to rewrite the rules, to push forward received understanding, and in the process you will become a kind of information warrior keen to establish and relay a new vision.

In your search for the big picture you may be tempted to look increasingly at the details and study them in ever decreasing circles of introspection and inspection of minutiae, but this will simply tire you out. For you, understanding the big picture involves a degree of letting go and allowing it to impress itself on you through experience, your senses and your intuition rather than through obsessive research into the minutiae of details.

Ultimately you're seeking belief in a higher power, and you'll seek to experience this through relying on—and trusting in—your own abilities, especially your psychic, intuitive and extra-sensory faculties. You'll undertake research and experimentation involving mind techniques such as meditation to attain altered states of awareness. For the same reason you also risk dabbling in drugs and intoxicants, which will only deaden your sensory antennae.

In everyday life you may appear forgetful, head in the clouds and even oddball, but the net result of all your hard work and research will push forward the boundaries of human understanding.

You are aware already that your contribution makes a difference and this in itself is how deeply you understand the laws of the universe. Every decision, thought and action has an impact, and your purpose in life is to understand this more fully. Not only on an extra-sensory level, but on an applied level where you can put your vision to good use realistically and in the present.

Perspective

Sensitive, experimental, perceptive, perfectionist, critical, aware, introspective

Talents

Research, writing, mathematics, teaching, philosophy

Interests

Cognitive science, meditation, spirituality, competitive sport, philosophy, human relations, psychic ability, poetry, mysteries, collecting

Challenge

To embrace the big picture

Potential pitfalls

Vagueness, indecision, lack of trust, intoxication

Affirmation

I am a fountain of knowledge.

Career and direction

Head in the clouds or a true visionary? You may wonder yourself sometimes so you'll also understand why people may question your ideas from time to time. But once you mature and people get to know you they'll see that even though you have bright ideas that are frequently way beyond your time, they're rooted in a sense of realism that can only come from a bright and progressive mind—and not from pure fantasy alone.

You're a visionary at heart. For you life itself is an invention. And treading the fine line between life being what you make it and life being simply what it is will be your life work. You'll learn a great deal yourself in the process, principally about how to distinguish fact from fiction.

You're able to put your ideas into practice relatively easily, and to enlist the help of powerful people in the process. Your fertile imagination knows no bounds, in fact it's there for you to use for the benefit of all. You'll be driven to express your unique world vision in your career through film, fiction, art, advertising or work with illusion in one form or another such as performance. You'll also show just how precise you can be through scientific work, editing and administration, for example.

You're one of life's philosophers, but make no mistake, you are no idle philosopher. Words from your lips will be backed by truths and facts. You may be drawn to study physics because you study life, matter, energy, force and motion, their causes and effects.

During your career and your life more broadly, circumstances will ask you to sacrifice an idea, a job or your career, a relationship or a role, or even your status in life. Retrospectively you will discover that you did not in fact sacrifice anything. On the contrary you benefitted from the experience and gained a deeper understanding, which is, after all, your prime motivation.

You'll come to learn that for you sacrifice is not a chore or a mere duty. It is something that enriches your life on a deep level, but if you fight against circumstances that at first appear to require a sacrifice your victim- or martyr-like tendencies can surface, and you're unlikely to learn—still less show—the deep understanding you're capable of.

By being level-headed you'll avoid being lost in a fantasy world. This is what gives you your unique ability to be both a visionary and a realist at the same time. And this represents your unique circumstance that straddles the world of what can be, and the world as it is.

Perspective

Visionary, dreamy, idealistic, discerning, perfectionist, realistic, methodical, original

Talents

Philanthropy, understanding, compassion, research, instigation, level-headedness

Type of career

Film, illusion, advertising, performance, science, domestic and property, philosophy, fiction and non-fiction, psychic, publishing, IT, health, naturopathy, art, troubleshooting

Challenge

To walk the fine line between reality and fiction

Potential pitfalls

Delusions, scattiness, lack of discrimination

Affirmation

I am a realistic visionary.

Goals, groups and humanitarianism

You'll chase many a spiritual rainbow and you'll land in many pots of gold because although you may appear to be one of life's dreamers and drifters you're also able to root your particular dreams in reality—and make pure gold out of seemingly nothing.

You're an invaluable addition to any group and will enjoy working with organisations and clubs even if you feel you risk losing your own identity in the process. Nevertheless you have the self-discipline and work ethic to see the completion of successful projects through and you'll enjoy working collaboratively towards a common goal.

You can appear critical of others, but your comments are generally designed to create a positive outcome and are not intended as negative comment for the sake of it. You will make an ideal mentor or guardian. You will do the end-line caring for those who have been left to fend for themselves.

You have the propensity to idolise people especially those you are close to emotionally, and believe they're your saviour or that they are perfect. The resulting disappointment can cause you to feel disillusioned. In this mind-set you risk being critical of others due to their perceived lack of perfection and you can be self-critical because you misjudged them in the first place.

Still, you knew all along that no-one and nothing is perfect in this perfectly imperfect world. But you'll enjoy dreaming that it is, that rainbows are perfect, that life is perfect because, if it isn't, what will you strive for?

You'll enjoy working—and relaxing—with people of like minds. Dreamers, philosophers, writers, readers, children, mums and dads who are all in their own way seeking the pot of gold at the end of the rainbow.

Perspective

Idealistic, pedantic, philosophical, unrealistic, distracted, practical, self-critical, playful

Talents

Creativity, inclusivity, self-discipline, organisational skills

Interests

Film, theatre, acting, art, advertising, self-development, voluntary work, healing, psychic ability, romance, literature, music, art

Challenge

To be part of a group and an individual at the same time

Potential pitfalls

Self-criticism, criticism, idolisation, fanaticism

Affirmation

My dreams take root in reality.

The secret you

As a consummate philosopher you may happily state that we are all living in a dream. Modern physics certainly suggests that we cannot ignore the impact our own perception has on the world, and our interaction with the world makes us at one with it. So the questions, 'Are we living in a dream?' and, 'What is reality? Is it something we invent?' are valid.

You'll enjoy contemplating what life is all about, and what your dreams and intuition tell you about your deeper concerns rather than what your physical senses tell you. But you'll also be very conscious that physical reality dictates that you must be hands-on and realistic about your day-to-day routine and practices if only to survive.

You'll go through phases in your life where you're oblivious to the deeper meaning of life and will become fascinated with everyday existence, schedules, duties and work. At these times you'll positively shun any mention of the metaphysical, preferring to stick to strict schedules and the details of practical life.

Shunning your metaphysical interests will tend to push them deeper, and only make your spiritual realisations all the more forceful and life-changing when they do eventually come. Your reticence to pursue deeper meaning in life will be due to a fear of the unknown or, more precisely in your case, a fear of the known. This is especially true if you've already been hurt physically or psychologically by interests in the otherworldly or in the unknown via drugs, intoxicants or through dalliances with notorious or nefarious characters.

As a result you may go through phases when the only thing you trust is what is tangible, and you will become analytical to the point of ignoring what your heart is telling you. You may also fear being lost in a fantasy world and becoming delusional, especially as there truly is a fine line between what we believe and what is—if there 'is' one at all.

Essentially yours is a fear of letting go and of loss, and more specifically a fear of losing yourself. You're aware that you soak up environments and atmospheres so it's in your interest to choose them carefully. Your impressionability can also lead you to believe that you may easily become ill and as a child you may be particularly prone to hypochondria.

You will eventually find that pursuing and trusting your deeper insights is what will truly fulfil you if only because you have the ability—more so than many—to profoundly understand the mysteries of life. And when you balance your sharp mind with your deep insight you overcome your fear of being lost in the precipice of life's deep mysteries. You'll dare to acknowledge and accept the validity of your insights, and avoid getting stuck in one-track analytical thinking that can lead to the obsessive thoughts that potentially lead you astray.

Your inner conflict between holding back and being overtly analytical while still being sensitive to life's mysteries can be all-consuming until you realise that your search for an ideal and for perfection begins and ends with your own particular life force. This is what is perfect. All else is coincidental—alluring and wonderful as it may be.

Your compassionate and uplifting approach to life will always prevent your fears and doubts from overpowering you. You know that people can help each other and work toward the common good and you honour both the sacrifices you make in your life as well as the sacrifices people close to you make. This knowledge may have come about because you have someone in your home or environment who requires help and attention above and beyond the usual.

You'll feel truly fulfilled in your lifetime by bringing your deeper insights out, by making your interest in fantasy more real by expressing your ideas, writing them down and by sharing them with the world. Your research may even be groundbreaking, but you'll only know if you give it the light of day in a realistic format—and become the true visionary you're destined to be.

Characteristics

Private, poetic, intuitive, philosophical, gentle, sensitive, fearful

Talents

Instinct, perception, insight, sixth sense, psychic ability, true compassion

Interests

Psychology, paranormal, gardening, the hidden areas of life, life's underbelly

Challenge

To trust your instincts and abilities

Potential pitfalls

Hypochondria, self-doubt, melancholia, delusional ideas, overt analysis, obsessive ideas, fear of losing identity

Affirmation

I'm awake and alive in mind, body and spirit.

How your sun sign informs your purpose in life

As your knowledge of yourself deepens through your understanding of astrology, you'll enjoy combining this understanding with the knowledge you already have, which for many of us begins with our sun signs.

In modern Western astrology your sun sign represents your core self. In the context of this book an understanding of your sun sign will inform how you're likely to approach your deeper purpose in life, and consequently how you'll succeed and feel fulfilled.

The following information will give you an insight into the way your individual sun sign contributes to your understanding of your purpose in life. When you mentally overlap the information you've just read about your north node with information about your sun sign you'll be well on your way to a deeper understanding of yourself.

Then if your interest in astrology deepens you can add layers to your understanding by finding out other signs such as your moon sign, which is likely to be different from your moon's north node sign, or your rising sign, which will tell you about your salient personality traits . . . and the list goes on. But for now find out how your core self (sun sign) is likely to inform your purpose in life (north node).

ARIES

You're the zodiac's go-getter. You're likely to enjoy developing a strong sense of purpose in a proactive, energetic way. There will be little to hold back your dynamic nature and willingness to initiate exciting projects that will, as you progress through life, bring dramatic results.

It is vital that you avoid seeing your spiritual path or purpose in life in the same way you approach a competition, or as a way to be better than your peers. And avoid making rash decisions and initiating plans that run out of steam halfway through.

Your purpose in life is not another means to be first or the best. It's a way to find happiness on a deep soul level, and for many Aries sun signs the lasting source of happiness is compassion and inclusivity as opposed to exclusivity and competitiveness.

TAURUS

You'll gain self-worth and self-esteem through the attention and focus you place on developing a strong sense of purpose. You'll approach your spiritual path in a practical and earthy, although sometimes stubborn way.

You'll be considerate and respectful of others who express their own dreams, desires and wishes, especially people at work and home. Yet you can become fixed on one particular aspect of your life including your purpose, and must take additional steps to free yourself from rigid or stubborn thought patterns or behavioural traits.

You may invest deeply in your spiritual life, and endeavour to encourage others to do the same. You'll feel nurtured when you express your spirituality or your higher purpose, and will feel moved to nurture those who wish to do the same. You may feel motivated to earn respect or money via your understanding of your spirituality and soulful life.

GEMINI

Your adaptable Gemini self will encourage you to approach your tasks in life in a light-hearted, fun and flexible way. You will enjoy discussing, communicating and expressing yourself in myriad ways that will promote diversity in your life, and encourage you to investigate the many different avenues that will take you towards your higher purpose.

You may initially approach finding your true purpose in life from many different perspectives and try many different avenues. Mentally you will be attracted to concepts alone simply because an open mind is one of your traits.

You'll enjoy incorporating a sense of spirituality in your many exploits, but you do risk spreading yourself too thin and being distracted from your purpose by the many interests, duties and delights you indulge in throughout your life. Taking time to focus on your purpose in life early on will help you to attain your many goals so much more efficiently.

CANCER

Your natural predisposition as a caring, supportive individual could predispose you to putting your spiritual path and purpose in life second to everything else. Unless you specifically take steps to put your spirituality at the top of your to-do list, you can paradoxically be less effective as a nurturer. This is especially true when you're under stress, which is when a strong sense of purpose is most needed.

It's therefore in your interest to ensure you invest your energy in yourself when possible, and this will include taking the time to develop self-care and self-fulfilment so that when you're under pressure you will flower and be useful, and not flounder.

You'll allow your inner strength and conviction to hold sway as opposed to circumnavigating what's truly important in your life by indulging a little more in your soul's needs.

LEO

As the powerful person you are you'll approach your purpose in life in a proactive way, although when you're younger a deeper appreciation of your spirituality may take second place to your ego and your intrinsically high regard for your conscious self.

Once you master the art of understanding that knowledge of your soul's purpose can only improve your path to success and empower you, you will embrace this vital aspect of your life. Know that, in the same way that you and your ego, your vitality and your generosity generate enjoyment in your life, so too will your spirituality and purpose generate a more complete picture in which you can safely embrace the uniqueness and importance of yourself—and others too.

Virgo

Virgo sun signs are generally characterised as hard workers and practical people with the ability to be well organised to the point of meticulousness. As such you'll take practical steps to incorporate your soul's purpose in life methodically and will endeavour to gain a deeper understanding of yourself.

You'll actively pursue methods to achieve this by way of retreats or meditation or by researching your options and quietly studying. The practical steps you take will enhance your life's purpose, and you may be drawn to teach in-depth what you discover on the way.

Your strong leaning towards a healthy mind, body and spirit will encourage you to meticulously analyse the information in this book to understand both yourself and people around you better.

Libra

Your search for harmony will motivate you to embrace your north node sign as another tool in your box of life-enhancement skills. You'll actively search for ways to incorporate your spiritual awareness in life in the hope that this will help you find more balance, beauty and wisdom.

Your life can be punctuated with potent phases of indecision, which can become stultifying. Knowledge of your purpose in life will prove an invaluable key toward establishing harmony during these periods when mental or intellectual debate and indecision can cause insecurity or even inaction.

With the security you gain from knowing your true purpose in life you'll find that your indecision and mental debate will take less of your energy as you gain certainty and self-confidence. Decision-making will become easier as you gain direction and inner knowing.

SCORPIO

Your passionate approach to life suggests that you'll embrace your purpose in life with dynamism and intensity, and you'll know instinctively that deeper knowledge of yourself and others can only add to your enjoyment and appreciation of the life experience.

Your understanding of life tends to go much deeper than many other sun signs, and you're naturally predisposed to delve profoundly into life's many experiences. The extra understanding you gain from having purpose will appeal to your lust for life.

The adage 'still waters run deep' applies to you. You'll dig deep into ways and means to effect the many changes and ideas your north node experience will present to you, and you'll enjoy finding ways to strengthen and deepen your knowledge too.

SAGITTARIUS

As the truth seeker of the zodiac you will embrace the inherent knowledge and wisdom that a spiritual path offers you. And as an intrinsically spiritual person—someone who actively pursues knowledge and wisdom through study, travel, higher education and physical endeavour—you will apply much of your learning about your purpose in life directly into your activities. You will act upon what you learn as you go along, effectively creating and gathering momentum that further facilitates learning and progress through life.

For you knowledge of your north node will be an investment of the highest order. You will travel, study and investigate many avenues to gain further insight into the reasons you're really here, and you'll aim high in order to gain utmost insight and knowledge leaving very few stones unturned in your quest.

CAPRICORN

Practical and hands-on, your journey through life is characterised by your ability to attain the goals you set yourself—and then some. Although you're generally characterised as a materialistic, status-orientated character, the bigger picture is that you have an appreciation for stability in life, and a desire to be the cornerstone in your own life and that of the people you love. As such, if you do appear materialistic it derives from your knowing that you must have the basics such as a roof over your head and a square meal or two to bank on.

You're likely to approach your purpose in life in a rational, end-game way, and will appreciate its value as a tool to gain the stability and wisdom you seek. But you can also risk approaching your spiritual path in a goal-oriented way, which will detract from your enjoyment of the actual path and journey itself.

AQUARIUS

Innovative yet conscious of traditions, the idea of finding your purpose in life will appeal to the Aquarian intellect. Applying your purpose to your everyday life will appeal to your ability to apply your great ideas in practical ways to real-life scenarios.

You're known as the quirky sign of the zodiac and anything otherworldly or avant-garde will make you sit up and take notice, but you must always see the practical applications of your quirky ideas.

You'll find that knowledge of your north node will put the icing on the cake of your bright ideas, and seal the deal with your more practical admiration for anything that actually works in reality and not just in your mind. Self-fulfilment, here you come!

PISCES

Better known as the zodiac's truly philosophical sign, your more outgoing and adventurous character is sometimes overlooked. But to those who know and admire you, you are the most expansive and broad-minded of zodiac signs. As such, a knowledge of your true purpose in life will fit you like a glove.

Your gentle appreciation of life's delicate balancing act—an alchemical concoction of karma and faith—will launch you into your own search for meaning in life. Knowing that you have purpose and are a spiritual being having an earthly experience will appeal to your sense of wonder and delight, helping you derive knowledge and understanding in your journey through life.

Take care not to lose sight of the practicalities and realities of life while striving for your particular nirvana and the sky's the limit!

Notes for budding astrologers

For additional insight and deeper understanding of your life and personality, a complete understanding of your astrological birth chart is recommended. Your astrological birth chart displays where the planets were at the time, place and date of your birth, and will reveal layers of additional insight.

In particular, knowing the placement of your north and south node in relation to celestial bodies and their house signs can give even more insight into your soul's path.

In the spirit of understanding how the position of the planets and celestial bodies influence your north node and your life's purpose, the following is given as additional information for budding and practising astrologers.

> NOTE: *not everyone had a planet aligning with their north or south nodes when they were born, and this is something that you will discover should you decide to draw up your birth chart or if you have done so already.*

WHEN THE SUN WAS CONJUNCT (OR OPPOSITE) YOUR NORTH NODE

Your spiritual path is closely connected with the development of your ego and sense of self. This can be a difficult path and yet, if you accept the challenge to improve yourself, you'll forge ahead with seemingly miraculous success.

Your parents will have a strong influence, especially your father or a father figure. Depending on the sign of your north node your quest could be to understand your relationship with your parents. This will be of particular help to you in this lifetime as you may have the task of changing the course of your family's collective direction.

You will learn that following your calling will help you shine all the more brightly, but the risk is that your ego overshadows your spiritual quest, making self-fulfilment harder to attain. Yet once you feel your sense of purpose is ignited, you could attain your goals more smoothly than many.

WHEN THE MOON WAS CONJUNCT (OR OPPOSITE) YOUR NORTH NODE

Your emotional life is closely intertwined with your potential for self-fulfilment so you'll find you express yourself very much emotionally, especially as a youngster. You may have particularly powerful and distracting emotions, which can be confusing as emotions have a tendency to run away with you leaving you feeling drained.

This can result in a blurring of the line between knowing what will truly fulfil you emotionally and what will fulfil you on a soul level. Meditation and other calming practices such as yoga and swimming can help realign your emotions with your soul purpose so you can progress more confidently.

Once you feel you're on an even keel this placement can indicate an exceptional psychic and healing skill and talent.

Your mother or a mother figure will be more influential in your life than for many.

WHEN MERCURY WAS CONJUNCT (OR OPPOSITE) YOUR NORTH NODE

You'll gain a particular sense of purpose from the way you communicate and learn, yet your communication skills are likely to be different from other people's.

You'll actively set out to study and gain knowledge as you instinctively know that information and learning will make your life path much more fulfilling. Travel may feature strongly in your lifetime too. One or both parents will be markedly adept—or lacking—in communication skills, and finances may play a relevant role in your life lessons.

WHEN VENUS WAS CONJUNCT (OR OPPOSITE) YOUR NORTH NODE

Your love life, values and potentially also your finances will be tied to your quest for self-fulfilment—more so than for many.

You may find you are drawn to people and events as if by a magnet. Your love life will change your world radically as it may transform your values or financial status simultaneously, for example.

Your values will also be a prominent feature of your life either because you are criticised for them or because you must take a stand for your principles in a poignant way at some point.

The pitfall for you is that you mistake fulfilling your financial and physical desires for being fulfilled spiritually. Distinguishing between the two will help you gain a sense of purpose.

You're likely to be attracted to art and music at a young age, and to have some form of artistic or musical talent yourself.

WHEN MARS WAS CONJUNCT (OR OPPOSITE) YOUR NORTH NODE

You'll passionately seek true purpose, actively creating a dynamic and proactive life. You'll feel fulfilled by pursuing your interests and abilities fervently and your feistiness may be so extreme that you risk alienating yourself.

It's imperative with this placement that you find out what is the most productive path in life for you because Mars will help you attain your goals swiftly. If you do lack direction, though, this position could cause you to be misdirected throughout your life by impulsive, imprudent actions.

Children may seem particularly aggressive, and extra care to channel this energy into productive pursuits, such as sports, will help solve belligerent tendencies.

WHEN JUPITER WAS CONJUNCT (OR OPPOSITE) YOUR NORTH NODE

Your pursuit of happiness and self-fulfilment could become all-consuming. You seek to empower yourself with the feeling that you are following your spiritual path toward a deeper understanding or even towards becoming enlightened.

You may find that you become a teacher, a life coach or mentor. You'll attract larger-than-life personalities and are likely to be one yourself.

Care must be taken to keep life events in perspective and with solid groundwork your ability both to attract joy and project it will be remarkable.

Travel and study are likely to be a prominent feature throughout your life. You may be perceived as a generally lucky person, unless other astrological traits predominate.

WHEN SATURN WAS CONJUNCT (OR OPPOSITE) YOUR NORTH NODE

You will take a disciplined approach to finding your true life purpose. You will be methodical and realistic about your abilities and being the best person you can.

You may find that a cynical lack of belief in your own talents and a tendency to dismiss the esoteric side of life diverts you from your true life purpose when young, and you may only begin to pursue a real sense of purpose later in life.

As a child a parental figure (usually a father or authoritarian figure) will be significantly disciplinarian or influential or the opposite, lacking in discipline or even absent.

WHEN URANUS WAS CONJUNCT (OR OPPOSITE) YOUR NORTH NODE

You will adopt an inspired and sometimes unconventional approach to understanding yourself and could present as an unusual person.

Technology will figure in some way along your spiritual path, for example you may approach meditation through technological means, preferring to hook up to a brain gym rather than imagine creative visualisations.

A noticeable spiritual awakening could occur during your lifetime, which will put you on an irreversibly spiritual path. Your life will be accompanied by spontaneous bursts of awakening and understanding—either through sudden events and new circumstances or by way of your own unusual circumstances.

Your life course could be subject to unexpected and definitive changes of status.

WHEN NEPTUNE WAS CONJUNCT (OR OPPOSITE) YOUR NORTH NODE

You will approach your life with a great deal of devotion or an inability to focus and concentrate.

You're likely to feel that being self-fulfilled is a priority, it's just a matter of actually getting down and doing something about it.

If you're a devotee you'll find meditation and guided visualisations particularly enriching and illuminating. If you're easily distracted you'll find practical discipline such as sticking to a timetable and a routine effective.

Either way you have a deep well of human understanding, creativity and inspiration at your fingertips. It's just a case of jumping in.

You're likely to be particularly artistic, romantic or spiritually inspired, and you may also have psychic abilities.

WHEN PLUTO WAS CONJUNCT (OR OPPOSITE) YOUR NORTH NODE

Your spiritual quest and sense of purpose in your lifetime will take you through intense periods of transformation.

You have a deep insight into the human condition, and will experience an intense sense of purpose. This may be through dramatic events that open your eyes to new realities and truths in life, or through your own efforts to transform yourself into a more effective, compassionate and productive human being.

You may achieve much of your deep understanding of the human life cycle through intense experiences with death, the dying or the funeral process.

You are likely to have one parent—most probably your mother—who is a particularly significant or strong figure in your life.

WHEN CHIRON WAS CONJUNCT (OR OPPOSITE) YOUR NORTH NODE

You'll move forward in life through understanding the pain and/or vulnerabilities of others, and through potentially sensitive situations you experience yourself. You may feel, as a result, that you become wounded psychologically or physically at a young age. Due to this you will learn to self-heal and self-nurture in many ways, which other people may not have the opportunity to experience. In turn, you may choose to become a healer yourself.

NOTE TO ASTROLOGERS: *when celestial bodies are conjunct (or opposite) your north or south node at the time of your birth they can manifest in the various ways I've described above.*

If these celestial bodies are in a square, or 90-degree angle to the north node, the circumstances described under each heading may be more challenging, creating tension in life because events initially present themselves as hurdles. However, as some people only attain their true potential through adversity, a challenging aspect such as a square can actually contribute to self-fulfilment and happiness.

When planets are in a trine, or a 120-degree angle to your north node, the planet in question can be helpful to the development of your life path and the fulfilment of your purpose.

A final word

I trust that you have enjoyed reading this book and that you will find fulfilment in your life.

For additional insight into your life and personality, a complete understanding of your astrological birth chart is recommended. Your astrological birth chart displays where the planets were at the time, place and date of your birth, revealing layers of additional insight too vast for the scope of this book.

If you decide to pursue further investigation into your astrological chart, please feel free to contact me at www.patsybennett.com. I will be delighted to hear from you.

Bibliography

Borstein A K 2004, *The Moon's Nodes: A Churning Process of the Soul*, Cresentia Publications, USA.

Campion N 2008, *The Dawn of Astrology: A Cultural History of Western Astrology*, Continuum, London, UK.

Carter C E O 2009, *The Principles of Astrology*, The Astrology Center of America, Bel Air MD, USA.

Marks T 2008, *The Astrology of Self-discovery*, Ibis Press, Florida, USA.

Michelsen N 1997, *The American Ephemeris for the 21st Century: 2000 to 2050 at Noon*, Starcrafts Publishing, Kensington, USA.

Michelsen N 1991, *The American Ephemeris for the 20th Century: 1900–2000 at Midnight*, ACS Publications, San Diego, California, USA.

Ronngren D 2005, *Lunar Nodes: Keys to Emotions and Life Experience*, ETC Publishing, Reno, NV, USA.

Schulman M 1975, *Karmic Astrology: The Moon's Nodes and Reincarnation*, Samuel Weiser Inc, Maine, USA.

Solar Fire computer program (available online at www.esotech.com. au).

ABOUT THE AUTHOR

Patsy Bennett is an astrologer, psychic medium and journalist. She began reading palms and tarot at age 14, experiencing medium insights as young as 12.

Patsy has worked as a professional astrologer for nearly 20 years. Her trusted insights are incredibly accurate and are highly regarded.

Born in New Zealand, she relocated to the UK in the 1980s where she worked as an editor for women's and fashion magazines including *Woman's Own* and *ELLE* (UK), later becoming a reporter.

Having gained a Master of Arts degree in romance languages and literature at the University of London, Patsy studied astrology at the Faculty of Astrological Studies in London and taught French at the University of California, Berkeley.

Patsy then moved to Australia in 1998 where she worked as a reporter for local newspapers in northern NSW. Her articles have also been published in national newspapers and magazines such as *Take 5* and *Practical Parenting*.

She continues to practise as an astrologer and journalist, and her horoscopes are published in national newspapers and magazines including *Nature & Health*. She also provides astrology and psychic readings in northern NSW where she presents astrology and psychic development workshops.

Patsy is a member of the Queensland Federation of Astrologers and the International Psychics Association. For more information, visit www.patsybennett.com

Astrology
Reading Cards

Alison Chester Lambert

This 36-card deck with accompanying
guidebook will help you fulfill your desire
to truly understand astrology.
The cards make learning quick and easy
through your interaction with the Zodiac
Signs, House and Planet cards. Something that
was once complicated, will now become fun!

ISBN: 978-1-921878-77-0

ROCKPOOL
PUBLISHING

Available at all good bookstores or online at
www.rockpoolpublishing.com.au

Explore the world of
DREAMS

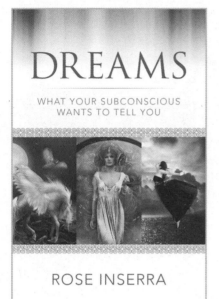

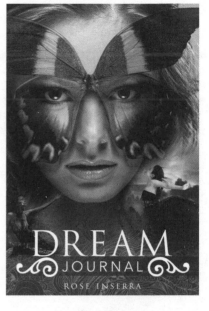

Dreams
Rose Inserra

Dreams is a comprehensive and practical guide to all aspects of dreaming. Discover how you can intuitively interpret your dream symbols and on waking, use practical self-help remedies to recall the dream's message. You can learn to unlock your dreams and bring them to your conscious mind to process.

ISBN 978-1-925017-17-5

Dream Journal
Rose Inserra

The *Dream Journal* is more than just a diary – it's a tool to jog your memory and give you greater insight into your subconscious mind. Using the *Dream Journal* will assist you in remembering and interpreting your dreams with accuracy and detail – and help you realise what they reveal about your inner world.

ISBN 978-1-921295-85-0

ROCKPOOL
PUBLISHING

Available at all good bookstores or online at
www.rockpoolpublishing.com.au

The Path of the
EMPRESS

· ·

Christine Li, Ulja Krautwald

The Path of the Empress *explores the feminine power of transformation and how women can harness their power and sexuality.*

Over a thousand years ago, the concubine Wu Zhao became China's most powerful woman. Her intelligence and erotic aura, combined with her knowledge of the art of war, led her to become empress – and the only woman who ever officially ruled ancient China. Her faithful adviser was the wise shaman and doctor Sun Simiao, guardian of age-old secrets of feminine wisdom and power.

Inspired by Wu Zhao and ancient Chinese texts, *The Path of the Empress* describes the ten important stages of a woman's life, and focuses on exercises and magical herbal elixirs that open up the mind and soul to new insights and solutions.

ISBN 978-1-925017-51-9

Available at all good bookstores or online at
www.rockpoolpublishing.com.au